A Guide to Places

on the

Colorado Prairie

1540–1975

A Guide to Places on the Colorado Prairie

1540–1975

By Ray Shaffer

PRUETT  PUBLISHING COMPANY
3235 Prairie Avenue   Boulder, Colorado 80301

© 1978 by Ray Shaffer
All rights reserved, including those to reproduce this book or parts thereof in any form without permission in writing from the Publisher.

Library of Congress Cataloging in Publication Data

Shaffer, Ray, 1929-
 A guide to places on the Colorado prairie, 1540-1975.

 Bibliography: p.
 Includes index.
 1. Cities and towns, Ruined, extinct, etc. — Colorado — History.   2. Colorado — History, Local.   I. Tital.
F776.S5   917.88   78-1741
ISBN 0-87108-513-5

First Edition
1 2 3 4 5 6 7 8 9

Printed in the United States of America

Acknowledgements

I wish to express a heartfelt thanks to the library staff of the Colorado Historical Society, the twenty-eight County Clerks and their staffs, E. J. Haley, the Burlington Northern Railroad, and the hundreds of people who provided information about their special place on the prairie. A special thanks is due Dudley Enos for his editing, Marjorie Hook for her assistance, the A & D Typing and Copy Service for their very professional approach, and my family for their encouragement and assistance through the last nine years.

Preface

Adena, A Place on the Colorado Prairie. As in the case of many of the other thirteen hundred places which have been on the maps of eastern Colorado, little remains of Adena now. The abandoned gas pump, the unmended fences, and the foundations which protrude through a cover of tumbleweeds—all attest to livelier times in Adena. Perhaps one should feel a little remorseful about years gone by. But I suspect that a more appropriate feeling would be one of gratitude to the Adenas for having been there at all.

Contents

Chapter

1 From the Beginning *1*
2 Bits and Pieces *7*
3 Adams County *11*
4 Arapahoe County *27*
5 Baca County *41*
6 Bent County *53*
7 Boulder County *63*
8 Cheyenne County *77*
9 Crowley County *85*
10 Denver County *89*
11 Douglas County *103*
12 Elbert County *115*
13 El Paso County *125*
14 Huerfano County *145*
15 Jefferson County *159*
16 Kiowa County *173*
17 Kit Carson County *179*
18 Larimer County *187*
19 Las Animas County *203*
20 Lincoln County *227*
21 Logan County *235*
22 Morgan County *247*
23 Otero County *259*
24 Phillips County *267*
25 Prowers County *273*
26 Pueblo County *285*
27 Sedgwick County *307*
28 Washington County *313*
29 Weld County *323*
30 Yuma County *355*
Selected Bibliography *365*
Index *369*

Abstract

In the early 1540s when the conquistadores under the command of Francisco Coronado left the region of Kansas after their unsuccessful search for the mythical land of Quivera, they probably crossed the southeastern corner of Colorado. If the Spaniards did travel across a part of the state, they were the first white men to touch upon the soil of Colorado. This book is the result of an effort on the part of the author to identify the places that have appeared on the prairie of Colorado from the time of Coronado's journey to 1976.

Limitations

The types of places presented in the ensuing chapters are limited to the following: (a) battlegrounds, (b) civilian forts, (c) military establishments, (d) noted landmarks of explorers, (e) platted towns, (f) post offices, (g) railroad sidings, (h) stage stations, (i) trading posts, (j) unincorporated metropolitan areas, and (k) way-stops.

Indian places and topographical features are deserving of attention under separate cover and, therefore, are not included in the types of places presented in this book.

Presentation

The places are divided by present-day counties and are presented under the following headings: (a) Still on the map, (b) Places in the Past, and (c) Some Whistlestops. The railroads are included for each county because of their direct relationship to the origin of many places on the Colorado prairie. The railroads are presented under the heading "Some Railroad Tracks," and a chronological list of company names is included for each railroad. The heading "Whistlestops" refers to those places next to railroads which did not have a post office and were probably little more than sidings.

Each place included under the headings of "Still on the Map" or "Places in the Past" is listed by the most recent name used for the place; the name is immediately followed by a term in parentheses which best describes the major function of the place, such as "platted town." Likewise, each place listed under the heading of "Whistlestops" is listed by its most recent name, and each name is immediately followed by the parenthesized initials of the railroad near which the place was established.

The post offices are divided into the following categories: (a) early post offices (1850s or 1860s), (b) railroad post offices, and (c) rural post offices. The term "rural post offices" refers to those post offices which were not established next to a railroad nor within a metropolitan area.

The maps which are presented in conjunction with each county depict the major highways and roads according to a 1968 geological survey map of Colorado. For most counties, places which are listed as "Still on the Map," "Places in the Past," and "Whistlestops" are shown on one map. However, it was necessary to use several maps for the larger counties.

Most post offices on the Colorado prairie were named after local topography or after the person who applied for the office, and most railroad sidings were named for the former owners of the land, railroad officials, or local topography. Therefore, except in the case of platted towns, no particular attention is given to the origin of place names.

Sources of Information

With the exception of the large cities, there has been relatively little written about places on the prairie of Colorado as compared to places in the Colorado mountains. Thus, in order to obtain sufficient information about many of the places, it was necessary to refer to a variety of sources. Most of the information presented in this book was obtained from government documents, published maps of Colorado, town plats, on-site visitations, and related literature.

GOVERNMENT DOCUMENTS. A review of the "United States Official Postal Guides" and the *Colorado Yearbooks* was useful in obtaining information about the size, length of existence, and function of many places on the Colorado prairie.

MAPS. A primary source of information used in this book was the maps of Colorado on file at the library of the State Historical Museum, the United States Geological Survey Office in Denver, and the regional office of the Burlington Northern Railroad. Additional information was obtained from road maps of various oil companies and maps in related literature.

TOWN PLATS. Another valuable source of information was the town plats which are on file at the county court houses. A review of the town plats revealed such information as the exact location, the filer of the plat, and the date of filing for most of the platted towns on the Colorado prairie. Some of the original town plats are more than a hundred years old, and viewing these was a realistic glance at Colorado history. Many of these plats are in a state of deterioration and will not be available for public scrutiny beyond the next few years.

VISITATIONS. In addition to the visits made to the twenty-eight county court houses, much information was obtained by specific visits to other locales. Some of the general locations visited by the author were as follows: (a) portions of all the major stage routes, (b) a majority of the immigrant trails, (c) the routes of many discontinued railroads, (d) most of the railroads which are still in operation, (e) almost all of the places which are still on the map, and (f) hundreds of "whistlestops" and sites of "places in the past." The numerous visits to various locations on the Colorado prairie were helpful in correcting misinformation and obtaining information not available from other sources.

LITERATURE. The major source of information about most of the places presented in this book was in related literature. A review of this literature, which revealed the need for a single source of information about the places on the prairie of Colorado, reaffirmed the purpose for writing this book. However, many excellent books have been written about specific types of places and specific places on the Colorado prairie, and this book is presented as an overview, not a supplement, of the related literature.

*Dedicated to
The People of the Prairie*

Chapter 1

From the Beginning

Before the white man entered the region which is now Colorado, the Indians gave names to their hunting grounds, campsites, landmarks, and religious places. The first white men to touch the soil of the Colorado region were probably the Spaniards under Coronado during the mid-1500s; however, there is no record of their having named any places in the area. It was not until the late 1600s that white men again reached the soil of Colorado. Sometime in the mid-1600s, a small group of Spanish soldiers from New Mexico pursued a band of Indians into southeastern Colorado. The conflict between the Indians and the Spaniards again led white men into Colorado several times in the late 1600s and the early 1700s, but the forays did not produce any recorded place names for the area.

The French entered the Colorado region in 1739 when the Mallet brothers traveled the Platte River into the area. It was the Mallet brothers who gave the river the name "Platte" after the flat-bottomed boats that they used to travel the river. The French made several trading ventures into the Colorado region before they ceded all rights in the region to Spain in 1763, at the conclusion of the French and Indian War.

The Spaniards did little with their new acquisition except for an exploratory expedition into the Colorado mountains by Fathers Dominquez and Escalante during 1776. The Spaniards

From the Beginning

continued their pursuit of rebellious Indians into Colorado during the late 1700s, but, still, no names were recorded for the prairie of Colorado. In 1800 the French again obtained possession of the Louisiana Territory from Spain and sold the territory to the United States in 1803.

The United States knew little about the land involved in their Louisiana Purchase and sent several expeditions to explore the area in the early 1800s. Lieutenant Zebulon Pike was dispatched into the Louisiana Territory in 1806. His reference to the "Big Timbers" along the Arkansas River was among the first places on the Colorado prairie to be named by white men. "Big Timbers" is the starting place for names that are used in this book; most of the places on the Colorado prairie, however, were not started until after the 1850s.

After the Louisiana Purchase and subsequent explorations, the Colorado prairie was merely a passageway for fur trappers and traders, with the exception of isolated trading posts established to capitalize on the traffic. The honor of being the first permanent place on the Colorado prairie belongs to the famous Bent's Fort. Charles and William Bent and Ceran Saint Vrain built their enormous trading post near the site of present-day La Junta during 1832 and 1833. Bent's Fort became the center for a small furtrading empire and led to the establishment of several other fort-like trading posts on the prairie of Colorado, especially along the Platte River. Fort Jackson was established a few miles north of the site of present-day Fort Lupton in 1837. Fort Lupton was established just north of present-day Fort Lupton in 1836 by Lancaster Lupton. Fort Saint Vrain was established by Marcelline and Ceran Saint Vrain in 1837, and was located about four miles west of the site of present-day Gilcrest. Fort Vasquez was established about one mile south of the site of present-day Platteville by Louis Vasquez and Andrew Sublette in 1836.

The furtrapping and trading industry had subsided sufficiently by the 1840s so that most of the smaller trading forts were closed by 1850. Few names were added to the list of places on the Colorado prairie in the early 1850s; however, Jules Beni rerouted a portion of the Oregon Trail to his trading

Places on the Colorado Prairie

post in what is now the tip of northeastern Colorado during the 1850s, thus starting the first of four Julesburgs. The prairie had remained virtually unpopulated until William Green Russell started the Colorado gold rush in 1858. Soon after the news of Russell's discovery of gold reached the midwest, the gold seekers started their rush to the "Pikes Peak" region. Russell's Auraria, Boulder City, Arapahoe City, Denver City, and Colorado City were among the many places that emerged at the base of the Rockies; most of these served as supply camps for the gold seekers. Stage routes to the Rockies were established beginning in 1859, and the names of stage stations such as American Ranch, Virginia Dale, and Living Springs began to appear on the early maps of Colorado.

The mass arrival of the white man on the Colorado prairie led to an Indian uprising in the early 1860s, and Fort Latham, Fort Collins, Fort Morgan, and other fortifications were erected in a defense against the uprising. The Battle of Summit Springs, the Sand Creek Massacre, and the Battle of Beecher Island were three of the most noted engagements between the military and the Indians on the plains of Colorado. The Indian uprising had lost much of its momentum by the end of the 1860s, when the maps of Colorado were about to be considerably altered by the arrival of the railroad.

The first railroad to reach Colorado was the Union Pacific line which was built to Julesburg in 1867. A parade of railroads followed the Union Pacific to Colorado in the 1870s and 1880s. The railroads brought a flood of new names to the maps of Colorado, and most of the places that have managed to stay on the map owe their existence to the railroad. The most prolific town-maker in Colorado was the Lincoln Land Company, which was established to begin towns along the Burlington railroads. In Colorado the Lincoln Land Company filed town plats for at least twenty towns: Akron, Amherst, Brush, Bryant, Derby, Eckley, Fleming, Grover, Haxtun, Hillrose, Holyoke, Hyde, Keota, Leslie, Peetz, Pinneo, Raymer, Sligo, Vallery, Willard, and Wray. Certainly, the most unusual origin of names along the railroads in Colorado is found on the Missouri Pacific railroad. The Missouri Pacific railroad in Colorado was built by the Pueblo and State Line

From the Beginning

Railroad, and the honor of naming places along the line was given to Jessie Thayer, the daughter of the railroad's president. Jessie Thayer chose to name the places in alphabetical order: Arden, Brandon, Chivington, Diston, Eads, Fergus, Galatea, Haswell, Inman, Joliet, and Kilburn (Fergus became Hawkins and Joliet became Arlington).

At about the same time the railroads were making their entrance onto the Colorado prairie, the colony towns were popular in eastern Colorado. Longmont, Green City, and Greeley are examples of colony towns on the prairie.

The cattle industry in Colorado was at its zenith in the 1870s, and several of today's towns began their existence as cattle shipping stations. Brush and Iliff, both in northeastern Colorado, were named after local cattle barons.

By the late 1880s, Colorado was gaining some attention for pursuits other than mining; for that reason, land promoters were successful in inducing many easterners to settle on the Colorado prairie. The newcomers to the prairie were hesitant about completely severing their former ties, and many named their new communities after their hometowns, such as Springfield, Boston, Minneapolis, Brookfield, and Stonington (in Baca County). There were dozens of new names on the maps of southeastern Colorado by the early 1890s; however, the drought of the 1890s left those same maps almost barren of names by 1900, and most of the places in southeastern Colorado disappeared along with the glowing promises of the land promoters.

The land boom in southeastern Colorado had a sister boom around Denver at about the same time, and such names as Aurora, Sullivan, Clark Colony, and Leetsdale began showing up on the maps; however, most of the places near Denver were as ill-conceived as those in Baca County and soon disappeared from—or never even appeared on—the maps.

Until several years after the turn of the century, there were not many new names added to the maps because of the disastrous drouth of the 1890s. However, the development of the windmill for use on the prairie in 1900 was sufficient reason to start a trickle of new names on the maps, as illustrated by Mildred, New Haven, Omer, and Plains. The

Places on the Colorado Prairie

increased interest in agriculture throughout Colorado was enhanced by the building of many sugar refineries, especially along the fertile South Platte River Valley, in the early 1900s. The sugar industry initiated Ovid, Beetland, and Sugar City, and it gave new impetus to Brush, Brighton, Fort Lupton, and Holly, among others. As agriculture increased on the prairie, the need for water increased. Many places were therefore initiated in conjunction with the building of reservoirs, such as Padroni near the Sterling Reservoir, Hasty near the John Martin Reservoir, and Queen City near the King Reservoir.

Between the early 1900s and the 1920s, the prairie of Colorado received an abundance of names in the form of farm or ranch post offices which were usually named after the owner of the ranch or farm, as illustrated by Blaine, Wages, Witherbee, and Kalous. As the automobile was improved, the need for the rural type post office decreased, and many of the names that appeared on the maps of Colorado in the 1920s were gone by the 1930s.

The depression in the early 1930s staggered many of the places on the prairie, but the dust bowl in the mid-1930s literally blew a lot of places off the maps of Colorado, particularly in southeastern Colorado. If the 1930s curtailed the starting of new places on the prairie, World War II brought it to a standstill. After World War II, rural life was less appealing to many, and few places—with the exception of metropolitan areas—were started.

The 1950s, '60s, and '70s brought a building boom to the perimeters of the large cities in Colorado, and the names of Thornton, Northglenn, Applewood, Cimmaron Hills, and Western Hills are just a few of the names that appeared on Colorado maps for the first time. From the time of Bent's Fort in the 1830s until the building boom in the 1970s, more than fourteen hundred places appeared on the maps of the Colorado prairie. Today, only a few hundred are left.

Chapter 2

Bits and Pieces

This book about places on the Colorado prairie does not deal primarily with the origin of place names; however, the origins of the names for platted towns and some other places were included in the discussion of those places—they warrant some attention here. This is not an attempt to list all of the places named for girls, creeks, and famous men; rather, it is bits and pieces about the names of some places on the Colorado prairie.

The town of Merino was named after merino sheep, and the plat for Merino was filed by a cattle company. Merino was first called "Buffalo."

One of the most unusual names to appear on the maps of Colorado is Toonerville, named after the mythical town in the newspaper comic strip entitled "Fontaine Fox." Appropriately, Toonerville was strictly a recreational community.

There was a place on the prairie called "Hoopup." Now, who would have named a place Hoopup? Nobody seems to know, but it could have been a Mr. Hoopup.

The stage stations across the Colorado prairie were usually named after a nearby water supply or the local topography. Some of the most appealing station names were American Ranch, Cheyenne Wells, Lillian Springs, Living Springs, Hole-In-The-Prairie, Hole-In-The-Rock, and Virginia Dale. In Bent County, there was a place called "Boggsville." What

7

Bits and Pieces

makes Boggsville worth noting is that three of the most important men in early Colorado history lived there: Thomas Boggs, Kit Carson, and John Prowers.

The prairie is not noted for an abundance of water; however, two of the places on the Colorado prairie which were instrumental in the development of early Colorado were islands. Henderson's Island and Hadfield's Island were located in the South Platte River and were the respective homes of Colonel Jack Henderson and Uncle Billy Hadfield, who were noted pioneers in their counties.

More often than not, optimism turned into hope for survival on the prairie, as evidenced by the fact that "Happyville" was later called "Heartstrong." Maybe the place called "Loco" was closer to the truth. One of the most dynamic men in Colorado's mining history had three given names, for which the initials were H.A.W.

One of the most dynamic men in Colorado's railroad history also had three given names; these initial letters were W.A.H. The two men, H.A.W. Tabor and W.A.H. Loveland, had a little more than their notoriety in common.

Some of the most descriptive names which have appeared on the maps of the Colorado prairie are Burnt Mill, Crow's Roost, Deer Trail, Double Adobe, Eagle's Nest, Flat Top, Hog Back, Lone Tree, New Stage Station, Old Stage Station, Prairie, Rocky Ford, Sugar City, and Wild Horse.

The shortest name on the maps of Colorado was a post office in El Paso County which was given only the initials of its postmaster, Old Zounds. It was known as O.Z.

First in line, first on the list, and first almost any place would have to be A. A. Aaby, who filed a plat for Aaby in Cheyenne County. One of the most confusing names was a place in El Paso County shown on the map as "Gwilliamsville" which somewhat defies the rules of spelling.

What's in a name? Arickaree, California Ranch, Bluebell, Easyville, Jimmy Camp, Ninaview, Punkin Center, Red Lion, Trinchera Plaza, and Uncle Jack Moore's.

Finally, we come to Adena. It was about sixteen miles southwest of Fort Morgan, but is little more than an abandoned gas pump now. A review of the plats at the Morgan County

Court House reveals that a plat was not filed for Adena, but just for its cemetery. At least, someone was looking ahead in Adena.

Chapter 3

Adams County

Still on the Map

Adams City
Aurora
Barr
Bennett
Brighton
Commerce City
Coronado
DuPont
Eastlake
Federal Heights
Fitzsimons
Henderson
Irondale
Leader

Northglenn
North Washington
Perl Mack
Rocky Mt. Arsenal
Shaw Heights
Shaw Heights Mesa
Sherrelwood
Strasburg
Thornton
Watkins
Welby
Western Hills
Westminster

Places in the Past

Antero
Avoca City

Bashor
Berlin

Adams County

Bird	Living Springs
Box Elder	Lyman
Bunell	Munroe Park
Comanche	Nine Mile House
Dairy Place	North Swansea
Derby	Oleson
Duff	Pierson
Eskdale	Quimby
Frost	Rose Hill
Fulton	Sable
Gramercy Park	Scranton
Hazeltine	Simpson
Hillsborough	Swimford
Hohnville	Thedalund
Kiowa	

Some Railroad Tracks

Burlington Northern Railroad (three parts)

Colorado Eastern Railroad

Denver & Interurban Railroad

Denver, Laramie & Northwestern Railroad

Denver, Utah & Pacific Railroad

Union Pacific Railroad (three parts)

Some Whistlestops

Antees	Manila
Celeryvale	Mesa
Cox	Pate
Darlow	Patron
Eno	Quimby Station
Gallup	Rolla
Klink	Sand Creek
Magee	Utah Junction

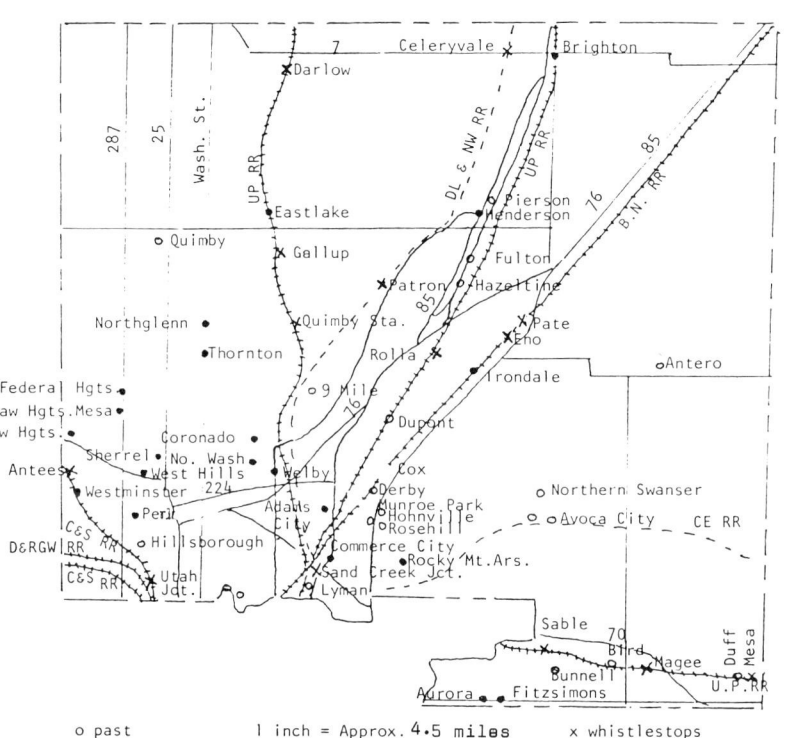

ADAMS COUNTY
(Western Part)

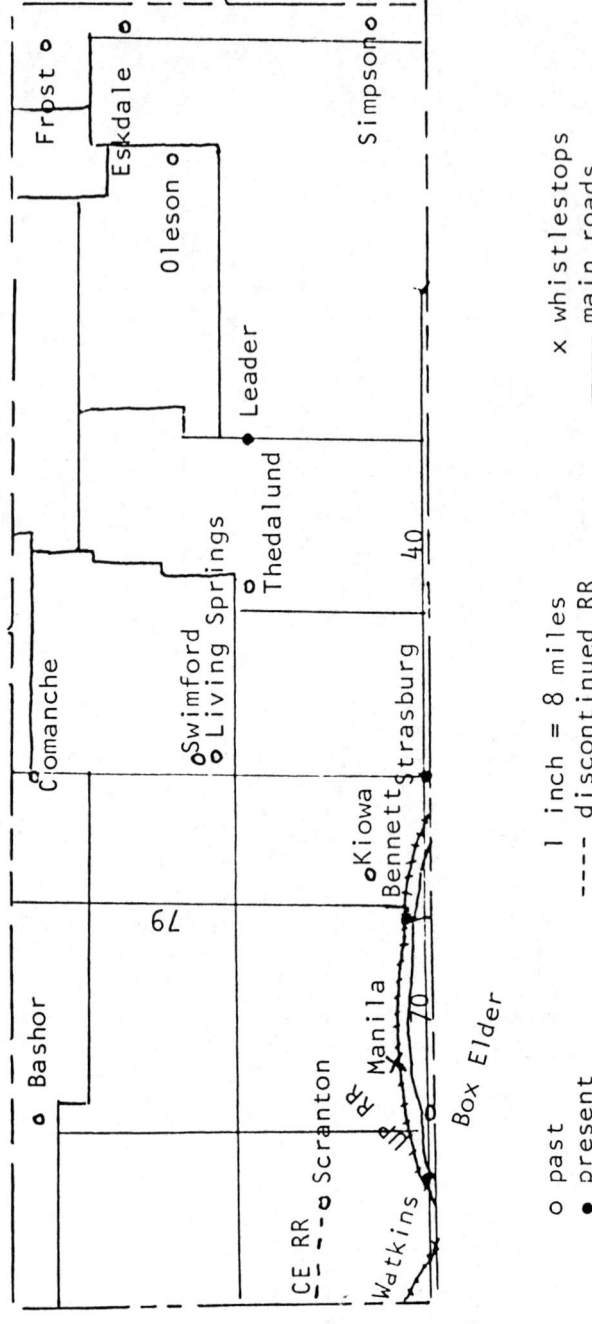

Still on the Map

ADAMS CITY (platted town) was named in reference to Alva Adams who was Governor of Colorado from 1887 to 1889, from 1897 to 1899, and in 1905. A town plat was filed for Adams City on August 27, 1903, by the Adams Land and Improvement Company; however, the Adams City post office wasn't established until 1923. Adams City was "pushed up" in the highly industrialized area north of Denver.

AURORA (platted town) was first called "Fletcher" in reference to Donald Fletcher, a land developer who established the community. The name of Fletcher's development was officially changed to "Aurora" when the Colfax Trust Company filed a plat for the area on April 1, 1890. Aurora means "dawn" or "beginning," but Aurora's lack of growth until the 1890s almost brought an early sunset to the town. Adams County was formed from a part of Arapahoe County in 1902, and Aurora found itself located in two counties; for that reason, Aurora incorporated in 1903 for some protection from two-county rule.

BARR (platted town) was named after a Mr. Barr who was a civil engineer for the Chicago, Burlington and Quincy Railroad. A town plat was filed for Barr on August 5, 1887, by W. E. Alexander, who also filed the plat for the Clark Colony. Barr Lake, which is next to the town of Barr, was constructed soon after the Burlington Railroad was built through the area in 1882. Barr Lake was enlarged in 1908, and that gave some impetus to the town of Barr; however, the town did not grow to any extent, and the Barr post office closed in 1952.

BENNETT (platted town) was established in the 1870s near the site of the Kiowa stage station. The Bennett post office was established in 1877 and was named after a Denver postmaster, H. P. Bennett. A town plat was filed for Bennett on May 8, 1911, by the Eastern Colorado Development Company; however, the Union Pacific railroad had made Bennett a well-established community some time prior to the filing of the plat.

Adams County

BRIGHTON (platted town) was preceded in the area by the Hughes stage station in the 1860s and the Hughes railroad station in 1870. Brighton was named after Brighton, Massachusetts, which was the hometown of Mrs. Carmichael, wife of Daniel Carmichael, who filed a plat for Brighton on February 19, 1881. Brighton was made County Seat of Adams County when the county was formed in 1902. The Kuner Canning factory and the Great Western Sugar factory were built at Brighton in 1889 and 1917, respectively.

COMMERCE CITY (platted town) was established and incorporated in 1952. Commerce City is predominantly an industrial community, and most of the people who work in Commerce City do not live there.

CORONADO (unincorporated metropolitan area) is located just south of Thornton and is shown on a 1975 map.

DUPONT (platted town) was named after the famous DuPont family who established a munitions storage plant in the area during the 1920s. A town plat was filed for DuPont on December 7, 1925, by Frank Henebry.

EASTLAKE (platted town) was named in reference to a nearby lake. The town plat for Eastlake was filed November 7, 1911, by the Eastlake Investment Company.

FEDERAL HEIGHTS (platted town) was named after its location next to Federal Boulevard. A town plat was filed for Federal Heights on June 18, 1940, and the town was incorporated in the same year.

FITZSIMONS ARMY HOSPITAL (military installation) was established on the eastern edge of Aurora in 1918. While the hospital was being built, it was serviced by Camp Fleer. Fitzsimons Hospital was named after Lieutenant William Fitzsimons, who was the first American officer killed in World War I.

16

Places on the Colorado Prairie

HENDERSON (platted town) was named after Colonel Jack Henderson who became the first permanent white settler in what is now Adams County when he settled on an island in the Platte River in 1858. A post office was established near Henderson's Island in 1872 and was called "Island Station." The Island Station post office was renamed "Henderson" in 1894, and a town plat was filed for Henderson on January 23, 1900, by the Davis Investment Company.

IRONDALE (platted town) was platted next to the Burlington railroad, and the plat was filed on March 5, 1889, by the Irondale Land and Improvement Company. The Irondale post office closed in 1895, but the railroad has kept Irondale on the map.

LEADER (rural post office) is located about twelve miles northeast of Byers, and the Leader post office was in operation from 1910 to 1940.

NORTHGLENN (platted town) was named after its location, which is north of Denver. The Northglenn post office opened in 1962, and Northglenn was incorporated in 1969. Northglenn is one of many communities which resulted from the housing boom around Denver after World War II.

NORTH WASHINGTON HEIGHTS (unincorporated metropolitan area) is located just south of Coronado and is shown on a 1975 map.

PERL MACK (unincorporated metropolitan area) is located just southeast of Westminster and south of the Valley Highway and is shown on a 1975 map.

ROCKY MOUNTAIN ARSENAL (federal installation) was established just northeast of Denver in 1942. The Rocky Mountain Arsenal was used for storage of extremely dangerous materials, such as nerve gas, and gained much attention because the dangerous materials were being stored so near Denver; however, steps were instituted to minimize the danger.

Adams County

SHAW HEIGHTS (unincorporated metropolitan area) is located just northwest of Westminster and is shown on a 1975 map.

SHAW HEIGHTS MESA (unincorporated metropolitan area) is located just east of Shaw Heights and is shown on a 1975 map.

SHERRELWOOD (unincorporated metropolitan area) is located just southeast of Federal Heights and is shown on a 1975 map.

STRASBURG (platted town) is located in both Arapahoe and Adams Counties. The Union Pacific Railroad established the Strasburg siding in the 1870s and named it after John Strasburg who built the railroad through the Strasburg area. D. H. Weaver laid out the lots for Strasburg in 1890; however, the Strasburg post office did not open until 1908.

THORNTON (platted town) was named in reference to Dan Thornton who was governor of Colorado when the town was established in 1952. Thornton's population was in excess of 11,000 by 1960. Thornton resulted from the post-World War II housing boom in and around Denver.

WATKINS (platted town) was named after a local rancher, L. A. Watkins. The Watkins post office opened in 1878, and a town plat was filed for Watkins on March 2, 1888, by John Fetzer and several others.

WELBY (platted town) was named after General Welby, who was president of the Denver, Laramie and Northwestern Railroad which built through the area in 1909. A town plat was filed for Welby on September 10, 1909, by the Northwestern Land and Development Company.

WESTERN HILLS (unincorporated metropolitan area) is located just south of Sherrelwood and is shown on a 1975 map.

WESTMINSTER (platted town) was first called "Harrisburg," then "Harris Park," then "Harris," and finally "Westminster" in 1908. A town plat was filed for "Harris Park" on June 27, 1890,

Places on the Colorado Prairie

by Henry Lowe and T. Hagerman. Westminster was named after nearby Westminster University which was founded in 1891. Westminster University closed in 1917, and the property was purchased by the Pillar of Fire Church in 1920.

Places in the Past

ANTERO (platted town) was little more than the plat which was filed on May 3, 1909, by the Antero Townsite Company. The land description on the Antero plat places the town about seven miles northeast of Irondale.

AVOCA CITY (platted town) was platted next to the Denver-Scranton railroad which had been discontinued several years before the plat was filed. A town plat was filed for Avoca City on July 21, 1922, by Louis E. Kriege. Avoca City was never shown on the map, and it did not obtain a post office.

BASHOR (rural post office) is shown about fourteen miles east of Brighton on a 1914 map. The Bashor post office was in operation from 1909 to 1918; however, the location of the post office is now covered by Horse Creek Reservoir.

BERLIN (platted town) was platted next to the Colorado Eastern railroad (Denver-Scranton) shortly after the line was constructed in 1896. A town plat was filed for Berlin on January 4, 1890, by E. Beller and W.A. Beller. Berlin was not shown on the map, and it did not obtain a post office.

BIRD (railroad post office) is shown next to the Union Pacific railroad and about four miles northeast of the Aurora site on an 1884 map. The Bird post office was in operation during 1880.

BOX ELDER (stage station) was located southeast of the Watkins site and on the Smoky Hill North stage route. Box Elder, also listed for Adams County, was named in reference to a nearby creek.

19

Adams County

BUNELL (rural post office) was located just east of Aurora. The Bunell post office was in operation from 1919 to 1921.

COMANCHE (rural post office) is shown about seventeen miles north of Strasburg on 1916 and 1920 maps. The Comanche post office was named after a nearby creek. It was in operation from 1911 to 1923.

DAIRY PLACE (platted town) was platted just northwest of the site of the Union Stockyards. The plat was filed by Thomas Anderson in November of 1898. However, Dairy Place was not shown on the map, and it did not obtain a post office.

DERBY (platted town) was named after Derby, England. The Lincoln Land Company and George McCullough filed a plat for Derby on November 15, 1889. Derby became part of Commerce City in 1952.

DUFF (railroad post office) was located next to the Union Pacific railroad and about six miles east of Sable. The Duff post office operated from 1884 to 1896.

ESKDALE (rural post office) was located about twenty-five miles southeast of Fort Morgan. The Eskdale post office was in operation from 1911 to 1933.

FROST (rural post office) was located about nine miles southwest of Gary. The Frost post office was in operation from 1899 to 1901.

FULTON (rural post office) was located near the site of Henderson and was located on the portion of the Overland stage route which was used before the Fort Morgan Cut-off. The Fulton post office was in operation in 1866 and 1867 and is shown on an 1866 map.

GRAMERCY PARK (platted town) was platted just northwest of the site of the Union Stockyards, and the plat was filed in 1889; however, Gramercy Place did not obtain a post office, and it was not shown on the map.

Adams County

NORTHERN SWANSEA (platted town) was platted just east of Derby, and the plat was filed on April 10, 1894, by J. M. Gore. Northern Swansea did not obtain a post office nor was the town shown on the map.

OLESON (rural post office) was located about twenty-five miles south of Fort Morgan. The Oleson post office was in operation from 1916 to 1931.

PIERSON (stage station) was located on the Overland stage route and about two miles northeast of the site of Henderson. Pierson was also called "Fifteen Mile House" in reference to its distance from Denver.

QUIMBY (rural post office) was located about two miles southwest of the site of Eastlake. The Quimby post office was in operation from 1895 to 1900.

ROSE HILL (platted town) was platted about two miles east of the site of Commerce City, and the plat was filed on December 22, 1884, by Matthew Cochrane. Rose Hill did not obtain a post office nor was the town shown on the map.

SABLE (platted town) was first called "Schuyler" in reference to Captain Howard Schuyler who was an engineer for the Kansas-Pacific Railroad which built a line through the area in 1870. The Bird post office was established near the Schuyler site in 1880 but closed in the same year. The site of Schuyler is shown as "Magnolia" on 1892 and 1902 maps and is shown as "Sable" on a 1909 map. The town plat for Sable was filed by G. W. Talmage; however, there was no date on the plat. Sable did not obtain a post office.

SCRANTON (railroad post office) was the terminus of the Denver and Scranton railroad which was built to the Scranton coal mine in 1886 by the Denver Railroad and Land Company. The Scranton post office was in operation from 1887 to 1888. The Denver and Scranton Railroad was abandoned in 1915.

Places on the Colorado Pr

HAZELTINE (railroad post office) was located on the Union Pacific railroad and about three miles southwest of Henderso The Hazeltine post office was in operation from 1893 to 190 Hazeltine was first called "Washburn."

HILLSBOROUGH (platted town) was platted near Westminste and the plat was filed on March 21, 1928, by Rosa Hirser. Hillsborough did not obtain a post office, and it was not shown the map.

HOHNVILLE (platted town) did not obtain a post office nor was t town shown on the map; however, a town plat was filed for Hohnville on November 30, 1887 by G. Hohn.

KIOWA (stage station) was named after a nearby creek and wa located on the Fort Morgan Cut-off and near the Cut-off's junctio with the Smoky Hill North stage route.

LIVING SPRINGS (stage station) was located on the Fort Morg Cut-off stage route and about ten miles north from the site of Strasburg. The post office of Living Springs was in operation onl from 1865 to 1867, but the place name stayed on the map into the 1900s.

LYMAN (railroad post office) is shown in the same location a Sand Creek Junction on 1884 through 1902 maps. The Lyman po office was in operation from 1885 to 1895.

MUNROE PARK (platted town) did not obtain a post office, and i was not shown on the map; however, a town plat was filed fo Munroe Park on March 10, 1892, by the Massachusetts Town and Development Company. Munroe Park was platted next to Hohnville.

NINE MILE HOUSE (stage station) was named after its distance from Denver on the Overland stage route and was located about three miles from the site of Thornton. Nine Mile House was sometimes called "Sand Creek Station."

Places on the Colorado Prairie

SIMPSON (rural post office) was located about eleven miles west of the site of Last Chance. The Simpson post office was in operation from 1917 to 1926.

SWIMFORD (rural post office) was located about ten miles north of Strasburg. Its post office was in operation from 1912 to 1913.

THEDALUND (rural post office) was located about five miles northeast of Byers. The Thedalund post office was in operation from 1917 to 1926.

Some Railroad Tracks

BURLINGTON NORTHERN from Weld County to Denver:

1881–1908 Burlington & Colorado RR
1908–1970 Chicago, Burlington & Quincy RR
1970– Burlington Northern RR

BURLINGTON NORTHERN from Denver to Jefferson County:

1870–1890 Colorado Central RR
1890–1898 Union Pacific, Denver & Gulf Ry.
1898–1908 Colorado & Southern Ry.
1908–1970 Chicago, Burlington & Quincy RR
1970– Burlington Northern RR

BURLINGTON NORTHERN from Denver to Jefferson County:

1886–1890 Denver, Marshall & Boulder Ry.
1890–1898 Union Pacific, Denver & Gulf Ry.
1898–1908 Colorado & Southern Ry.
1908–1970 Chicago, Burlington & Quincy RR
1970– Burlington Northern RR

23

Adams County

COLORADO EASTERN from Scranton to Denver:
    1886–1887 Denver Railroad & Land Co.
    1887–1888 Denver Railroad, Land, & Coal Co.
    1888–1894 Colorado Eastern Ry.
    1894–1915 Colorado Eastern RR

DENVER & INTERURBAN from Denver to Jefferson County:
    1906–1926 Denver & Interurban RR

DENVER, LARAMIE & NORTHWESTERN from Weld County to Denver:
    1909–1917 Denver, Laramie & Northwestern RR

DENVER, UTAH & PACIFIC from Boulder County to Denver:
    1881–1889 Denver, Utah & Pacific RR
    1889–1908 (used Denver, Marshall & Boulder Ry.)

UNION PACIFIC from Arapahoe County to Denver:
    1870–1880 Kansas Pacific Ry.
    1880–   Union Pacific RR

UNION PACIFIC from Weld County to Denver:
    1909–   Union Pacific RR

UNION PACIFIC from Weld County to Denver:
    1880–1890 Colorado Central RR
    1890–   Union Pacific RR

Some Whistlestops

ANTEES (BN) is shown about two miles northwest of Westminster on a 1924 map.

CELERYVALE (DL&N) is shown about one mile west of Brighton on a 1916 map.

COX (BN) is shown about four miles northeast of Derby on a 1924 map.

Places on the Colorado Prairie

DARLOW (UP) is shown about six miles west of Brighton on a 1920 map.

ENO (BN) is shown about five miles northeast of Derby on 1916 through 1940 maps.

GALLUP (UP) is shown about one mile north of the Thornton site on a railroad map.

KLINK (BN) is shown about five miles east of Brighton on 1909 through 1942 maps.

MAGEE (UP) is shown about three miles east of Aurora on a railroad map.

MANILA (UP) is shown about five miles west of Bennett on a railroad map.

MESA (UP) is shown about six miles west of Watkins on 1909 through 1920 maps.

PATE (BN) is shown about six miles northeast of Adams City on a 1924 map.

PATRON (DL&NW) is shown about two miles west of Hazeltine on a railroad map.

QUINBY STATION (UP) is shown about four miles north of Welby on a railroad map.

ROLLA (UP) is shown about four miles east of Thornton on a railroad map.

SAND CREEK JUNCTION (BN) is shown about one mile southwest of Adams City on 1916 and 1920 maps.

UTAH JUNCTION (BN) is shown about six miles east of Arvada on a 1924 map.

Chapter 4

Arapahoe County

Still on the Map

Aurora
Broadway Estates
Buckley Naval Air Station
Byers
Cherry Hills Village
Cherry Knolls
Cherrywood Village
Columbine
Columbine Valley
Deer Trail
Dream House Acres
Englewood

Glendale
Greenwood Village
Littleton
Lowry Air Force Base
Nob Hill
Peoria
Ridgeview
Sheridan
Southglenn
South Wind
Southwood
Strasburg

Places in the Past

Alexandria
Benham
Bijou Springs

Box Elder
Brooklyn
Cherrylyn

Arapahoe County

Cherry Creek	Nine Mile House
Cherry Valley	Oakesdale
Clark Colony	Petersburg
Coal Creek	Salem
Fisk's	Seventeen Mile House
Hawthorn	Sheridan Park
Hillside	Sullivan
Logantown	Toll Gate
Melvin	Twelve Mile House
Military Park	Wynetka
Montana Diggins	

Some Railroad Tracks

Atchison, Topeka & Santa Fe Railway
Colorado & Southern Railway (two parts)
Denver & Rio Grande Western Railroad

Some Whistlestops

Chatfield	Macrose
Junction	Mooreville
Kenwood	Wolhurst

Still on the Map

AURORA (platted town) is discussed under Adams County.

BROADWAY ESTATES (unincorporated metropolitan area) is located just east of Littleton and is shown on a 1975 map.

ARAPAHOE COUNTY
(Eastern Part)

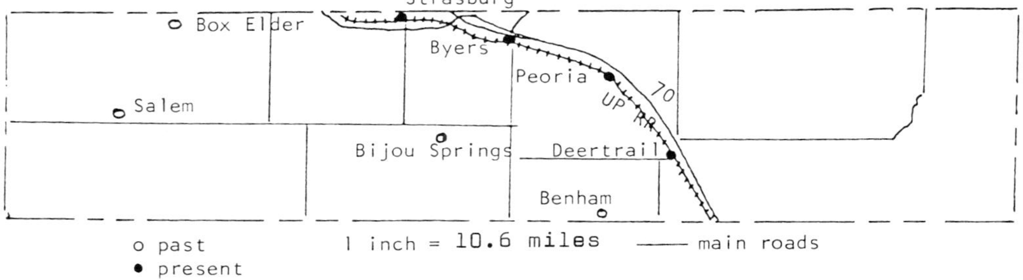

Strasburg
Box Elder
Byers
Peoria
I 70
UP RR
Deertrail
Salem
Bijou Springs
Benham

o past
● present

1 inch = 10.6 miles   ——— main roads

INSERT

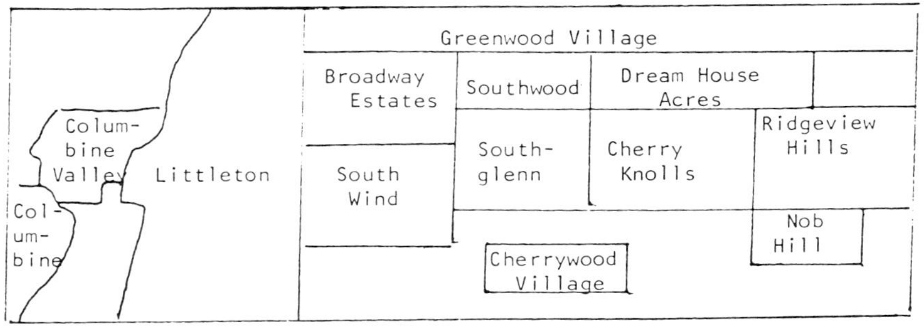

Greenwood Village
Broadway Estates
Southwood
Dream House Acres
Ridgeview Hills
South Wind
Southglenn
Cherry Knolls
Nob Hill
Cherrywood Village
Littleton
Columbine Valley
Columbine

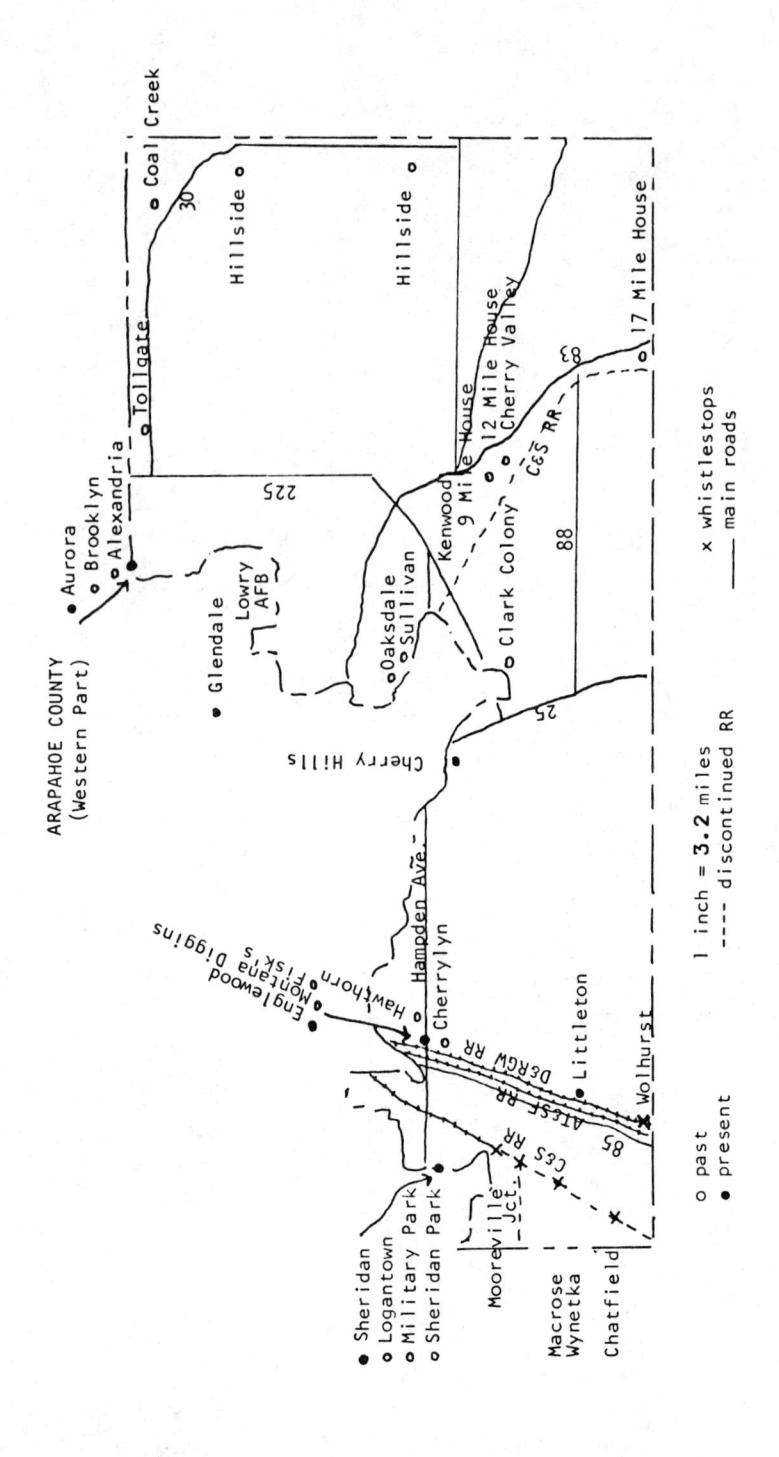

ARAPAHOE COUNTY (Western Part)

- Aurora
- Brooklyn
- Alexandria
- Tollgate
- Coal Creek
- 30
- Hillside
- Hillside
- Hillside
- Glendale
- Lowry AFB
- 225
- Oaksdale
- Sullivan
- Kenwood
- 12 Mile House
- 9 Mile House
- Cherry Valley
- C&S RR
- 83
- 17 Mile House
- Clark Colony
- 88
- 25
- Cherry Hills
- Hampden Ave.
- Englewood
- Montana Diggins
- Hawthorn
- Fisk's
- Cherrylyn
- D&RGW RR
- AT&SF RR
- Littleton
- Wolhurst
- 85
- Sheridan
- Logantown
- Military Park
- Sheridan Park
- C&S RR
- Mooreville Jct.
- Macrose
- Wynetka
- Chatfield

1 inch = 3.2 miles
x whistlestops
—— main roads
---- discontinued RR
o past
• present

Places on the Colorado Prairie

BUCKLEY NAVAL AIR STATION (military installation) was established as a naval air station and bombing range in 1942. Buckley Air Station became the home base for the Colorado Air National Guard.

BYERS (platted town) was established in 1868 by Oliver Wiggins, a former frontier scout, and was first called "Bijou" in reference to a nearby creek. The community of Bijou was renamed "Byers" soon after the Kansas Pacific Railroad laid track through the area in 1870. Byers was named after William Byers, noted editor of the *Rocky Mountain News* in Denver. He was also a land agent for the Kansas Pacific Railroad. A town plat was not filed for Byers until John Fetzer and L. McDonnell did so on May 2, 1889.

CHERRY HILLS VILLAGE (platted town) was named after orchards which were once prevalent in the area. In 1940, the county commissioners zoned the Cherry Hills area for one-half to two and one-half acre homesites; thus, the incorporation of Cherry Hills Village in 1945 led to an exclusive community which emulated Henry Ford's Greenfield Village.

CHERRY KNOLLS (unincorporated metropolitan area) is located just east of Southglenn and is shown on a 1975 map.

CHERRYWOOD VILLAGE (unincorporated metropolitan area) is located just southeast of Littleton and south of Southglenn and is shown on a 1975 map.

COLUMBINE (unincorporated metropolitan area) is located just southwest of Columbine Valley and is shown on a 1975 map.

COLUMBINE VALLEY (platted town) is located just west of Littleton and the Platte River. Columbine Valley incorporated 600 acres in 1959 with a population of about 275. Columbine Valley was platted as an exclusive community.

Arapahoe County

DEER TRAIL (platted town) was named after the many deer which watered nearby. The Kansas Pacific Railroad filed a town plat for Deer Trail on November 29, 1875. Deer Trail has managed to survive many disastrous floods on nearby East Bijou Creek.

DREAM HOUSE ACRES (unincorporated metropolitan area) is located just south of Greenwood Village. It is shown on a 1975 map.

ENGLEWOOD (platted town) was first settled in 1859 by Thomas Skerritt and others. The Englewood area became noted for Fisk Gardens, which was a recreation area. The Englewood area was called "Orchard Place" in reference to the extensive orchards of Jacob Jones who later became Englewood's first mayor. A town plat was filed for Englewood on June 27, 1887, by D. G. Peabody and W. McGavock. The town was named in reference to Englewood, Illinois, which was the hometown of one of the aldermen for the new town.

GLENDALE (platted town) was established when William F. Perkins filed a plat for the town in 1882. Glendale became encircled by Denver, and it incorporated in 1952 to avoid being annexed.

GREENWOOD VILLAGE (platted town) was established in 1950 when residents of the area sought incorporation to deter undersirable housing in the area. Greenwood Village was named after the many trees which once grew in the area.

LITTLETON (platted town) was named after Richard Little who settled in the area sometime in 1862. In 1867, Little and J. C. Lilley started the Rough and Ready Flour Mill, and the success of the mill led Little to file a town plat for Littleton on June 3, 1872. Littleton became the seat of Arapahoe County when Denver withdrew to become a county within itself in 1902; however, official recognition of the county was not bestowed until 1904.

Places on the Colorado Prairie

LOWRY AIR FORCE BASE (military installation) is located between Denver and Arapahoe Counties. It was established in 1938 on land that was donated by the city of Denver. The post-war growth in east Denver and Aurora caused the discontinuation of air traffic at the base, and Lowry is now almost totally a ground training base.

NOB HILL (unincorporated metropolitan area) is located just southeast of Cherry Knolls and is shown on a 1975 map.

PEORIA (railroad post office) is located next to the Union Pacific railroad and about six miles southeast of Byers. The Kansas-Pacific railroad was built to the site of Peoria in 1870; however, the Peoria post office was not started until 1906.

RIDGEVIEW (unincorporated metropolitan area) is located just east of Cherry Knolls and is shown on a 1975 map.

SHERIDAN (platted town) was established by combining several communities which were clustered near Fort Sheridan (now Fort Logan). Isaac McBroom filed a plat for Sheridan on November 18, 1887; its boundaries encompassed Logantown, Military Park, Petersburg, and Sheridan Park. A plat was filed for "The Town of Sheridan" on May 1, 1888, by George Timerman and L. D. Stocking. The land description on the plat placed it just north of Sheridan.

SOUTHGLENN (unincorporated metropolitan area) is located just south of Southwood and is shown on a 1975 map.

SOUTH WIND (unincorporated metropolitan area) is located just south of the southwestern end of Southglenn and is shown on a 1975 map.

SOUTHWOOD (unincorporated metropolitan area) is shown just southwest of Greenwood Village's western portion on a 1975 map.

Arapahoe County

STRASBURG (platted town) is located in both Adams and Arapahoe Counties and is discussed in detail under Adams County.

Places in the Past

ALEXANDRIA (platted town) was located near Aurora in the area that is now the northeast corner of Lowry Air Force Base. A town plat was filed for Alexandria on October 23, 1894, by Henry W. Betts; however, the town did not obtain a post office, and it was not shown on maps.

BENHAM (stage station) was located on the Smoky Hill North stage route about nine miles southwest from the site of Deer Trail. The Benham station was between the Fairmont and Bijou Springs stations.

BIJOU SPRINGS (stage station) was located on the Smoky Hill North stage route about five miles from the site of Byers. Bijou Springs was near West Bijou Creek.

BOX ELDER (stage station) was located on the Smoky Hill North stage route about three miles southeast from the site of Watkins. Box Elder was near Box Elder Creek.

BROOKLYN (platted town) wasn't named in reference to the famed eastern borough. It was named after Henry Brooks who filed a plat for the town on January 16, 1888. Brooklyn didn't obtain a post office, and it was not shown on the maps. Aurora absorbed the community of Brooklyn.

CHERRY CREEK (stage station post office) was operated in conjunction with the Twelve Mile House stage station. The Cherry Creek post office was in operation from 1869 to 1886 and was named in reference to the nearby creek that gained fame in the 1858 gold discovery.

Places on the Colorado Prairie

CHERRYLYN (rural post office) was located south of Englewood and was eventually absorbed by Englewood. The Cherrylyn post office was in operation from 1894 to 1916. The horse-drawn streetcar to Cherrylyn was famous because the horse rode on the streetcar during the downhill portions of the route.

CHERRY VALLEY (stage station) was one of the earlier stage stations on the Smoky Hill South stage route and was the forerunner of Twelve Mile House. The Cherry Valley stage station was located about two miles south of the famous Twelve Mile House.

CLARK COLONY (platted town) was founded by Rufus (Potato) Clark and W. E. Alexander in 1892. The construction of the Arapahoe Ditch encouraged Clark and Alexander to file a plat for Clark Colony on April 1, 1892, and they promoted the area as a potential garden spot; however, Clark Colony never obtained a post office, and it did not reach the maps.

COAL CREEK (stage station) was located between the Box Elder and Toll Gate stations on the Smoky Hill North stage route. Coal Creek was named after a nearby creek.

FISK'S BROADWAY GARDENS (platted town) was named after its founder, Eugene Fisk, and its location on Broadway. The Fisk family was determined to pay homage to the Colorado plant life: Archie Fisk established a pleasure park which was called "Fisk's Garden," and he also filed a plat for Fisk Orchard Place, which was north of Arvada.

HAWTHORN (platted town) was founded by Thomas Fitzgerald who filed a plat for the town on June 3, 1887. Hawthorn never obtained a post office and was absorbed by Englewood.

HILLSIDE (platted town) was located about eight or nine miles southwest of Watkins. A town plat was filed for Hillside on September 12, 1892, by Thomas Laurbie. Hillside didn't obtain a post office. It was not shown on the maps. The location of

Arapahoe County

Hillside wasn't close enough to Denver for Laurbie to capitalize on the land boom near the capital city in the 1890s.

LOGANTOWN (unincorporated metropolitan area) was named after nearby Fort Logan and was incorporated into the town of Sheridan in 1890.

MELVIN (railroad post office) was located next to the Colorado and Southern Railroad through Parker. The Melvin post office was in operation around 1890 and was named after Johnnie Melvin who operated the Twelve Mile House on the Smoky Hill stage route.

MILITARY PARK (unincorporated metropolitan area) was named after nearby Fort Logan and was incorporated into the town of Sheridan in 1890.

MONTANA DIGGINS (place name) was the brief settlement of the St. Charles Company near Little Dry Creek before it relocated in the area that eventually became Denver.

NINE MILE HOUSE (stage junction) was a single cabin near the junction of the Middle Smoky Hill Trail and the Smoky Hill South stage route. The site of Nine Mile House is now covered by Cherry Creek Reservoir.

OAKESDALE (platted town) was a small community just a short distance northwest of where Cherry Creek Dam is now located. A town plat was filed for Oakesdale on June 12, 1890, by J. L. Oakes. The Oakesdale post office was closed in 1905, and the name left the maps shortly afterward.

PETERSBURG (platted town) was one of several communities that were formed into the present town of Sheridan. The town plat for Petersburg was filed on September 20, 1873, by Peter Magnus. Sheridan was formed in 1887.

SALEM (rural post office) was located about seven miles southwest of Watkins. The Salem post office was in operation from 1894 to 1919.

Places on the Colorado Prairie

SEVENTEEN MILE HOUSE (rural tavern) was located on the Smokey Hill South stage route but catered to the local community more than to the stage line. The Seventeen Mile House was named in reference to its distance from Denver and was operated by the Doud family in the 1870s.

SHERIDAN PARK (unincorporated metropolitan area) was named after nearby Fort Sheridan and, in 1890, was incorporated into the town of Sheridan.

SULLIVAN (platted town) was named after Dennis Sullivan, a Denver banker, who promoted the town. A town plat was filed for Sullivan on February 16, 1891, by the Zang Brewing Company and seventeen others. Sullivan was located on the Union Pacific, Denver and Gulf (Colorado and Southern) railroad, but never obtained a post office.

TOLL GATE (stage station) was located on the Fort Morgan Cut-off of the Overland stage route. The Toll Gate station was located next to Eight Mile Creek, and toll was collected for crossing the creek; thus, the name of Eight Mile Creek was changed to Toll Gate Creek.

TWELVE MILE HOUSE (stage station) was located on the Smoky Hill South stage route and was operated by Johnnie Melvin. The Twelve Mile House was noted for its large hotel and barroom. Mr. Melvin provided four white horses for the final part of the stage run into Denver.

WYNETKA (platted town) was located west of Littleton. A town plat was filed for the community on February 6, 1890, by Charles E. Hill and Joseph Bowles. A post office was not listed for Wynetka, and it was not shown on maps; however, the area is still called Wynetka.

Arapahoe County

Some Railroad Tracks

ATCHISON, TOPEKA & SANTA FE from Denver to Douglas County:

    1887–1900 Denver & Santa Fe RR

    1900–   Atchison, Topeka & Santa Fe Ry.

COLORADO & SOUTHERN from Denver to Douglas County:

    1881–1886 Denver & New Orleans RR

    1886–1890 Denver, Texas & Gulf RR

    1890–1898 Union Pacific, Denver & Gulf Ry.

    1898–1936 Colorado & Southern Ry.

COLORADO & SOUTHERN from Denver to Jefferson County:

    1873–1889 Denver, South Park & Pacific Ry.

    1889–1898 Denver, Leadville & Gunnison Ry.

    1898–   Colorado & Southern Ry.

DENVER & RIO GRANDE WESTERN from Denver to Jefferson County:

    1870–1886 Denver & Rio Grande Ry.

    1886–1921 Denver & Rio Grande RR

    1921–   Denver & Rio Grande Western Ry.

Some Whistlestops

CHATFIELD (C&S) is shown about three miles southwest of Littleton on 1892 and 1897 maps.

JUNCTION (C&S) is shown about three miles northwest of Littleton on 1882 and 1884 maps.

KENWOOD (C&S) is shown near the site of present-day Cherry Creek Dam on a 1902 map. Kenwood was named in reference

Places on the Colorado Prairie

to nearby Kenwood Dam which preceded the Cherry Creek Dam in the area.

MACROSE (C&S) is shown about two miles west of Littleton on 1909 through 1920 maps.

MOOREVILLE (C&S) is shown about one mile northwest of Englewood on 1884 and 1892 maps.

WOLHURST (AT&SF) is shown about four miles southwest of Littleton on 1902 through 1927 maps. The Wolhurst estate was owned by Senator E. O. Wolhurst and later by Thomas Walsh, who owned the famous Camp Bird mine near Ouray.

Places to Meet

Leader, Adams County

South of Broomfield, Jefferson County

Chapter 5

Baca County

Still on the Map

Bartlett
Blaine
Campo
Deora
Edler
Lycan
Midway

Pritchett
Springfield
Stonington
Two Buttes
Utleyville
Vilas
Walsh

Places in the Past

Adams
Atlanta
Baker
Boston
Brookfield
Buckeye
Carriso
Carriso Springs

Carrizo
Cimmaron City
Clyde
Corinth
Decatur
Estelene
Graft
Holmes City

Baca County

Joycoy	Pride
Kirkwell	Progress
Kliesen City	Regneir
Konnantz	Richards
Lamport	Rodley
Mathews	Ruff
Maxey	Sand Arroya
Minneapolis	Setonsburg
Monon	Stevenson
Nowlinsville	Viena
Oklarado	Wentworth
Plymouth	

Some Railroad Tracks

Atchison, Topeka & Santa Fe Railway (two parts)

Some Whistlestops

Bisonte	Frick
Harbord	

Still on the Map

BARTLETT (platted town) was started in 1926 when a Santa Fe subsidiary, the Dodge City and Cimmaron Valley Railway, built through the area. A town plat was filed for Bartlett on December 20, 1926, by Melvin H. Frush, and a post office was opened two years later. Bartlett, like so many towns in Baca County, struggled against the drouth of the '30s, and the post office was forced to close in 1938.

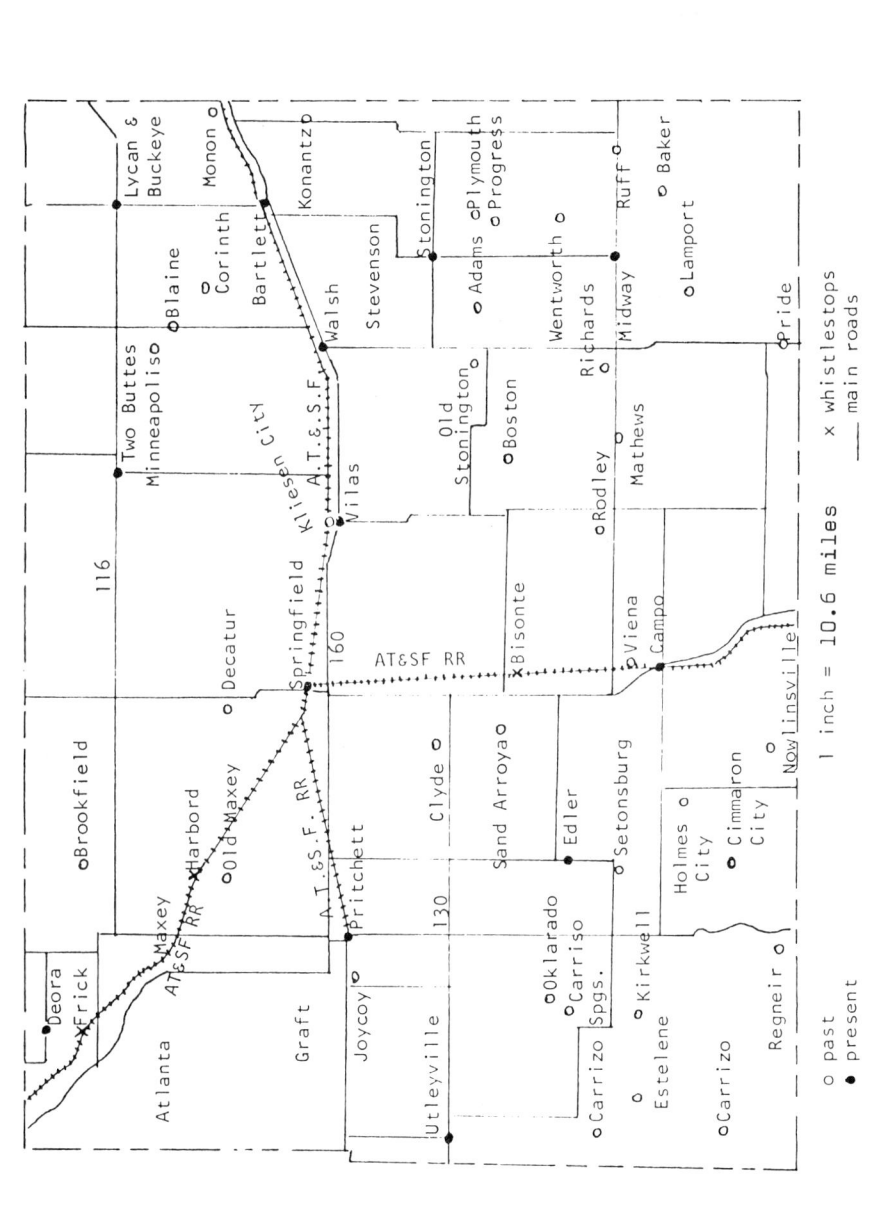

BACA COUNTY

Map of Baca County showing past (o) and present (●) towns, whistlestops (x), and main roads.

Towns and locations shown:
- Deora, Frick, Brookfield, Lycan & Buckeye, Monon
- Atlanta, Maxey, Harbord, Old Maxey, Blaine, Corinth, Bartlett, Konantz
- Two Buttes, Minneapolis, Decatur, Springfield, Kliesen City, Walsh, Stevenson, Stonington
- Graft, Pritchett, Vilas, Adams, Plymouth, Progress
- Joycoy, Clyde, Old Stonington, Wentworth, Midway, Ruff
- Utleyville, Sand Arroyoa, Bisonte, Boston, Richards, Baker, Lamport
- Oklarado, Carriso, Edler, Setonsburg, Rodley, Mathews
- Carrizo Spgs., Kirkwell, Holmes City, Cimmaron City, Viena, Campo
- Estelene, Carrizo, Regneir, Nowlinsville, Pride

Railroads: AT&SF RR, A.T.&S.F. RR

Roads: 116, 160, 130

1 inch = 10.6 miles

x whistlestops
— main roads
o past
● present

Baca County

BLAINE (rural post office) followed the land boom town of Minneapolis in the area. The Blaine post office was in operation from 1900 to 1939 and was named after the Blaine family. Blaine has remained as a rural landmark on Colorado State Highway 51.

CAMPO (platted town) was on the map for fourteen years before a plat was filed for the town. The Campo post office was opened in 1913. The name "Campo" means "field" in Spanish. A town plat for Campo was filed on September 16, 1927, by George W. Petty, but the major impetus for the area came from the Dodge City and Cimmaron Valley Railway which was built to Campo in 1937. Campo is almost a lone citadel in the sparsely populated area south of Springfield.

DEORA (rural post office) is located about four miles northeast of Frick. The Deora post office has been in operation since 1920. The name "Deora" means "of gold" in Spanish.

EDLER (rural post office) is located about fifteen miles northwest of Campo. The Edler post office was in operation from 1916 to 1948.

LYCAN (rural post office) is located on Colorado State Highway 116 and has maintained postal service since 1913. Lycan was named after the Lycan family who settled in the area during 1910.

MIDWAY (way-stop) is located on Colorado State Highway 51 and is about half-way between Stonington and the Oklahoma border.

PRITCHETT (platted town) is the terminus of the Santa Fe Railroad in the area. The railroad reached the site of Pritchett in 1926, and a town plat was filed for Pritchett on November 23, 1926, by J. H. Keefe. Pritchett was named after a railroad official, Henry Pritchett.

Places on the Colorado Prairie

SPRINGFIELD (platted town), like so many towns in Baca County, was a result of land promotion in the 1880s. A town plat was filed for Springfield on April 15, 1887, by the Windsor Town Company. Springfield was named after Springfield, Missouri, which was the hometown of Andrew Harrison who owned the site. Springfield was made county seat when Baca County was formed in 1889, and it was able to survive the drouth of the '90s when most other places in the country left the map.

STONINGTON (platted town) was named after Stonington, Massachusetts, which was the hometown of many settlers in the area. Stonington managed to survive the drouth of the '90s; however, in 1909 the town was moved six miles northeast of the original site.

TWO BUTTES (platted town) was named after the nearby buttes which dominate the otherwise barren landscape. A town plat was filed for Two Buttes on October 20, 1909, by A. N. Parrish who represented the Two Buttes Land Company. Parrish, a Lamar banker, was capitalizing on the nearby dam and recreation area when he filed the plat for Two Buttes. The town of Two Buttes was incorporated in 1911 but never attained the growth that usually accompanies incorporation.

UTLEYVILLE (rural post office) began postal operations in 1917. It is located on United States Highway 160, which runs from Kansas to Trinidad.

VILAS (platted town) began during the Baca County land boom. A town plat was filed for Vilas on July 18, 1887, by Martin D. Ryan, and the town was named after Senator Vilas of Wisconsin. Vilas and the nearby community of Boston were bitter rivals during the land boom, and Vilas lost several businesses to the flourishing Boston; however, Vilas made it through the drouth of the 1890s, but Boston disappeared from the map.

WALSH (platted town) grew up with the Santa Fe Railroad in the area. A Santa Fe subsidiary built into the site of Walsh in

45

1926, and a town plat was filed for Walsh on September 23, 1926, by the Santa Fe Land Company. Walsh was named after a baggage agent for the Railroad.

Places in the Past

ADAMS (platted town) preceded the original Stonington in the area; however, Adams did not have a post office, and it was not shown on the maps. A town plat was filed for Adams in August, 1887, by Hobart P. Vermilye.

ATLANTA (rural post office) was one of the more noted land-boom communities in Baca County. The Atlanta post office began in 1887 and was named after the hometown of many settlers in the area, Atlanta, Georgia. Atlanta was a vital link in the chain of communities between Springfield and Las Animas; for that reason, Atlanta was almost able to survive the drouth in the early '90s. The Atlanta post office closed in 1899.

BAKER (rural post office) was located southeast of Stonington, and the Baker post office was in operation from 1915 to 1921.

BOSTON (platted town) began and ended in the land boom. A town plat was filed for Boston on May 13, 1887, by John Beatty. The town was named after Boston, Massachusetts, which was the hometown of many settlers in the area. The similarity between Boston and other land-boom towns in Baca County ended with the manner in which the name was chosen—Boston was a lawless town and entertained the infamous Jennings gang with five saloons. The Boston post office was discontinued in 1893, along with most of the other activity in the area.

BROOKFIELD (platted town) was another Massachusetts contribution to the land boom. A town plat was filed for Brookfield on August 24, 1888, by the Brookfield Town Company, and the town was named after Brookfield, Massachusetts, which was the hometown of many settlers in the area. The Brookfield post office lasted until 1902.

Places on the Colorado Prairie

BUCKEYE (highway way-stop) was located on State Highway 116 just west of the Kansas border and is shown on a 1927 map.

CARRISO (platted town) started with a post office in 1887, and a town plat was filed for Carriso by E. C. Murray on October 3, 1888. The Carriso post office was discontinued in 1895. Carriso was about the only town in southwest Baca County during the 1880s, except for nearby Carriso Springs.

CARRISO SPRINGS (platted town) was located about six miles southwest of Carriso, and a town plat was filed for Carriso Springs on February 10, 1888, by William McClane. The Carriso Springs post office closed in 1890, but the name stayed on the map into the 1900s. The Carriso Springs area became known as "Tubs" because of the large wooden tanks that were used for watering livestock by the local ranchers. In early Baca County, most of the wagon roads in the western part of the county converged at either Atlanta or Carriso Springs.

CARRIZO (rural post office) is sometimes confused with the earlier town of Carriso, but was an entirely separate place. Carrizo was located about six miles south of Carriso Springs and was preceded in the area by the Townsite post office which operated from 1900 to 1902. The Carrizo post office was in operation from 1907 to 1916. Carrizo Creek was near Carrizo.

CIMMARON CITY (platted town) was named after the nearby Cimmaron River. Cimmaron City should have been the scene of a western saga, but it wasn't much more than a paper plat. C. H. Anderson filed the plat for Cimmaron City on March 5, 1927, and that was about the extent of it.

CLYDE (rural post office) was located about eight miles southwest of Springfield, and the Clyde post office was in operation from 1913 until the 1920s.

CORINTH (rural post office) was located about two miles east of Minneapolis. The Corinth post office was in operation for a

Baca County

short time in 1887; then the post office was moved to nearby Minneapolis. Corinth could have been the forerunner of Minneapolis; however, Minneapolis and Corinth are both shown on an 1897 map.

DECATUR (rural post office) was another of the "come and gone" post offices which sprang up during the Baca County land boom. The Decatur post office was in operation from 1888 to 1891.

ESTELENE (rural post office) should have gained some fame because it wasn't started during the land boom in Baca County. The Estelene post office was in operation from 1910 to 1927 and was located southeast of Utleyville.

GRAFT (rural post office) was located near Pritchett. The Graft post office was in operation from 1916 to 1935.

HOLMES CITY (platted town) began in 1887 when George Tromilitz filed a plat for the town on October 25. It appears that the fastest way for a town to disappear in Baca County was to add "City" to the name—Holmes City, Cimmaron City, and Kliesen City were never much more than town plats.

JOYCOY (rural post office) preceded Pritchett in the area, and the Joycoy post office was in operation from 1915 to 1927. When the railroad terminated at Pritchett, Joycoy came to an end.

KIRKWELL (rural post office) was located in southwestern Baca County and was in operation from 1917 to 1921; however, Kirkwell stayed on the map into the '40s.

KLIESEN CITY (platted town) was platted next to Vilas, and the plat was filed by W. T. Hurst on March 23, 1927. Kliesen City did not obtain a post office, and it was not shown on the map.

KONNANTZ (rural post office) was located near the Kansas state line and the site of the old Texas cattle trail. The Konnantz post office was in operation from 1898 to 1917.

Places on the Colorado Prairie

LAMPORT (rural post office) was located about eighteen miles southeast of Stonington, and the Lamport post office was in operation from 1908 to 1927.

MATHEWS (place name) is shown about eight miles northwest of Lamport on a 1902 map. Mathews did not have a post office and probably served as a farm or ranch landmark on the road from Ruff to Oklahoma.

MAXEY (rural post office) was located on the wagon road from Springfield to Atlanta which later became State Highway 101. The Maxey post office was in operation from 1889 to 1920.

MINNEAPOLIS (platted town) was one of the larger land-boom communities in Baca County during the 1880s and 1890s. A town plat was filed for Minneapolis on January 23, 1888, and the Minneapolis post office began in 1887. Minneapolis was an outgrowth of Butte City which was short-lived, and the town was named after Minneapolis, Minnesota, which was the hometown of many settlers in the area. Minneapolis struggled through the devastating drouth of the early 1890s, but the Minneapolis post office was discontinued in 1899 along with most of the activity in the area.

MONON (rural post office) was located next to the Kansas border. The Monon post office was in operation from 1901 to 1918.

NOWLINSVILLE (rural post office) was located southwest of Campo, and the Nowlinsville post office was in operation from 1916 to 1919.

OKLARADO (rural post office) was obviously named in reference to its location. The Oklarado post office was in operation from 1916 to 1935.

PLYMOUTH (place name) is shown on an 1892 map and has the earmarks of a land-boom community; but it didn't have a post office, and it was not shown on earlier maps. Since many of the

Baca County

communities in the land boom were named in reference to towns in Massachusetts, Plymouth was perhaps settled also by a group from the Bay state.

PRIDE (rural post office) was located near the Cimmaron River, and the Pride post office was in operation from 1914 to 1920. (There wasn't a "Prejudice" on the map.)

PROGRESS (rural post office) was located on the road to Stonington from Kansas, and the Progress post office was in operation from 1888 to 1895. (Now we have Pride and Progress.)

REGNEIR (rural post office) was located near the Colorado-Oklahoma state line. The Regneir post office was in operation from 1900 into the 1920s.

RICHARDS (rural post office) was located near the south fork of the Cimmaron River, and the Richards post office was in operation from 1912 to 1938.

RODLEY (rural post office) was located on the road from Vilas to Campo, and the Rodley post office was in operation from 1910 to 1937.

RUFF (rural post office) was located on the old wagon road from Progress to Oklahoma, and the Ruff post office was in operation from 1889 to 1896. Ruff was a typical land boom post office—lasting only a few years.

SAND ARROYA (rural post office) was named after the nearby arroya which dominates the landscape in the area. The Sand Arroya post office was in operation from 1915 to 1920.

SETONSBURG (rural post office) was first called "Seton" and was located southwest of Springfield. The Setonsburg post office was in operation from 1915 to 1920.

STEVENSON (rural post office) was born of the land boom and stayed on the map until the turn of the century; however, the

Places on the Colorado Prairie

Stevenson post office was in operation during a part of 1888 only.

VIENA (place name) is shown about twenty miles southwest of Vilas on an 1897 map. Viena did not have a post office, but is shown in the same location as Ruff.

WENTWORTH (rural post office) was located a short distance off State Highway 89, and the Wentworth post office was in operation from 1911 to 1921. Wentworth managed to stay on the map into the '40s.

Some Railroad Tracks

ATCHISON, TOPEKA & SANTA FE from Bent County to Oklahoma:
    1937–   Dodge City & Cimmaron Valley Ry.

ATCHISON, TOPEKA & SANTA FE from Kansas to Pritchett:
    1937–   Dodge City & Cimmaron Valley Ry.

Some Whistlestops

BISONTE (AT&SF) is shown about ten miles south of Springfield on 1956 and 1968 maps.

FRICK (AT&SF) is shown about seventeen miles northwest of Pritchett on 1956 and 1968 maps.

HARBORD (AT&SF) is shown about ten miles northwest of Springfield on a 1968 map.

Places to Live

Near Eastonville, El Paso County

Elizabeth, Elbert County

Chapter 6

Bent County

Still on the Map

Caddoa
Fort Lyon (1st)
Fort Lyon (2nd)
Four Corners
Hasty

Las Animas
McClave
Ninaview
Prowers
Toonerville

Places in the Past

Alkalai
Boggsville
Fredonia
Gem
Harbourville
Maine Ranch

Medford Springs
Mitchell Camp
Opal
Rixey
Rule

Some Railroad Tracks

Arkansas Valley Railway
Atchison, Topeka & Santa Fe Railway (three parts)

Bent County

Some Whistlestops

Beethurst	Lubers
Big Bend	Marlman
Cornelia	Martin
Gilpin	Melonfield
Hadley	Player
Hilton	Riverdale
Keesee	Ruxton
Kreybill	Waveland

Still on the Map

CADDOA (platted town) was named after nearby Caddoa Creek and the Caddoa Indians. A town plat was filed for Caddoa on May 8, 1888, by the Caddoa Town and Land Company. Caddoa consisted of three houses when John Prowers moved to the site in 1863. The site of Caddoa was flooded when the John Martin Reservoir was built in the 1940s, and the few houses and post office were moved a few miles to the south. The Caddoa post office was closed in 1958.

FORT LYON (FIRST) AND BENT'S SECOND FORT (military post) was established when William Bent abandoned Bent's Fort and moved forty miles downstream to establish a new fort in 1853. Bent's second fort was located north across the river from Prowers. In 1859, Bent leased his fort to the federal government, and the fort was renamed "Fort Fountleroy," then "Fort Wise," and finally "Fort Lyon" after General Lyon who was the first Union general to be killed in the Civil War. The Arkansas River began to cut away the bank near Fort Lyon, and the fort was moved twenty miles upstream in 1866.

55

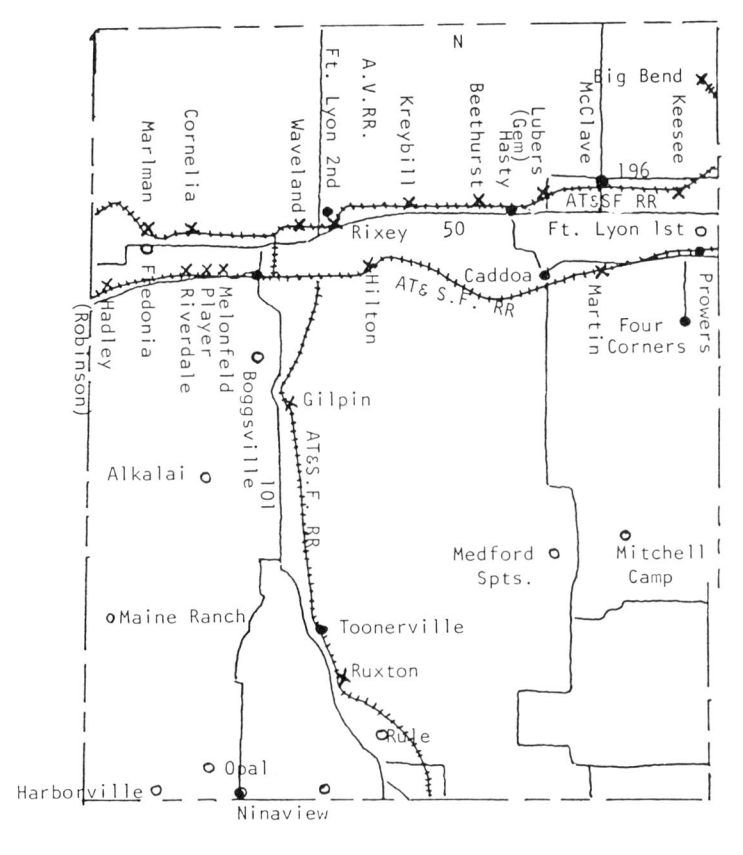

Bent County

FORT LYON (SECOND) (military post) was established in 1866 about five miles northeast of Las Animas. The second Fort Lyon was then a United States Army Post, later a Naval tuberculosis hospital, and since 1934 a Veterans Administration facility.

FOUR CORNERS CROSSING (place name) is shown about four miles south of Prowers on a 1968 map.

HASTY (platted town) was named after Lou Hasty, who was a pioneer in the area. A town plat was filed for Hasty on November 1, 1907, by Arthur Beymer. The town of Hasty did not grow to any size, but did experience a brief revival when the John Martin Reservoir was built nearby in the 1940s.

LAS ANIMAS (platted town) was named after the Las Animas River and was first located about six miles to the east of the present Las Animas. The first Las Animas was established in 1869. When the Arkansas Valley Railway built a line from Kit Carson to six miles west of Las Animas for the Kansas Pacific Railroad in 1873, the town of West Las Animas was established at the junction of the railroad and the Arkansas. A town plat was filed for West Las Animas on April 18, 1885, by a person unnamed on the plat, and the town was renamed "Las Animas" in 1886.

MCCLAVE (platted town) was named after B. T. McClave who filed a plat on October 7, 1907. B. T. McClave was instrumental in the development of Bent County. The major reason for the existence of McClave to date has been the McClave family.

NINAVIEW (rural post office) was located about thirty miles south of Las Animas, and the Ninaview post office was in operation from 1915 to 1965. Ninaview was named after the view that Nina Jones enjoyed from her home. Nina Jones was the wife of T. B. Jones, on whose ranch the post office was located.

PROWERS (railroad post office) was named after John Prowers who was instrumental in the growth of the Arkansas Valley. Prowers is located about ten miles east of Caddoa and next to the Santa Fe railroad. Prowers was first called "Meadows."

Places on the Colorado Prairie

TOONERVILLE (recreation site) is located about twenty-two miles southeast of Las Animas and was named in reference to the mythical town in the newspaper cartoon about Fontaine Fox. Toonerville was established in the 1930s and was the site of dances, baseball games, and other entertainment. Before the drouth, people flocked to Toonerville in such numbers that a tramway to the site was under definite consideration.

Some Places in the Past

ALKALAI (stage station) was located about fourteen miles southwest of Las Animas and on the Purgatoire stage route of the Santa Fe Trail. Albert Perry was the station master at Alkalai. The Alkalai post office was in operation from 1874 to 1875.

BOGGSVILLE (early community) was located about three miles southeast of the site of the present Las Animas. Boggsville was named after Thomas Boggs who founded the community, and was the home of Kit Carson and John Prowers. Thomas Boggs was noted as the father of the sheep industry in Bent County, and he later became the first sheriff in Bent County.

FREDONIA (rural post office) was located about six miles west of Las Animas. The Fredonia post office was in operation from 1892 to 1900.

GEM (railroad post office) was located about four miles west of McClave and next to the Santa Fe railroad. The Gem post office was in operation from 1907 to 1913 and was established by a Mr. Flynn (or Flinn) who took part in the Colorado gold rush. The railroad station at Gem is shown as "Lubers."

HARBOURVILLE (rural post office) was located about eight miles southwest of Ninaview. The Harbourville post office operated from 1915 to 1925.

Bent County

MAINE RANCH (rural post office) was located about twenty miles southwest of Las Animas. The Maine Ranch post office was in operation from 1872 to 1875. Maine Ranch could have been the next stop after Alkalai on the Purgatoire stage route.

MEDFORD SPRINGS (rural post office) was located about eighteen miles south of Caddoa. The Medford Springs post office was in operation from 1916 to 1922.

MITCHELL CAMP (place name) is shown about fifteen miles southeast of Caddoa on a 1916 map.

OPAL (rural post office) was located about three miles northwest of Ninaview. The Opal post office was in operation from 1913 to 1923.

RIXEY (platted town) was platted just south of the new Fort Lyon. The town plat for Rixey was filed on May 9, 1908, by E. C. Howe; however, Rixey never obtained a post office.

RULE (rural post office) was located about eight miles northwest of Opal. The Rule post office was in operation from 1909 to 1921.

Some Railroad Tracks

ARKANSAS VALLEY from Kiowa County to Otero County:
    1873–1878 Arkansas Valley Ry.

ATCHISON, TOPEKA & SANTA FE from Prowers County to Otero County:
  Prowers County to Keesee:
    1906–1912 Arkansas Valley Ry.
    1912–   Atchison, Topeka & Santa Fe Ry.
  Keesee to Otero County:
    1908–   Atchison, Topeka & Santa Fe Ry.

Prowers County to Big Bend:
1908– Atchison, Topeka & Santa Fe Ry.

ATCHISON, TOPEKA & SANTA FE from Las Animas to Baca County:
1937– Dodge City & Cimmaron Valley Ry.

ATCHISON, TOPEKA & SANTA FE from Prowers County to Otero County:
1875–1900 Pueblo & Arkansas Valley RR
1900– Atchison, Topeka & Santa Fe Ry.

Some Whistlestops

BEETHURST (AT&SF) is shown about five miles west of Hasty on 1909 through 1968 maps.

BIG BEND (AT&SF) is shown about five miles northwest of Wiley on 1909 through 1956 maps.

CORNELIA (AT&SF) is shown about three miles east of Marlman on 1909 through 1920 maps.

GILPIN (AT&SF) is shown about nine miles south of Las Animas on a 1968 map.

HADLEY (AT&SF) is shown about nine miles southwest of Las Animas on 1916 through 1927 maps. Hadley was preceded by Robinson in the area.

HILTON (AT&SF) is shown about seven miles east of Las Animas on 1909 through 1920 maps.

KEESEE (AT&SF) is shown about three miles east of McClave on 1909 through 1968 maps. Keesee was named after a local rancher.

Bent County

KREYBILL (AT&SF) is shown about four miles west of Beethurst on 1909 through 1920 maps.

LUBERS (AT&SF) is shown about two miles northeast of Hasty on a 1968 map. The post office at Lubers was called "Gem."

MARLMAN (AT&SF) is shown about four miles northwest of Las Animas on 1909 through 1920 maps.

MARTIN (AT&SF) is shown about three miles southwest of McClave on 1909 through 1920 maps.

MELONFIELD (AT&SF) is shown about three miles west of Las Animas on 1909 through 1916 maps.

PLAYER (AT&SF) is shown about four miles west of Las Animas on a 1902 map.

RIVERDALE (AT&SF) is shown about six miles west of Las Animas on 1909 through 1920 maps.

RUXTON (AT&SF) is shown about three miles southeast of Toonerville on a 1968 map.

WAVELAND (AT&SF) is shown about two miles north of Las Animas on 1909 through 1927 maps.

Places to Keep

Fort Morgan, Morgan County

Broomfield, Boulder County

Chapter 7

Boulder County

Still on the Map

Boulder
Broomfield
Eldorado Springs
Hygiene
Lafayette
Longmont
Louisville
Lyons
Marshall
Niwot
Superior
Valmont

Places in the Past

Altona
Boone's
Burlington
Canfield
Capitol Hill
Clarkston
Davidson
Fort Chambers
Irvington
Lakeside
Langford
Modoc
Noland
Northrop
Pella
Ryssby
Saint Vrain

Boulder County

Some Railroad Tracks

Burlington Northern Railroad (three parts)
Chicago, Burlington & Quincy Railroad
Colorado & Southern Railway (four parts)
Denver & Interurban Railroad (two parts)
Union Pacific
Union Pacific, Denver & Gulf Railroad

Some Whistlestops

Boettcher	Highland
Chapman	Liggett
Clifton	Mitchell
Dixons Mill	Tower Junction
Downer	Ward
Eversman	Whiterock
Fisher	

Still on the Map

BOULDER (platted town) was founded by Captain Thomas Aikens and his party of Nebraska gold-seekers in 1858, and was first called "Boulder City." In spite of the warnings by Chief Niwot, an Arapahoe Indian chief who was later involved in the Sand Creek Massacre, the tiny group from Nebraska established a post office, platted their community, and built their houses with some degree of permanence. Boulder was made County Seat of Boulder County when that county was formed in 1861. Both Boulder and Boulder County were named after the many large boulders near the town of Boulder. A town plat was filed for Boulder in 1859 and again on June 20, 1868, by a person unnamed on the plat. The construction of Colorado University in Boulder began in 1875.

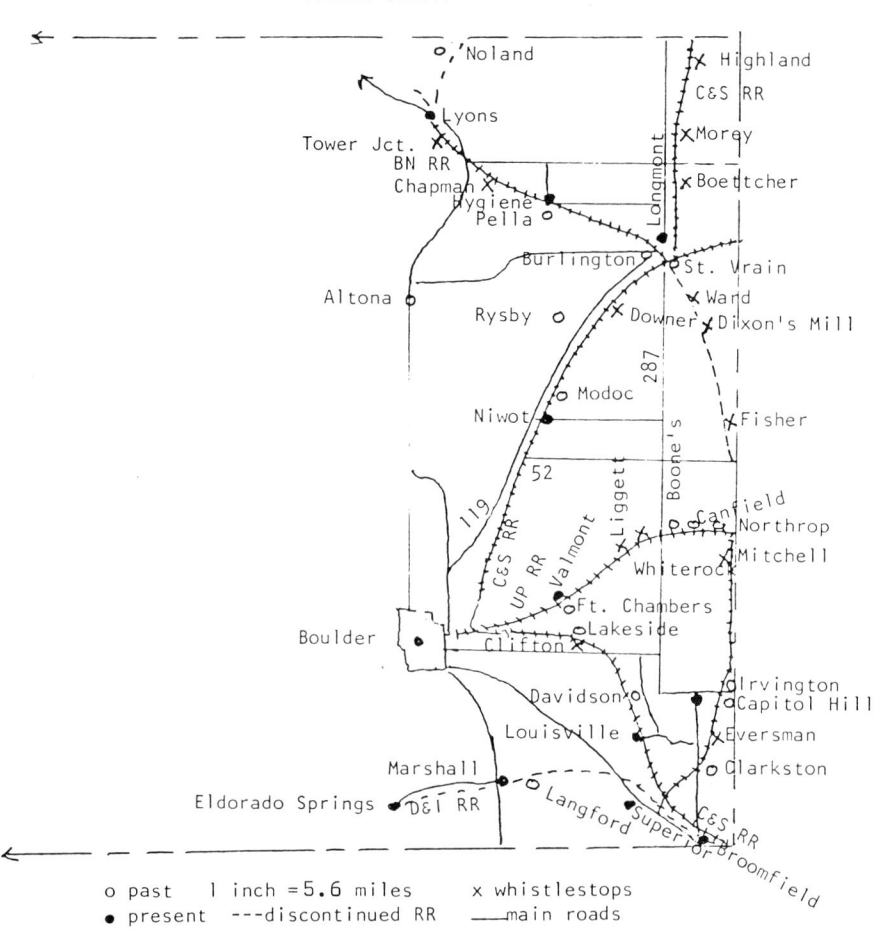

BOULDER COUNTY

o past　　1 inch = 5.6 miles　　x whistlestops
● present　---discontinued RR　___main roads

Boulder County

BROOMFIELD (platted town) originated as a stop on the Denver, Utah and Pacific railroad and was named in reference to the abundant broomcorn in the area. The Broomfield post office was established in 1890, but a town plat was not filed for the town until more than thirty years later. The Adolph J. Zang Investment Company filed a plat for Broomfield on August 21, 1923. Broomfield was incorporated in 1961 as a result of the postwar building boom in the area.

ELDORADO SPRINGS (platted town) was named after the famed "Eldorado" and springs in the area. The Hawthorne post office was established at the Eldorado Springs site in 1906, and a town plat was filed for Eldorado Springs on June 25, 1908, by the Moffat Lakes Resort Company. Eldorado Springs attracted many who built summer cottages at the foot of South Boulder Canyon, and the Eldorado Springs swimming pool became a major recreational facility in the area.

HYGIENE (railroad post office) is located next to the Burlington railroad and about five miles northwest of Longmont. Hygiene was named after the Hygiene Health Sanitarium which was established in the area by Jacob S. Flory in the 1880s. The Hygiene post office has been in operation since 1883. Many of the residents of nearby Pella moved to Hygiene when the Denver, Utah and Pacific railroad was extended to the Lyons quarry in 1885.

LAFAYETTE (platted town) began as a coal-mining community and was named after Lafayette Miller on whose land coal was found in 1884. A town plat was filed for Lafayette on January 5, 1888, by Mary Miller, wife of Lafayette Miller. The Denver, Marshall and Boulder railroad was built to Lafayette in 1888, and the town was incorporated in 1890.

LONGMONT (platted town) began as a colony town in the early 1870s and was named after Long's Peak. The Chicago-Colorado Colony, with Reverend Robert Collyer as president, selected a townsite next to the Saint Vrain River in 1871. Seth Terry, of the Chicago-Colorado Colony, filed a town plat for Longmont on February 26, 1872. The Colony filed a plat for the Chicago-

Places on the Colorado Prairie

Colorado Colony five months after the Longmont plat, but the name of Longmont prevailed for the town. Longmont became the center of a rich agricultural area, and the Great Western Sugar Company built a factory at Longmont in 1903.

LOUISVILLE (platted town) was named after Louis Nawatny who filed a plat for the town. C. C. Welch discovered coal in the Louisville area during 1877, but it was Louis Nawatny who led the first coal boring expedition on Welch's discovery. A town plat was filed for Louisville on October 24, 1878, by Louis Nawatny. Louisville has become well known for the many Italian restaurants in the town.

LYONS (platted town) was named after the Lyons family who was instrumental in developing the nearby sandstone quarry. The red sandstone from the quarry near Lyons was used in many buildings on the University of Colorado campus. A town plat was filed for Lyons in July 25, 1882, by the Evans Townsite and Quarry Company.

MARSHALL (railroad post office) was named after Joseph M. Marshall who developed a coal mine in the area. The Marshall post office was in operation from 1878 to 1880, from 1892 to 1893, from 1895 to 1899 under the name of "Langford," and from 1899 to 1942 under the name of "Gorham." The Denver, Marshall and Boulder Railroad was built to Marshall in 1885 and was discontinued from Boulder to Superior in the 1930s.

NIWOT (platted town) was named in reference to Chief Niwot, Arapahoe Indian chief, who greeted the first goldseekers to the Boulder area in 1858. Chief Niwot, or "Left Hand," was mistakenly reported killed in the famous Sand Creek Massacre of 1864, but lived to become the leading chief of the Southern Arapahoes. A town plat which embraced an unusual amount of land was filed for Niwot on March 30, 1875, by Ambrose Murray, Jr. and Porter Hinman; however, Niwot never reached the proportions indicated on the town plat.

Boulder County

SUPERIOR (platted town) was named after the nearby Superior coal mine which was named after Superior, Wisconsin. A town plat was filed for Superior on August 19, 1895, by William Hake, and the Superior post office opened a year later. The small coal-mining town of Superior was incorporated in 1904. The fortunes of Superior followed the decline of the coal industry after World War II, and the Superior post office was eventually discontinued.

VALMONT (railroad post office) began as one of the leading communities in Boulder County and was larger than Boulder in the 1860s; however, the success of Boulder lessened Valmont's role in the area. The Valmont post office was located next to the Union Pacific railroad and was in operation from 1865 to 1901. Valmont was named after nearby buttes.

Places in the Past

ALTONA (rural post office) was located at the mouth of Left Hand Canyon and was a supply center to the mining camps up the canyon. The Altona post office was in operation from 1879 to 1916.

BOONE'S (stage station) was located on the Overland stage route from Denver to Virginia Vale and next to Boulder Creek. Boone's Station was an intermediate station between Church's Station near the site of Broomfield and Saint Vrain Station near the site of Longmont.

BURLINGTON (rural post office) was located about one mile west of the site of Longmont, and the Burlington post office was in operation from 1862 to 1873. Burlington preceded Longmont in the area.

CANFIELD (platted town) was named in reference to the Canfield brothers who owned coal mines in the rich area near Canfield. A town plat was filed for Canfield on December 30, 1875, by

Places on the Colorado Prairie

William Wise and others. The Canfield post office was established in 1878 and discontinued in 1906.

CAPITOL HILL (platted town) was platted about one mile southeast of Lafayette, and the plat for Capitol Hill was filed on August 27, 1907, by the Colorado Coal Mining Company. Capitol Hill did not obtain a post office, and it was not shown on the map.

CLARKSTON (platted town) was named after C. A. Clark who filed a plat for the town on May 29, 1897. Clarkston was platted next to the Denver, Utah and Pacific railroad; however, Clarkston did not obtain a post office. It was not shown on the map.

DAVIDSON (platted town) was named after William Davidson who filed a plat for the town on July 31, 1874. William Davidson was president of the Davidson Coal and Iron Mining Company which developed coal-mining properties in the area. The Davidson post office closed in 1878, four years after the plat was filed for the town.

FORT CHAMBERS (military fort) was established just below Valmont during the uprising of Indians in the 1860s. Captain David Nichols was commissioned to recruit and train some one hundred men for protection against the uprising. Captain Nichol's detachment became noted for its victory over Chief Big Wolf and for its participation in the ill-famed Sand Creek Massacre.

IRVINGTON (platted town) was named after the Irvington Coal and Land Company which filed a plat for the town on October 5, 1905. Irvington was shown on the map, but it did not obtain a post office.

LAKESIDE (platted town) was platted next to the Colorado and Southern Railroad between Broomfield and Boulder and was named after its location. A town plat was filed for Lakeside in July of 1923, by Andrew Anderson; however, Lakeside did not obtain a post office, and it was not shown on the map.

LANGFORD (railroad post office) was located just east of Marshall on the Denver, Marshall and Boulder Railroad. The Langford post office was in operation at the Langford site from 1881 to 1892, when it was moved to Marshall. The Marshall post office closed in 1893 and reopened under the name of "Langford" in 1895. The Langford post office at Marshall had its name changed to "Gorham" in 1899.

MODOC (railroad post office) was located on the Colorado Central railroad and about one mile northeast of Niwot. The Modoc post office was in operation from 1874 to 1879, when it was moved to Niwot.

NOLAND (platted town) was located near the stone quarries which were developed northeast of Lyons. A town plat was filed for Noland on August 26, 1890, by E. C. Cox, and the Stone Mountain railroad was built to the area in the same year. The Noland post office opened in 1890 and closed in 1901.

NORTHROP (platted town) was platted just west of Erie, and the town plat was filed on February 7, 1888, by Reid Northrop, who named the town after himself. The town of Northrop was shown on the map, but it did not obtain a post office.

PELLA (rural post office) was named after Pella, Iowa, which was the hometown of many residents in the area. The Pella post office was in operation from 1871 to 1885. Many of the residents of Pella moved to Hygiene when the railroad was built to Hygiene instead of to Pella in 1885.

RYSSBY (Swedish community) was located about six miles southwest of Longmont and was founded in 1872 by a group from Ryssby Parish in Smoland, Sweden. The residents of Ryssby maintained their native customs and were noted for their festivals.

SAINT VRAIN (platted town) was named in reference to the nearby Saint Vrain River. The town plat for Saint Vrain was filed on June 11, 1887, by William Suydarn. The town of Saint Vrain was platted just south from the site of the Saint Vrain stage station which was located on the Overland stage route. The Saint Vrain stage station was built by Alonzo Allen. The town of Saint Vrain never obtained a post office.

Some Railroad Tracks

BURLINGTON NORTHERN from Weld County to Burns Junction:
1889–1908 Denver, Utah & Pacific RR
1908–1970 Chicago, Burlington & Quincy RR
1970– Burlington Northern RR

BURLINGTON NORTHERN from Longmont to Weld County:
1878–1880 Longmont & Erie RR
1881–1884 Denver, Longmont & Northwestern RR
1884–1908 Denver, Utah & Pacific RR
1908–1970 Chicago, Burlington & Quincy RR
1970– Burlington Northern RR

BURLINGTON NORTHERN from Lyons to Longmont:
1885–1908 Denver, Utah & Pacific RR
1908–1970 Chicago, Burlington & Quincy RR
1970– Burlington Northern RR

CHICAGO, BURLINGTON & QUINCY from Larimer County to Tower Junction:
1888–1908 Denver, Utah & Pacific RR
1908–1918 Chicago, Burlington & Quincy RR

COLORADO & SOUTHERN from Longmont to Jefferson County:
1873–1890 Colorado Central RR
1890–1898 Union Pacific, Denver & Gulf Ry.
1898– Colorado & Southern Ry.
    1888 (discontinued between Burns Junction and Jefferson County)

Boulder County

COLORADO & SOUTHERN from Larimer County to Longmont:
    1877–1890 Colorado Central RR
    1890–1898 Union Pacific, Denver & Gulf Ry.
    1898–   Colorado & Southern Ry.

COLORADO & SOUTHERN from Louisville to Lafayette:
    1888–1890 Denver, Marshall & Boulder Ry.
    1890–1898 Union Pacific, Denver & Gulf Ry.
    1898–   Colorado & Southern Ry.
    1951 (discontinued except for a two-mile spur)

COLORADO & SOUTHERN from Boulder to Jefferson County:
    1885–1890 Denver, Marshall & Boulder Ry.
    1890–1898 Union Pacific, Denver & Gulf Ry.
    1898–   Colorado & Southern Ry.
    1930s (discontinued from Boulder to Superior)

DENVER & INTERURBAN from Boulder to Jefferson County:
    1908–1926 Denver & Interurban RR

DENVER & INTERURBAN from Eldorado Springs to Main Line:
    1908–1908 Eldorado Springs Ry.
    1908–1926 Denver & Interurban RR

UNION PACIFIC from Weld County to Boulder:
    1870–1874 Denver & Boulder Valley RR
    1874–1880 Denver Pacific Ry.
    1880–   Union Pacific RR

UNION PACIFIC, DENVER & GULF from Valmont to Marshall:
    1877–1890 Golden, Boulder & Caribou RR
    1890–1890 Union Pacific, Denver & Gulf RR

Some Whistlestops

BOETTCHER (C&S) is shown about two miles north of Longmont on 1909 through 1920 maps.

CHAPMAN (BN) is shown about two miles northwest of Hygiene on 1902 through 1920 maps.

CLIFTON (UP) is shown about six miles east of Boulder on 1884 through 1892 maps.

DIXONS MILL (BN) is shown about two miles east of Longmont on 1909 through 1916 maps. It is also shown in Weld County.

DOWNER (C&S) is shown about four miles southwest of Longmont on 1909 through 1920 maps.

EVERSMAN (BN) is shown about three miles south of Lafayette on a 1909 map.

FISHER (DU&P) is shown about five miles south of Longmont on an 1892 map.

HIGHLAND (C&S) is shown about six miles north of Longmont on 1892 through 1959 maps.

LIGGETT (UP) is shown about six miles east of Boulder on a 1969 map.

MITCHELL (DU&P) is shown about one mile south of Erie on 1892 through 1902 maps.

MOREY (C&S) is shown about three miles north of Longmont on 1909 through 1916 maps.

TOWER JUNCTION (BN) is shown about one mile southeast of Lyons on a railroad map.

Boulder County

WARD (DU&P) is shown about four miles south of Longmont on an 1892 map.

WHITEROCK (UP) is shown about seven miles east of Boulder on 1892 through 1916 maps.

Places to Pray

Kiowa, Elbert County

Calhan, El Paso County

Chapter 8

Cheyenne County

Still on the Map

Arapahoe
Arena
Aroya
Cheyenne Wells

Firstview
Kit Carson
Wild Horse

Places in the Past

Aaby
Bent's Road Crossing
Big Springs
Chemung
Cheyenne Wells
David's Wells
Deering's Well

Dubois
Eureka
Grady's
Mayville
Medill
Mount Pearl
Sorrento

Some Railroad Tracks

Arkansas Valley Railway
Union Pacific Railroad

Some Whistlestops

Ascalon Rush Creek
Coronado Salis
Eureka Sand Creek
Namaouna

Still on the Map

ARAPAHOE (platted town) was named after the Arapahoe Indians. The Arapahoe post office began operations in 1906, and a town plat was filed on February 26, 1908, by G. W. Bailey and W. W. Howard. Arapahoe, like most of the towns in Cheyenne County, received its initial impetus from the Union Pacific railroad.

ARENA (railroad post office) is located next to the Union Pacific railroad and about six miles northeast of Kit Carson. The Arena post office was in operation from 1910 to 1923.

AROYA (platted town) was named after a deep ravine in the area. The Aroya post office was opened in 1889, and a town plat was filed for Aroya on June 20, 1907, by the Union Pacific Land Company. The Aroya post office was discontinued in 1965, and very little remains of the community today.

CHEYENNE WELLS (platted town) was named after Indian wells and the stage station close to the wells. The Kansas Pacific railroad reached the site of Cheyenne Wells in 1870. The Cheyenne Wells

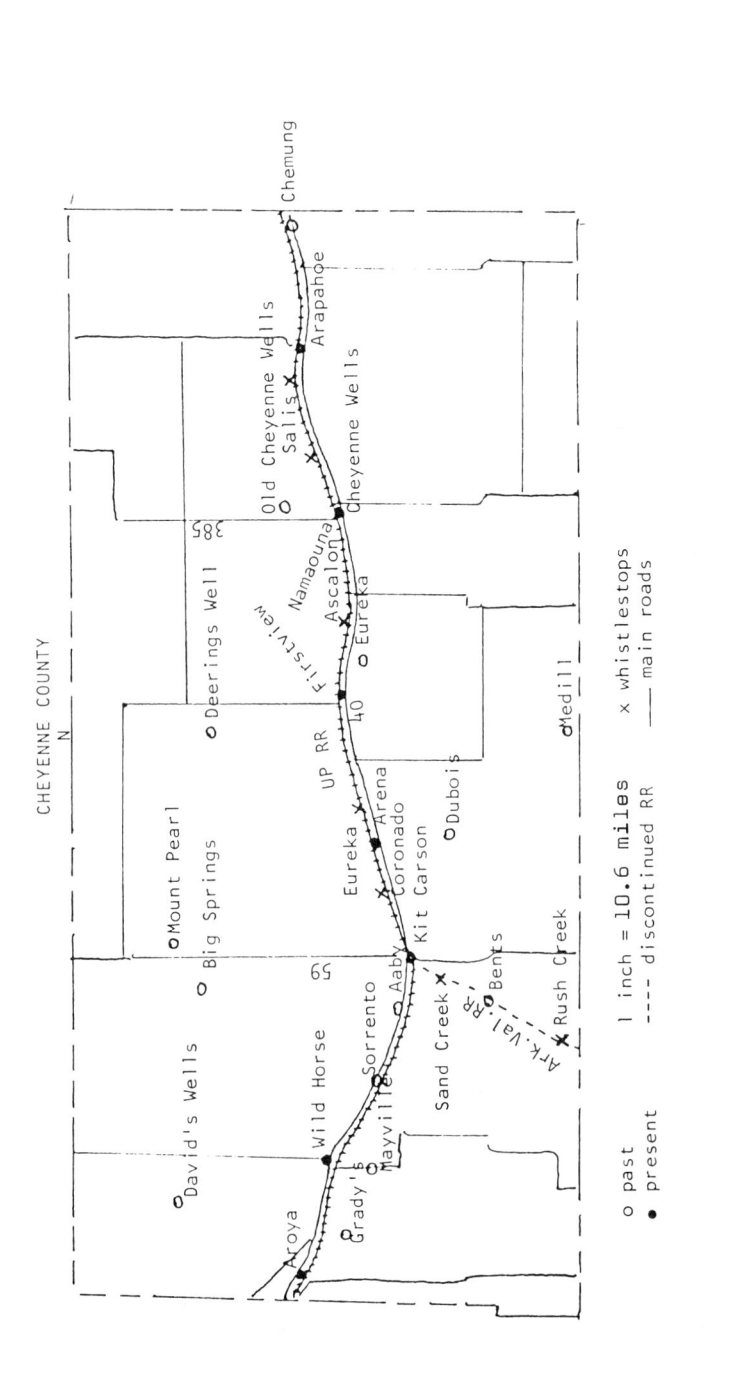

Cheyenne County

post office opened six years later. A town plat was filed for Cheyenne Wells on June 20, 1888, by the Cheyenne Wells Town and Investment Company. The town became county seat of Cheyenne County in 1889.

FIRSTVIEW (platted town) was named after the fact that the site afforded westward travelers one of the first views of Pikes Peak. The Firstview post office was established in 1907, and a town plat was filed for Firstview on September 11, 1911, by Mary Woodrow. The Firstview post office was discontinued in 1961.

KIT CARSON (platted town) was established in 1869 and was named after the famed pioneer scout, Kit Carson. The Kansas-Pacific railroad reached Kit Carson in 1870, and the Arkansas Valley railroad was built from Kit Carson to Las Animas in 1873. A town plat was filed for Kit Carson on June 16, 1888, by L. E. Smith and E. F. Madden.

WILD HORSE (platted town) was named in reference to nearby Wild Horse Creek which was the watering place for wild horses. A post office was established at Wild Horse in 1877, but closed in the same year. The Wild Horse post office reopened in 1904, and a town plat was filed for Wild Horse by Frederick Goodier on November 20, 1906. A fire almost destroyed the town of Wild Horse in 1917.

Places in the Past

AABY (platted town) was platted about eight miles southeast of Wild Horse, and the plat was filed by A. A. Aaby on June 22, 1907. However, the town of Aaby did not obtain a post office, and it was not shown on the map.

BENT'S ROAD CROSSING (road junction) is shown about six miles southwest of Kit Carson on 1882 and 1897 maps and was a wagon road junction.

Places on the Colorado Prairie

BIG SPRINGS (stage station) was located on the Smoky Hill North stage route and about twelve miles north from the site of Kit Carson.

CHEMUNG (railroad post office) was located about five miles east of Arapahoe and next to the Union Pacific railroad. The Chemung post office was in operation from 1906 to 1910.

CHEYENNE WELLS (stage station) was located about five miles north of the Cheyenne Wells townsite. Cheyenne Wells was an important junction station for the Smoky Hill North and the Smoky Hill South stage routes. The Smoky Hill stage routes were named after the nearby Smoky Hill River.

DAVID'S WELLS (stage station) was located on the Smoky Hill North stage route and about ten miles from the site of Aroya. The locating of stage stations near wells was a common practice, as is evidenced by David's Wells and Deering's Well.

DEERING'S WELL (stage station) was located on the Smoky Hill North stage route and about halfway between the Big Springs and Cheyenne Wells stage stations.

DUBOIS (stage station) was located on the Smoky Hill South stage route and about six miles southeast from the site of Kit Carson. Dubois was the third stage station in Colorado from Kansas on the Smoky Hill South stage route.

EUREKA (stage station) was located on the Smoky Hill South stage route and about two miles southeast of the site of Firstview. Eureka was named after nearby Eureka Creek.

GRADY'S (stage station) was located on the Smoky Hill South stage route and about one mile west from the site of Wild Horse. Grady's was on the north bank of the Big Sandy.

MAYVILLE (platted town) was platted about three miles southwest of Wild Horse. The plat for Mayville was filed on November 6,

Cheyenne County

1906, by Ida and George Webb; however, Mayville was not shown on the map, and it did not obtain a post office.

MEDILL (rural post office) was located about twelve miles south of Firstview. The Medill post office was in operation from 1910 to 1920.

MOUNT PEARL (rural post office) was located about fifteen miles north of Kit Carson. The Mount Pearl post office was in operation from 1911 to 1923.

SORRENTO (railroad post office) was located next to the Union Pacific railroad and about six miles northwest of Kit Carson. The Sorrento post office was in operation from 1907 to 1918.

Some Railroad Tracks

ARKANSAS VALLEY from Kit Carson to Kiowa County:
    1873–1877 Arkansas Valley Ry.

UNION PACIFIC from Kansas to Lincoln County:
    1870–1880 Kansas Pacific Ry.
    1880–   Union Pacific RR

Some Whistlestops

ASCALON (UP) is shown about six miles east of Firstview on 1902 through 1920 maps.

CORONADO (UP) is shown about five miles northeast of Kit Carson on an 1884 map.

EUREKA (UP) is shown about eight miles northeast of Kit Carson on 1882 through 1897 maps.

NAMAOUNA (UP) is shown about four miles northeast of Cheyenne Wells on an 1884 map.

RUSH CREEK (AV) is shown about ten miles southwest of Kit Carson on an 1897 map.

SALIS (UP) is shown about four miles west of Arapahoe on 1916 and 1920 maps.

SAND CREEK (AV) is shown about one mile south of Kit Carson on an 1882 map.

Places to Stop

Goodrich, Morgan County

Elbert, Elbert County

Chapter 9

Crowley County

Still on the Map

Crowley
Olney Springs
Ordway
Sugar City

Places in the Past

Double Adobe
Hester
Pultney

Some Railroad Tracks

Missouri Pacific Railroad

Some Whistlestops

Croft
King Center
Lolita
Numa

CROWLEY COUNTY

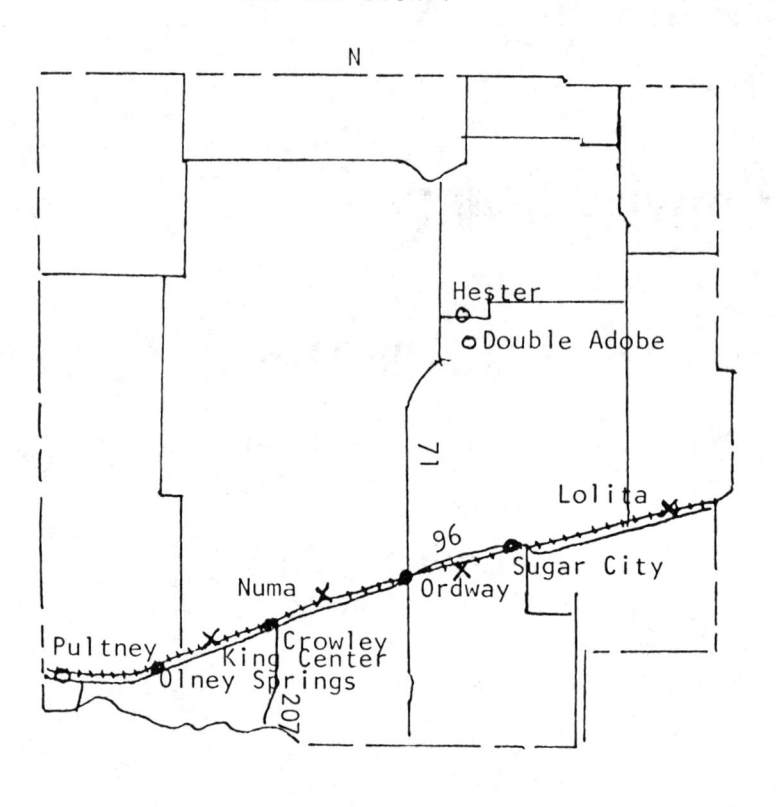

o past
● present

1 inch = 8 miles

x whistlestops
___ main roads

Still on the Map

CROWLEY (railroad post office) was named after Crowley County which was named after John Crowley, a state senator from Rocky Ford. Crowley is located next to the Missouri Pacific Railroad. The Crowley post office opened in 1914.

OLNEY SPRINGS (platted town) was named after a Mr. Olney who was an official of the Missouri Pacific Railroad which built through the area in 1887. A town plat was filed for Olney Springs on December 17, 1898, by Eugene Cronk. Olney Springs was called "Olney" until the post office name was changed in 1909.

ORDWAY (platted town) was named in reference to George Ordway, ex-alderman of Denver, who owned the townsite. Town plats were filed for Ordway in 1894 and again on April 23, 1895, by the Ordway Town and Land Company. Ordway was made the seat of Crowley County when the county was formed in 1911.

SUGAR CITY (platted town) was named in reference to the National Sugar Company which located a sugar factory on the site in 1899. A town plat was filed for Sugar City on December 26, 1899, by Piene Van Alstyne. Sugar City reflected the economic status of the factory until the factory was dismantled in the 1960s.

Places in the Past

DOUBLE ADOBE (place name) is shown about nine miles north of Sugar City on a 1916 map.

HESTER (rural post office) was located about fifteen miles north of Ordway, and the Hester post office was in operation from 1905 to 1912.

PULTNEY (railroad post office) was located about six miles west of Olney Springs and next to the Missouri Pacific Railroad. The

Crowley County

Pultney post office was in operation during 1890; however, Pultney was on the map into the 1920s.

Some Railroad Tracks

MISSOURI PACIFIC from Kiowa County to Pueblo County:
   1887–1909 Pueblo & State Line RR
   1909–   Missouri Pacific RR

Some Whistlestops

CROFT (MP) is shown about three miles northeast of Ordway on a railroad map. Meridian is shown in the same location as Croft on an 1897 map.

KING CENTER (MP) is shown about three miles southwest of Crowley on a 1968 map.

LOLITA (MP) is shown about five miles northeast of Sugar City on 1897 through 1940 maps.

NUMA (MP) is shown about three miles southwest of Ordway on 1897 through 1916 maps.

Chapter 10

Denver County

Still on the Map

Denver
Fort Logan

Places in the Past

Alcott
Annandale
Argo
Athens
Auraria
Barnum
Berkeley
Colfax
Elyria
Four Mile House
Globeville
Grafton

Harman
Highlands
Independence
Kingston
Kirkland
Leetsdale
Montclair
Sheffield
South Denver
University Park
Valverde
Villa Park

Denver County

Some Railroad Tracks

Associated Railroads
Atchison, Topeka & Santa Fe Railway (two parts)
Burlington Northern Railroad
Chicago, Rock Island & Pacific Railway
Colorado & Eastern Railroad
Colorado & Southern Railway (four parts)
Denver & Interurban Railroad
Denver & Rio Grande Western Railroad (two parts)
Denver, Laramie & Northwestern Railroad
Denver, Utah & Pacific Railroad
Metro Transit
Missouri Pacific Railroad
Union Pacific Railroad (two parts)

Some Whistlestops

Auraria
Burnham
Coronado
Pullman Shops
Roydale
Sandown

Still on the Map

DENVER (platted town) was first named "St. Charles" by the St. Charles Company which settled on the site in 1858. The site of St. Charles was taken over by the William Larimer party in November 1858 and was renamed "Denver City" in reference to Governor James Denver of the Kansas Territory who sponsored the Larimer party. Denver City was overshadowed by William Russell's "Auraria" on the south side of Cherry Creek for about a year;

DENVER COUNTY

o past
• present

1 inch = 4.2 miles   ____ main roads

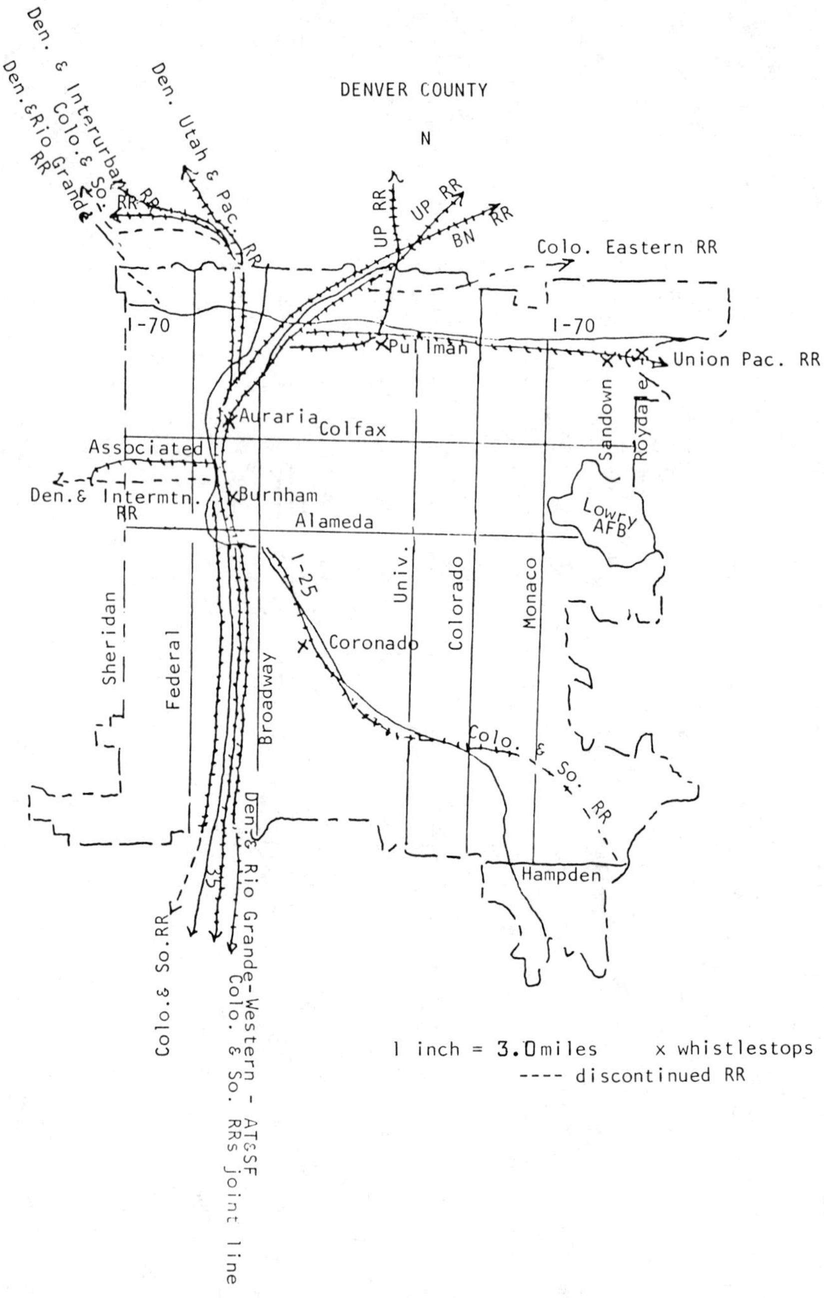

DENVER COUNTY
N
Den. & Interurban RR
Colo. & So.
Den. & Rio Grande RR
Den. Utah & Pac. RR
UP RR
UP RR
BN RR
Colo. Eastern RR
I-70
I-70
Pullman
Union Pac. RR
Sandown
Roydale
Auraria
Colfax
Associated
Den. & Intermtn. RR
Burnham
Alameda
Lowry AFB
I-25
Coronado
Sheridan
Federal
Broadway
Univ.
Colorado
Monaco
Colo. & So. RR
Hampden
Colo. & So. RR
Den. & Rio Grande-Western - AT&SF
Colo. & So. RRs joint line
1 inch = 3.0 miles
x whistlestops
---- discontinued RR

Places on the Colorado Prairie

however, Denver City became the selected rendezvous for the gold-seekers and was the dominant town of the two by 1860. Denver City was incorporated in 1861, and the post office name was shortened to "Denver" in 1866. Denver was made the seat of Arapahoe County when that county was formed in 1861. Denver obtained the position of Territory capital from Golden in 1867 and was made capital of Colorado when the state was formed in 1876. Denver County was formed in 1902.

FORT LOGAN (military installation) was established as "Fort Sheridan" in October 1887. It originally quartered two companies of the 18th Infantry. Fort Logan has served as headquarters for the 2nd Engineers, a citizens' military training camp, a reserve officers' military training camp, a U.S. Army reserve training camp, a national cemetery, and a mental health center.

Places in the Past

ALCOTT (platted town) was established in the 1890s, and the Alcott post office opened in 1896. Alcott was located just northwest of Denver in the 1890s, and the Alcott post office was made a Denver substation in 1904. Alcott was located just north of Elitch Gardens, an amusement park, which opened in 1890.

ANNANDALE (platted town) was platted just south of Denver. The plat was filed by William Harvey and H. C. Rider on April 7, 1888; however, Annandale did not obtain a post office. It was not shown on the map, either.

ARGO (platted town) was named after the nearby Argo Smelter which had been moved from Blackhawk in 1878. Argo was established when the smelter was built and was incorporated in 1880. The smelter was discontinued in 1889, and Argo was annexed to Denver in 1904. Argo was bounded by Broadway Boulevard, Pecos Street, 44th Avenue, and 49th Avenue.

Denver County

ATHENS (platted town) was established in the early 1890s. The Athens post office was opened in 1892. Athens, which was located just southwest of University Park, was short-lived, and the Athens post office closed in 1896.

AURARIA (early community) was established by William Russell and his party in 1858 and was located on the south side of Cherry Creek at its junction with the South Platte River. It dominated its neighbor, Denver City, until the 1860s. Denver City and Auraria were combined to form Denver City in 1861. Auraria was named after Auraria, Georgia, which was the hometown of Russell and many others in his party of gold-seekers. It was Russell who is credited with starting the Colorado gold rush.

BARNUM (platted town) was established in the 1880s and was named after the famous circus owner, P. T. Barnum, who owned land in the area. The town of Barnum, located just southwest of Denver, was incorporated in 1887 and annexed to Denver in 1896.

BERKELEY (platted town) was the name which was first used in the area when the present town of Mountain View was platted. The area just east of Mountain View was incorporated as "North Denver" in 1892; however, the name of North Denver was changed to Berkeley in 1896. A. C. Fisk platted a town northwest of Inspiration Point in 1896, and it was called "Berkeley" also; however, Berkeley, which was bounded by Sheridan Boulevard, Lowell Boulevard, 38th Avenue, and 52nd Avenue, was annexed to Denver in 1902 when Denver County was formed.

COLFAX (platted town) was named after Colfax Avenue and was established just west of Denver. Colfax was incorporated in 1891 and annexed in 1897.

ELYRIA (platted town) was established by A. C. Fisk in 1881. Elyria was incorporated in 1890 and annexed to Denver in 1897. The boundaries of Elyria were 55th Avenue, 46th Avenue, and from Colorado Boulevard to near the South Platte River.

Places on the Colorado Prairie

FOUR MILE HOUSE (stage station) was located on the Smoky Hill stage route and at the site of the intersection of Forest Street and Cherry Creek. Four Mile House was used as a freshening-up stop before entering Denver.

GLOBEVILLE (platted town) was established in 1889 and was named after the nearby Globe Smelter. Globeville was incorporated in 1891 and annexed to Denver in 1902. Globeville was bounded by 52nd Avenue, 44th Avenue, and from Broadway Boulevard to the South Platte River.

GRAFTON (platted town) was platted southeast of Denver and east of Englewood, and the plat was filed on July 9, 1883, by William Browning; however, Grafton neither obtained a post office nor was shown on the map.

HARMAN (platted town) was platted next to Cherry Creek and just south of University Boulevard in 1882. Harman was incorporated in 1886 and annexed to Denver in 1895. The Harman post office was discontinued in 1904.

HIGHLANDS (platted town) was established northwest of Denver in 1875 and was named after its location in relation to Denver. Highlands was incorporated in 1885 and annexed to Denver in 1888.

INDEPENDENCE (platted town) was platted just north of the site of the Denver airport, and the plat was filed on September 13, 1886, by the Platte Land Company. Independence was located near the Denver Scranton railroad. Independence did not obtain a post office, and it was not shown on the map.

KINGSTON (platted town) was platted just east of Happy Canyon Road and south of Hampden Avenue, and the plat was filed on January 13, 1890, by M. A. King. Kingston did not obtain a post office. It was not shown on the map.

Denver County

KIRKLAND (platted town) was platted just east of Englewood, and the plat was filed on July 3, 1890, by Samuel Kirkland. Kirkland did not obtain a post office, and it was not shown on the map.

LEETSDALE (platted town) was platted just east of Glendale. The plat was filed on October 19, 1892, by John Leet. The portion of Parker Road to Leetsdale from Colorado Boulevard was renamed Leetsdale Drive. Leetsdale did not obtain a post office, and it was not shown on the map.

MONTCLAIR (platted town) was established in 1885 by Mathias Cochrane and was incorporated in 1888. Montclair was a preconceived "utopia-suburb" and received most of its publicity from Baron Walter von Richthofen who built a castle-like home in the area for his second wife. Montclair was annexed to Denver in 1902.

SHEFFIELD (platted town) began as a post office in 1891. The name of the Sheffield post office was changed to "Denver Mills" in 1892. The Denver Mills post office was discontinued in 1918. A town plat was filed for Sheffield on September 26, 1926, by John Evans; however, a post office was not re-established in Sheffield. The town of Sheffield was located east of Elyria.

SOUTH DENVER (platted town) was established in 1874 by William Hodgson. South Denver was incorporated in 1886 and annexed to Denver in 1894. South Denver was located just northeast of Englewood.

UNIVERSITY PARK (platted town) was established in the 1880s near the University of Denver from which it took its name. The University Park post office began operations in 1890 and became a Denver station in 1915.

VALVERDE (platted town) was established in 1882 by the Valverde Town and Improvement Company. Valverde, which means "green valley" in Spanish, was incorporated in 1888 and annexed to Denver in 1902. Valverde was located just southwest of downtown Denver.

VILLA PARK (platted town) was advertised as a residential development in 1889. The Villa Park post office was in operation from 1890 to 1901. Villa Park (or Villapark) was located near Federal Boulevard and Colfax Avenue.

Some Railroad Tracks

ASSOCIATED RAILROADS from Denver to Jefferson County:
    1890–1904 Denver, Lakewood & Golden RR
    1904–1907 Denver & Intermountain Ry.
    1907–1909 Intermountain Ry.
    1909–1913 Denver & Intermountain RR
    1913–1914 Denver City Tramway Co.
    1914–1925 Denver Tramway Co.
    1925–1953 Denver Tramway Corp.
    1953–   Associated Railroads

ATCHISON, TOPEKA & SANTA FE from Larimer Street to Jewell Park (Overland Park):
    1881–1887 Denver Circle RR
    1887–1889 Atchison, Topeka & Santa Fe Ry.

ATCHISON, TOPEKA & SANTA FE from Denver to Arapahoe County:
    1887–1900 Denver & Santa Fe RR
    1900–   Atchison, Topeka & Santa Fe Ry.

BURLINGTON NORTHERN from Adams County to Denver:
    1881–1908 Burlington & Colorado RR
    1908–1970 Chicago, Burlington & Quincy RR
    1970–   Burlington Northern RR

Denver County

CHICAGO, ROCK ISLAND & PACIFIC from Adams County to Denver and from Denver to Arapahoe County:
    1888–1891 Chicago, Kansas & Nebraska Ry.
    1891–   Chicago, Rock Island & Pacific Ry.

(Union Pacific track was used from Adams County to Denver, and Denver and Rio Grande track from Denver to Arapahoe County.)

COLORADO & EASTERN from Adams County to Denver:
    1886–1887 Denver Railroad & Land Co.
    1887–1888 Denver Railroad, Land, & Coal Co.
    1888–1894 Colorado Eastern Ry.
    1894–1915 Colorado Eastern RR

COLORADO & SOUTHERN from Denver to Adams County (and Golden):
    1870–1890 Colorado Central RR
    1890–1898 Union Pacific, Denver & Gulf Ry.
    1898–   Colorado & Southern Ry.

COLORADO & SOUTHERN from Denver to Arapahoe County (and Waterton):
    1874–1889 Denver, South Park & Pacific Ry.
    1889–1890 Denver, Leadville & Gunnison Ry.
    1890–1898 Union Pacific, Denver & Gulf Ry.
    1898–   Colorado & Southern Ry.

COLORADO & SOUTHERN from Denver to Arapahoe County (and Parker):
    1881–1886 Denver & New Orleans RR
    1886–1887 Denver, Texas & Gulf RR
    1887–1890 Denver, Texas & Fort Worth RR
    1890–1898 Union Pacific, Denver & Gulf RR
    1898–   Colorado & Southern Ry.

Places on the Colorado Prairie

COLORADO & SOUTHERN from Adams County (and Boulder) to Denver:
1881–1885 Denver, Western & Pacific Ry.
1885–1890 Denver, Marshall & Boulder Ry.
1890–1898 Union Pacific, Denver & Gulf Ry.
1898– Colorado & Southern Ry.

DENVER & INTERURBAN from Adams County to Denver:
1907–1926 Denver & Interurban RR

DENVER & RIO GRANDE WESTERN from Denver to Arapahoe County:
1871–1886 Denver & Rio Grande Ry.
1886–1921 Denver & Rio Grande RR
1921– Denver & Rio Grande Western RR

DENVER & RIO GRANDE WESTERN from Denver to Jefferson County:
1902–1912 Denver, Northwestern & Pacific RR
1912–1947 Denver & Salt Lake RR
1947– Denver & Rio Grande Western RR

DENVER, LARAMIE & NORTHWESTERN from Adams County to Denver:
1909–1910 Denver, Laramie & Northwestern Ry.
1910–1917 Denver, Laramie & Northwestern RR

DENVER, UTAH & PACIFIC from Adams County to Denver:
1881–1884 Denver, Utah & Pacific RR
1884–1889 Denver, Utah & Pacific RR
(Denver, Marshall & Boulder track was used after 1889.)

Denver County

METRO TRANSIT within the city and county of Denver:
    1867–1872 Denver Horse RR
    1872–1896 Denver City Ry.
        1896 Denver City Ry., Denver City Cable Ry., and Denver City Electric Rys. formed Denver City RR #2
    1896–1898 Denver City RR #2
        1898 Denver City RR #2 and West End RR formed Denver City Traction Co. in 1898
    1898–1899 Denver City Traction Co.
        1899 Denver City Traction Co. and Denver Consolidated Tramway formed Denver City Tramway in 1899
    1899–1914 Denver City Tramway
    1914–1925 Denver Tramway Co. #2
    1925–1972 Denver Tramway Corp.
    1972–   Metro Transit
        1891 Denver & Berkeley Park Rapid Transit, Highlands St. RR, and Park Ry. formed Metro Ry.
        1890 South Denver Cable Ry. and Denver Tramway Extension Co. absorbed by Denver Tramway Co. #1
        1893 Denver Tramway Co. #1 and Metro Ry. formed Denver Consolidated Tramway
        1913 Denver & Northwestern Ry. and Denver & Intermountain RR absorbed by Denver City Tramway
        University Park Ry. and Denver & Westside Cable Ry. probably formed into Metro Ry.

Places on the Colorado Prairie

MISSOURI PACIFIC from Denver to Arapahoe County:
    1887–   Missouri Pacific Ry. used Denver & Rio Grande Western track.

UNION PACIFIC from Adams County to Denver:
    1870–1880 Denver Pacific Ry.
    1880–1898 Union Pacific Ry.
    1898–   Union Pacific RR

UNION PACIFIC from Adams County to Denver:
    1870–1880 Kansas Pacific Ry.
    1880–1898 Union Pacific Ry.
    1898–   Union Pacific RR

Some Whistlestops

AURARIA (C&S) is shown within Denver on an 1892 map.

BURNHAM (AT&SF) is shown just south of the Valley Highway and 6th Avenue on a railroad map.

CORONADO (C&S) is shown about two miles southeast of Harman on 1884 through 1902 maps.

PULLMAN SHOPS (UP) is shown as Jersey on 1882 through 1892 maps.

ROYDALE (UP) is shown about two miles east of Sandown on a railroad map.

SANDOWN (UP) is shown just northwest of Stapleton airport on a railroad map.

Chapter II

Douglas County

Still on the Map

Castle Rock
Franktown
Greenland
Larkspur

Louviers
Parker
Sedalia

Places in the Past

Acequia
Case
Cherry
Douglas
Golddale
Hilltop
Huntsville
Irving
New Memphis

Pine Grove
Rockford
Rock Ridge
Russellville
Spring Valley
Sulphur Gulch
Table Rock
Twenty Mile House
Virginia

Douglas County

Some Railroad Tracks

Atchison, Topeka & Santa Fe Railway
Colorado & Southern Railway
Denver & Rio Grande Railroad (two lines)
Denver & Rio Grande Western Railroad (two lines)

Some Whistlestops

Citadel	Madge
Gann	O'Briens
Glade	Plateau
Hathaways Quarry	Spruce
King	Struby
Lehigh	Tomah

Still on the Map

CASTLE ROCK (platted town) began as a post office station on the Denver and Rio Grande Railroad in 1871 and was named in reference to a nearby rock formation. A town plat was filed for Castle Rock on April 25, 1874, and the Douglas County Seat was moved to Castle Rock from Franktown in the same year.

FRANKTOWN (rural post office) is one of the oldest communities in Douglas County. Franktown was first known as "California Ranch" and was a stop on the stage line from Denver to Colorado City. The Franktown post office opened in 1862 and was named after J. Frank Gardner who pioneered in the area. Franktown's early growth suffered because it was not serviced by a railroad; therefore, Franktown lost the county seat to Castle Rock in 1874.

DOUGLAS COUNTY

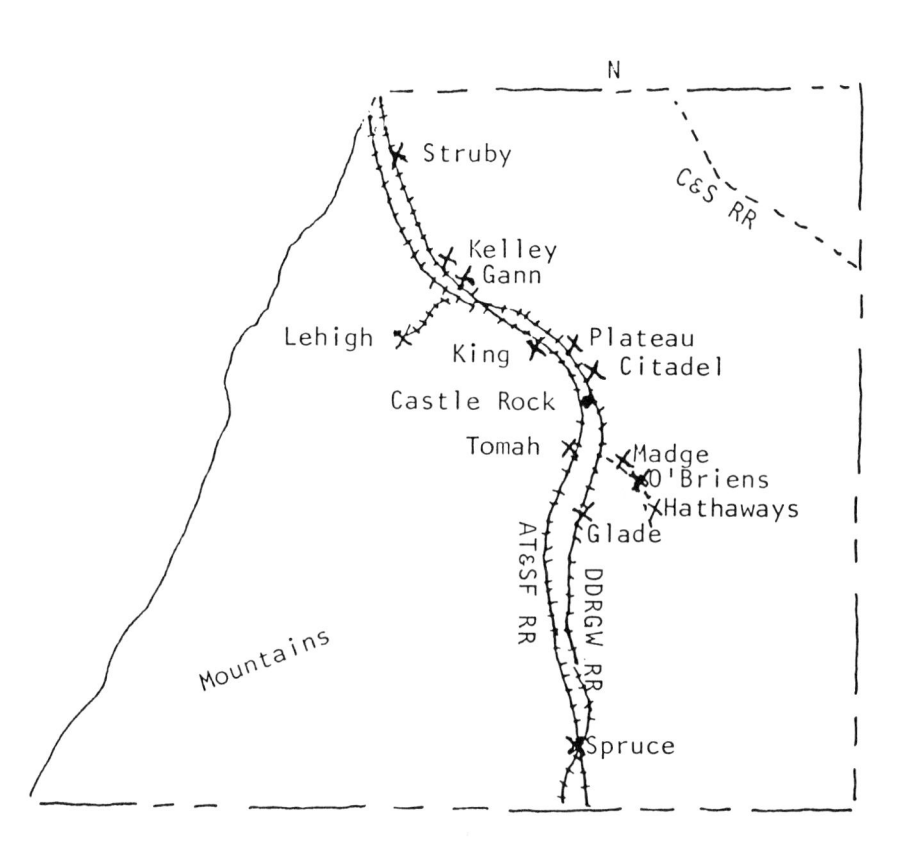

1 inch = 8 miles
---- discontinued RR   x whistlestops

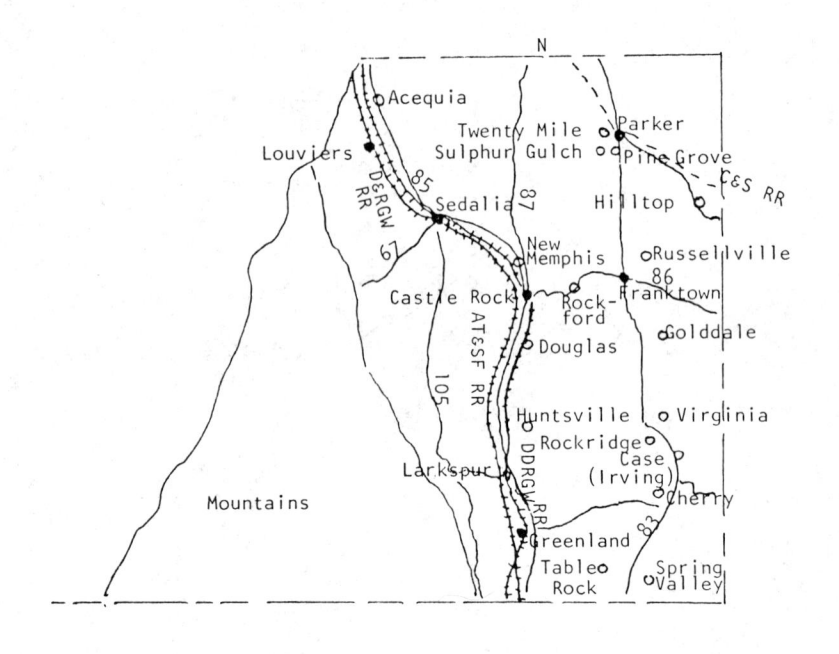

o past   1 inch = 10.6 mi.   ___ main roads
● present   ----discontinued RR

Places on the Colorado Prairie

GREENLAND (platted town) was named by the famous author, Helen Hunt Jackson, after the surrounding countryside. A town plat was filed for Greenland in September 1875 by Fred Salamon; however, the Greenland post office had opened two years earlier. Greenland began as a Rio Grande railroad town.

LARKSPUR (railroad post office) was named in reference to the many delphiniums in the area. The Larkspur area was first serviced by "Clay Pit" on the stage route to Denver from the Colorado Springs area. After the Denver and Rio Grande built through the area, the Larkspur post office was started in 1871.

LOUVIERS (company post office) is the name which is used for the explosive plant, the company community, and post office, all of which were started in 1906 and 1907 by the DuPont Company. Louviers was named after Louviers, Delaware, the home of the DuPonts' first woolen plant and a step in their financial empire. Louviers, Delaware, was named after the woolen capital of the world, Louviers, France.

PARKER (stage and railroad post office) was named after James S. Parker, who took over the famous Twenty Mile House on the Smoky Hill South stage route in 1874. When Parker moved to Twenty Mile House, he brought the post office from nearby Pine Grove, and the post office carried the name of "Pine Grove" until the name was changed to "Parker" in 1882. The Denver and New Orleans railroad was built through the area in 1881, and Parker was a station until the line was discontinued in 1936.

SEDALIA (platted town) was first called "Round Corral" and then "Plum." A Mr. Craig founded Round Corral in 1865, but the name was changed to "Plum" in reference to nearby Plum Creek when Jonathan House purchased the site in 1870. Plum was renamed "Sedalia" when the National Land and Improvement Company filed a town plat for the site on May 15, 1882. Sedalia was named after Sedalia, Missouri, which was the hometown of H. M. Clay, who was an early resident in the area.

Douglas County

Places in the Past

ACEQUIA (platted town) was named after a nearby ditch and was another of the communities which were platted by the National Land and Improvement Company. A town plat was filed for Acequia on June 28, 1881; however, the Acequia post office began in 1874. The Denver and Rio Grande and Santa Fe railroads sustained Acequia until the Acequia post office closed in 1900.

CASE (rural post office) was named after the nearby Case Creamery. The Case post office was in operation from 1897 to 1913.

CHERRY (rural post office) was named in reference to nearby West Cherry Creek. The Cherry post office was in operation from 1900 to 1920. Cherry was located about ten miles east of Larkspur.

DOUGLAS (platted town) was located on the Denver and Rio Grande railroad and was a shipping point for the nearby Madge Stone Quarry. The Douglas post office began operations in 1874, and the National Land and Development Company filed a town plat for Douglas on July 28, 1880; however, the Douglas post office was discontinued in 1884. Douglas was named after the county and stayed on the map into the 1920s.

GOLDDALE (rural post office) was located about six miles southeast of Franktown. The Golddale post office was in operation from 1882 to 1885. Golddale was located in the same area as Russellville, which was the scene of some gold-searching; thus, Golddale could have been named in reference to the early gold activity.

HILLTOP (railroad post office) was located on the Colorado and Southern railroad and was named in reference to its location. The Hilltop post office was in operation from 1896 to 1944, some nine years after the railroad was discontinued. Hilltop stayed on the map into the 1960s.

Places on the Colorado Prairie

HUNTSVILLE (rural post office) was one of the earliest communities in Douglas County. The Huntsville post office began operations in 1860, but it was discontinued in favor of nearby Larkspur when the railroad was built through the area in 1871. Huntsville is shown as a railroad station on an 1877 map.

IRVING (rural post office) began operating when the Case post office ceased operations in the area in 1913. The Irving post office was discontinued in 1920.

NEW MEMPHIS (railroad post office) was named in reference to Memphis, Tennessee, and began operations in 1872. The New Memphis post office was discontinued when most of the residents moved to nearby Castle Rock in 1874. New Memphis was on the Rio Grande line.

PINE GROVE (stage station post office) was first located about one and one-half miles south of Twenty Mile House and began operating in 1873. Jim Parker moved the Pine Grove post office to Twenty Mile House in 1874; however, the name "Pine Grove" was retained for the post office until it was changed to "Parker" in 1882.

ROCKFORD (place name) is shown on the wagon road to Franktown from Castle Rock on an 1897 map of Colorado.

ROCK RIDGE (rural post office) was once the summer home of George Crofutt who wrote *Crofutt's Guide to Colorado*. The Rock Ridge post office was in operation from 1872 to 1892 and was named after the nearby terrain.

RUSSELLVILLE (stage station) was a junction station where the Jimmy Camp Road and the Cherokee stage route came together just below Franktown. Russellville was named after William Green Russell who found some gold in the area while enroute to his famous strike at "Little Dry Creek." Russellville had postal service in 1862 only.

SPRING VALLEY (rural post office) began as a station on Cherokee stage route. A small fort for refuge from Indian attacks was located

Douglas County

near the station. The Spring Valley post office was in operation from 1865 to 1885 and serviced the area north of Palmer Lake and Monument. Spring Valley's importance to the area can be attested to by the fact that it was shown on the map into the 1900s.

SULPHUR GULCH (stage station) was located a mile southwest of the site of Parker. The Sulphur Gulch and Cherry Valley stations were two of the earlier stage stations on the Smoky Hill South stage route and were later replaced by the Twelve and Twenty Mile Houses as stage stops.

TABLE ROCK (place name) is shown about six miles east of Greenland on a 1902 map. Table Rock was named after a nearby rock formation.

TWENTY MILE HOUSE (stage station) was one of the most noted stations on the Smoky Hill South stage route. Twenty Mile House was built by George Long in 1864. Nelson Doud acquired Twenty Mile House in 1870, and he operated the station until James Parker took over in 1874. Parker moved the nearby Pine Grove post office to Twenty Mile House station. The post office retained the name of "Pine Grove" until it was changed to "Parker" in 1882.

VIRGINIA (stage station) was located on the Cherokee stage route and was named after its location on the Virginia Ranch. The Virginia post office was in operation from 1869 to 1871.

Some Railroad Tracks

ATCHISON, TOPEKA & SANTA FE from Arapahoe County to El Paso County:
    1887–1900 Denver & Santa Fe RR
    1900–   Atchison, Topeka & Santa Fe Ry.

Places on the Colorado Prairie

COLORADO & SOUTHERN from Arapahoe County to Elbert County:
1881–1886 Denver & New Orleans RR
1886–1890 Denver, Texas & Gulf RR
1890–1898 Union Pacific, Denver & Gulf Ry.
1898– Colorado & Southern Ry.

DENVER & RIO GRANDE from Douglas to Madge Quarry:
1881–1886 Denver & Rio Grande Ry.
1886–1902 Denver & Rio Grande RR

DENVER & RIO GRANDE from Lehigh Junction to Lehigh:
1883–1886 Denver & Rio Grande Ry.
1886–1890 Denver & Rio Grande RR

DENVER & RIO GRANDE WESTERN from Arapahoe County to El Paso County:
1871–1886 Denver & Rio Grande Ry.
1886–1921 Denver & Rio Grande RR
1921– Denver & Rio Grande Western RR

DENVER & RIO GRANDE WESTERN from Castle Rock to O'Briens:
1882–1886 Denver & Rio Grande Ry.
1886–1921 Denver & Rio Grande RR
1921–1924 Denver & Rio Grande Western RR

Some Whistlestops

CITADEL (D&RGW) is shown about one mile north of Castle Rock on an 1877 map. Citadel was named in reference to nearby Castle Rock.

Douglas County

GANN (D&RGW) is shown about three miles northeast of Sedalia on 1909 through 1924 maps.

GLADE (D&RGW) is shown about four miles north of Larkspur on 1882 through 1897 maps.

HATHAWAYS QUARRY (D&RGW) is shown about five miles southeast of Castle Rock on an 1892 map.

KING (AT&SF) is shown about four miles east of Sedalia on 1887 through 1968 maps.

LEHIGH (D&RG) is shown about five miles west of Sedalia on 1892 through 1916 maps. Lehigh was a coal mine.

MADGE (D&RG) is shown about five miles south of Castle Rock on a 1916 map. Madge was a rock quarry.

O'BRIENS (D&RGW) is shown about six miles southeast of Castle Rock on 1892 through 1902 maps. O'Briens was a rock quarry.

PLATEAU (D&RGW) is shown about five miles east of Sedalia on 1892 through 1920 maps.

SPRUCE (D&RGW) is shown about four miles southwest of Greenland on 1916 and 1920 maps.

STRUBY (AT&SF) is shown about five miles southwest of Littleton on 1909 through 1920 maps.

TOMAH (AT&SF) is shown about five miles southwest of Castle Rock on 1909 through 1968 maps.

Places to Wait

Strasburg, Adams and Arapahoe Counties

Eaton, Weld County

Chapter 12

Elbert County

Still on the Map

Agate
Buick
Elbert
Elizabeth
Fondis
Kiowa

Kutch
Matheson
Resolis
River Bend
Simla

Places in the Past

Benham Springs
Bijou Basin
Bijou Creek
Bland
Bluebell
Cedar Point

Chenoweth
Claud
Clermont
Fairmont
Gomer's Mills
Graceland

Elbert County

Hargisville	Orsburn
Holtwold	Reed's Springs
Kanza	Running Creek
Keysor	Schley
Kuhn's Crossing	Well's Ranch
Norton	Wolf Creek

Some Railroad Tracks

Colorado & Southern Railway
Chicago, Rock Island & Pacific Railway
Union Pacific Railroad

Some Whistlestops

Barnwell	Lowland
Cameron	Rock Butte
Cedar Point	Sidney
Doby	

Still on the Map

AGATE (platted town) was named after either a gate in local stock pens or the large amount of agate in the area. The Agate post office, which opened in 1882, was preceded by the Gebhard post office, which operated in 1881 and was named after a local rancher, Henry Gebhard. A town plat was filed for Agate on December 4, 1919, but the filer was not named on the plat. Agate received its impetus from the Union Pacific railroad.

ELBERT COUNTY

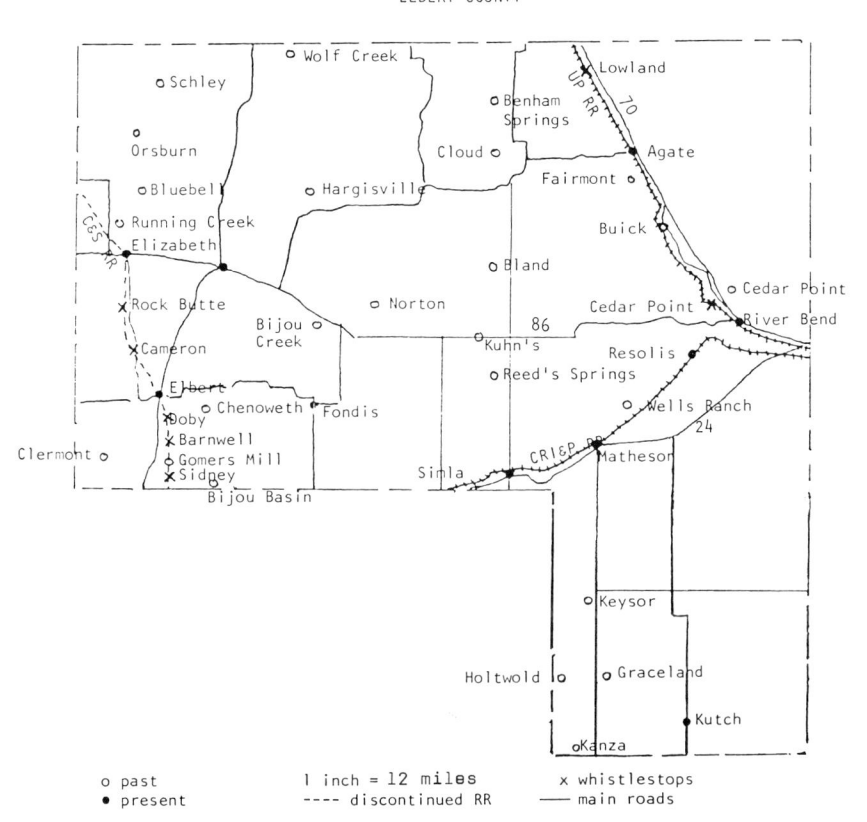

Elbert County

BUICK (railroad post office) was first called "Godfrey," which is shown on 1873 through 1916 maps. The Godfrey post office operated in 1908. The Beuck post office which was named after a local rancher, August Beuck, opened in 1916; however, the name was changed to "Buick." The post office at Buick was closed in 1925.

ELBERT (platted town) was named in reference to Samuel Elbert who was a territorial governor of Colorado. Elbert was initiated by the Elbert Townsite, Road, and Coal-Mining Company. The Elbert post office first opened in 1875. The Elbert post office closed in 1880, but when the Denver and New Orleans railroad was built through the area in 1881, the post office reopened. A town plat was filed for Elbert on February 18, 1884, by Susan Lipscomb. Elbert was an important stop on the railroad until the line was discontinued in 1936.

ELIZABETH (platted town) was named by Governor John Evans in honor of his sister-in-law, Elizabeth Hubbard. The Denver and New Orleans Railroad reached the site of Elizabeth in 1881, and a town plat was filed for Elizabeth on June 19, 1882 by Thomas Phillips. Elizabeth was incorporated in 1890.

FONDIS (rural post office) is located about eleven miles east of Elbert, and the Fondis post office was in operation from 1895 to 1954. Fondis was named after an Italian hotel by the wife of a Mr. Burns, first postmaster in Fondis.

KIOWA (platted town) was first called "Middle Kiowa" in reference to a nearby creek, and began as a stage station on the Smoky Hill South stage route. The Kiowa post office opened in 1868, and Kiowa was made the seat of Elbert County when the county was formed in 1874. Kiowa was platted; however, the plat for Kiowa was not on file in the Elbert County court house in Kiowa.

KUTCH (rural post office) was first located three miles south of its present location, and the first Kutch post office operated in

Places on the Colorado Prairie

1899. Kutch was named after Ira Kutch who operated the first post office and store on the site. A Mr. Anderson started the new Kutch store, and the new Kutch post office began operating in 1905.

MATHESON (platted town) was named after Duncan Matheson, one of the most noted pioneers in Elbert County. The Rock Island Railroad built through the area in 1886 and incorrectly spelled the siding "Mattison." A town plat was filed for Matheson on January 14, 1889, by the Rock Island town filer, C. F. Jilson. The name of the "Mattison" post office was finally renamed "Matheson" in 1915.

RESOLIS (platted town) was another Rock Island Railroad town, and the town plat for Resolis was filed by the Rock Island town-maker, C. F. Jilson, on November 9, 1888. The Resolis post office was discontinued in 1914.

RIVER BEND (platted town) was named in reference to its location on the Big Sandy. The River Bend post office opened in 1875; however, a town plat was not filed for the town until 1909. The Union Pacific Land Company filed a plat for River Bend on June 21, 1909. The River Bend post office was discontinued in the late 1930s.

SIMLA (platted town) was established in 1907 when Mike Altman, a saloon keeper in Ramah, was encouraged to leave Ramah. He moved down the tracks to the site of Simla. A town plat was filed for Simla on January 30, 1909, by the Simla Town Company; William Robinson was its president. Simla was incorporated in 1913.

Places in the Past

BENHAM SPRINGS (stage station) was located on the Smoky Hill North stage route and about seven miles south of the site of Deer Trail.

119

Elbert County

BIJOU BASIN (rural post office) was located next to the El Paso and Elbert county line. The Bijou Basin post office was in operation from 1869 to 1907.

BIJOU CREEK (stage station) was located on the Smoky Hill South stage route and about eighteen miles southeast of the site of Kiowa.

BLAND (rural post office) was located about five miles north of Kuhn's Crossing. The Bland post office was in operation from 1882 to 1921.

BLUEBELL (platted town) was platted about five miles northeast of Elizabeth, and the plat was filed on September 7, 1910, by William Charles Wheeler; however, Bluebell did not obtain a post office, and it was not shown on the map. Bluebell was platted on one of the prettiest locations in Elbert County.

CEDAR POINT (stage station) was located a few miles east of the Cedar Point railroad siding and on the Smoky Hill North stage route. A small fort was located near the Cedar Point stage station and was in use during the 1860s.

CHENOWETH (rural post office) was located about five miles west of Fondis. The Chenoweth post office was in operation from 1897 to 1900.

CLAUD (rural post office) was located about ten miles south of Deer Trail, and the Claud post office was in operation from 1882 to 1888.

CLERMONT (rural post office) was located about ten miles southwest of Elbert. The Clermont post office was in operation from 1881 to 1883.

FAIRMONT (stage station) was located about two miles northwest of the site of Buick and on the Smoky Hill North stage route.

Places on the Colorado Prairie

GOMER'S MILLS (rural post office) was located about seven miles south of Elbert, and the Gomer's Mills post office was in operation from 1870 to 1882. Gomer's Mills was named after P. P. Gomer who settled next to nearby Running Creek in 1869. Gomer established several sawmills in the area, and the mills provided much of the lumber for early Denver. Gomer's Mills was made a siding when the Denver and New Orleans Railroad was built through the area in 1881.

GRACELAND (rural post office) was located about fourteen miles south of Matheson, and the Graceland post office was in operation from 1908 to 1911. Graceland was established by Ed Young.

HARGISVILLE (rural post office) was located about eight miles northeast of Kiowa, and the Hargisville post office was in operation from 1908 to 1915. Hargisville was named after the Hargis brothers, who were local residents.

HOLTWOLD (rural post office) was located about fifteen miles southwest of Matheson, and the Holtwold post office was in operation from 1889 to 1917. The Holtwold post office was located in El Paso County after 1902.

KANZA (rural post office) was located about eleven miles south of Keysor; its office was in operation from 1907 to 1917.

KEYSOR (rural post office) was located about ten miles south of Matheson, and the Keysor post office was in operation from 1906 to 1938. Keysor was named in reference to the Keysor brothers, who were instrumental in starting the community.

KUHN'S CROSSING (rural post office) was located about eighteen miles west of River Bend, and the Kuhn's Crossing post office was in operation from 1879 to 1920. Kuhn's Crossing was named after Charley Kuhn, who owned the nearby XK ranch. Kuhn's ranch was bought by the Richards. Mrs. Richards wrote a book, *The Tenderfoot Bride*, which described her life at the ranch.

Elbert County

NORTON (rural post office) was located about twelve miles southeast of Kiowa, and the Norton post office was in operation from 1889 to 1896.

ORSBURN (rural post office) was located about seven miles north of Elizabeth, and the Orsburn post office was in operation from 1885 to 1896.

REED'S SPRINGS (stage station) was located about three miles south of the site of Kuhn's Crossing and on the Smoky Hill South stage route.

RUNNING CREEK (rural post offce) was located about three miles north of Elizabeth, and the Running Creek post office was in operation from 1868 to 1883. Running Creek was named after a nearby creek and was the site of the Ruthton stage station on the Smoky Hill South stage route.

SCHLEY (rural post office) was located about fifteen miles northeast of Elizabeth, and the Schley post office was in operation from 1899 to 1913. The Schley post office was preceded in the area by the Clemmons post office, which was in operation from 1882 to 1898.

WELL'S RANCH (stage station) was located on the Smoky Hill South stage route and about one mile south of the site of Resolis.

WOLF CREEK (rural post office) was located about fifteen miles northeast of Kiowa, and the Wolf Creek post office was in operation from 1910 to 1919. Wolf Creek was named after a nearby creek.

Some Railroad Tracks

COLORADO & SOUTHERN from Douglas County to El Paso County:
    1881–1886 Denver & New Orleans RR

Places on the Colorado Prairie

1886–1890 Denver, Texas & Gulf RR
1890–1936 Colorado & Southern Ry.

CHICAGO, ROCK ISLAND & PACIFIC from Lincoln County to El Paso County:
1888–1891 Chicago, Kansas & Nebraska Ry.
1891– Chicago, Rock Island & Pacific Ry.

UNION PACIFIC from Lincoln County to Arapahoe County:
1870–1880 Kansas Pacific Ry.
1880–1898 Union Pacific Ry.
1898– Union Pacific RR

Some Whistlestops

BARNWELL (CRI&P) is shown about five miles south of Elbert on a 1902 map.

CAMERON (C&S) is shown about three miles northwest of Elbert on 1887 through 1916 maps.

CEDAR POINT (UP) is shown about three miles northwest of River Bend on 1882 through 1968 maps.

DOBY (C&S) is shown about three miles south of Elbert on a railroad map.

LOWLAND (UP) is shown about eight miles southeast of Deer Trail on 1919 through 1956 maps.

ROCKE BUTTE (C&S) is shown about eight miles southwest of Kiowa on 1882 through 1897 maps.

SIDNEY (C&S) is shown in about the same location as Gomer's Mills on 1892 through 1916 maps and just inside El Paso County on a 1920 map.

123

Places to Think

Northeast of Golden, Jefferson County

Calhan, El Paso County

Chapter 13

El Paso County

Still on the Map

Black Forest	Palmer Lake
Broadmoor	Peyton
Buttes	Pikeview
Calhan	Ramah
Cimmaron Hills	Rush
Colorado Springs	Security
Eastonville	Stratmoor Hills
Ellicott	Stratmoor Valley
Ent Air Force Base	Stratton Meadows
Falcon	Truckton
Fort Carson	U.S. Air Force Academy
Fountain	Wigwam
Ivywild	Yoder
Monument	

North American Air Defense Command (NORAD)

El Paso County

Places in the Past

Air Force Base
Albano
Allan Ranch
Amo
Bassetts
Big Sandy
Brookside
Burt
Chico Basin
Colorado City
Crow's Roost
Drennan
Edgerton
Edison
El Paso
Elsmere
Franceville
Franceville Junction
Gleneath
Glenn
Granger
Gwilliamsville
Hanover
Holtwold
Husted
Jimmy Camp

Kelker
La Vergne
Little Buttes
Loraine
Love
Lytle
Majors
Mosby
Newfield
Papeton
Piedmont
Roswell
Southwater
Squirrel Creek
Suffolk
Surber
Table Rock
Teachouts
Union Hill
Wayne
Weissport
Wheatland
Widefield
Willow Springs
Woodburn

Some Railroad Tracks

Atchison, Topeka & Santa Fe Railway
Chicago, Rock Island & Pacific Railway
Colorado & Southern Railway
Cripple Creek & Colorado Springs Railroad

126

Places on the Colorado Prairie

Denver & Rio Grande Western Railroad
Midland Terminal Railroad (two parts)
Midland Terminal Railway (Golden Cycle)

Some Whistlestops

Aetna	Jimmy Camp
Bierstadt	McConnelisville
Breed	Pring
Carlton	Skinners
Crews	Sommers
Hall	Tip Top
Henkel	Widefield
Holmes	Woodmen

Still on the Map

BLACK FOREST (rural post office) is located about eight miles southwest of Eastonville, and the Black Forest post office has been open since 1960. Black Forest was named for its location in the Black Forest.

BROADMOOR (hotel) was built in 1918 by Spencer Penrose. The Broadmoor Hotel does not meet the scope of places which are included in this book; however, Colorado Springs and the Broadmoor Hotel are interwoven in discussion of the area. The Broadmoor has gained world-wide attention as an exclusive hotel and for its ice-skating facility.

EL PASO COUNTY

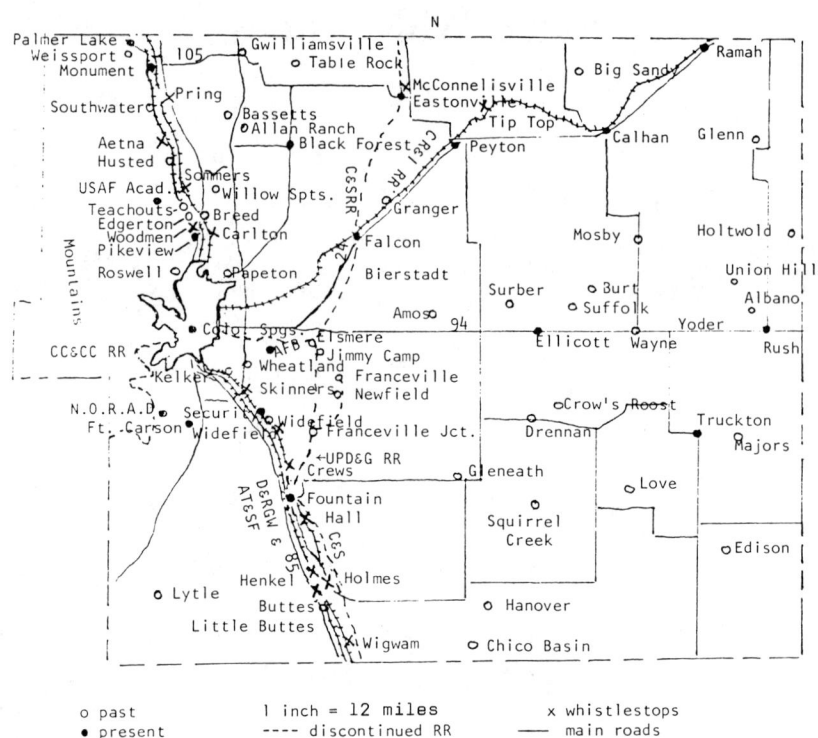

o past
• present

1 inch = 12 miles
---- discontinued RR

x whistlestops
— main roads

EL PASO COUNTY
(Colorado Springs)

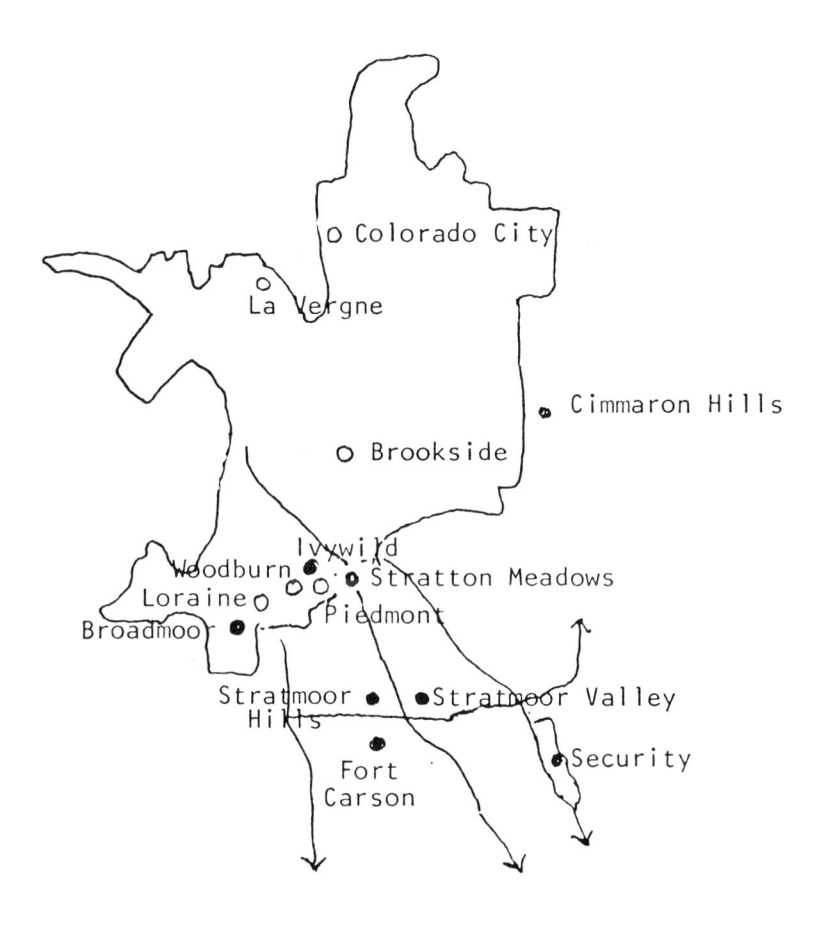

- Colorado City
- La Vergne
- Cimmaron Hills
- Brookside
- Ivywild
- Woodburn
- Stratton Meadows
- Loraine
- Piedmont
- Broadmoor
- Stratmoor Hills
- Stratmoor Valley
- Security
- Fort Carson

o past
● present

1 inch = 2.6 miles

——— main roads

El Paso County

BUTTES (railroad post office) is located next to the Denver and Rio Grande Western railroad and is about eight miles southeast of Fountain. The Buttes post office was in operation from 1895 to 1922 and was preceded by the El Paso post office, which was in operation from 1862 to 1893. El Paso was one of the earliest post offices in El Paso County and is one of the few places in the county which is shown on an 1866 map.

CALHAN (platted town) was established when the Rock Island Railroad built to the site in 1888. A town plat was filed for Calhan on April 17, 1895, by Ely Woodring. Calhan was named after a Mr. Calhan who was a contractor for the Rock Island Railroad.

CIMMARON HILLS (unincorporated metropolitan area) is located just east of Colorado Springs and is shown on a 1975 map.

COLORADO SPRINGS (platted town) was named after the many springs in the area. Colorado City dominated the area at the head of Ute Pass until General William Palmer routed his Denver and Rio Grande railroad east of Colorado City in 1871. General Palmer established Colorado Springs through the Fountain Colony in July 1871, and a town plat was filed for the "Springs" in September of the same year. Colorado City couldn't compete with Colorado Springs and General Palmer, and the seat of El Paso County was moved from Colorado City to the "Springs" in 1873. General Palmer was instrumental in the establishment of Colorado College, which started under control of the Congregational Church. After the discovery of gold in nearby Cripple Creek during 1891, Colorado Springs became the home of many millionaires. Colorado Springs annexed Colorado City in 1917.

EASTONVILLE (platted town) was first called "Easton," and the Easton post office opened in 1872. The Denver and New Orleans railroad was built to Easton in 1881, and Easton was renamed "Eastonville" in 1883. A town plat was filed for Eastonville on November 6, 1886, by Joel Westfall. The Eastonville post office closed in 1932, and the railroad was discontinued to Eastonville in 1936.

Places on the Colorado Prairie

ELLICOTT (rural post office) is located about twenty-four miles east of Colorado Springs, and the Ellicott post office was in operation from 1895 to 1916.

ENT AIR FORCE BASE (military installation) was established as the Colorado Springs Air Force Base during World War II; however, the air force base was renamed "Ent" after the war. The headquarters for the air base is located within Colorado Springs, and the air traffic is handled at Peterson Field southeast of the "Springs." When the North American Air Defense Command was established in Colorado Springs, it was headquartered at Ent Air Force Base.

FALCON (platted town) was platted next to the Rock Island Railroad when it was built through the area in 1888 by the Chicago, Kansas and Nebraska Railway. A town plat was filed for Falcon on September 18, 1888, by the Falcon Town and Land Company. The Falcon post office closed in 1942.

FORT CARSON (military installation) was established just south of Colorado Springs in 1942 and was first called "Camp Carson." In 1954, Camp Carson was renamed "Fort Carson," and the installation has grown to become the largest military establishment in Colorado.

FOUNTAIN (platted town) was named after nearby Fountain Creek which in turn was named after the soda springs or Fountaine-Qui-Bouille. Fountain was started as a Quaker colony by Terrell and Hutchin, who filed a plat for Fountain on January 14, 1871; however, the Fountain post office had opened seven years earlier. The Rio Grande railroad was built to Fountain in 1872, and the Santa Fe railroad reached Fountain in 1887. In 1888, a carload of powder on the Santa Fe railroad exploded and destroyed the town of Fountain; however, the town was rebuilt by the Santa Fe Railway Company.

IVYWILD (platted town) was located two miles south of Colorado Springs when the Ivywild post office was opened in 1871. A town

El Paso County

plat was filed for Ivywild on February 11, 1888, by William B. Jenkins. Ivywild was eventually absorbed by Colorado Springs; however, Ivywild is still shown on the map.

MONUMENT (platted town) was named after a nearby rock formation. The Monument post office opened in 1869, and the Rio Grande railroad was built to Monument in 1871. The railroad station at Monument was first called "Henry's" in reference to Henry Limbach, who filed the plat for Monument on January 5, 1874. Charles Adams was also responsible for the platting of Monument.

NORTH AMERICAN AIR DEFENSE COMMAND (military installation) was established in the Colorado Springs area for the primary purpose of detecting enemy aircraft or missiles which might be directed toward an attack upon North America. The North American Air Defense Command (NORAD) is deemed so vital to the defense of the United States that the operational section of the command is built underground in Cheyenne Mountain, which is located just southwest of Colorado Springs.

PALMER LAKE (platted town) was named in reference to General William Palmer, whose Rio Grande railroad was built to the site of Palmer Lake in 1871. The first railroad station at the site of Palmer Lake was called "Divide," and a post office was established at nearby Weissport in 1875. A town plat was filed for Palmer Lake on December 1, 1883, by David Dodge, and the Weissport post office was changed to Palmer Lake in 1887.

PEYTON (platted town) was named after George Peyton who filed the town plat for Peyton on February 29, 1889. The site of Peyton was first called "Mayfield," and the name was changed shortly after the Rock Island railroad was built to the site in 1888.

PIKEVIEW (railroad post office) is located about six miles north of Colorado Springs and next to the Denver and Rio Grande Railroad. The Pikeview post office was in operation from 1902 to 1957. Pikeview was named after the view of Pikes Peak from the site.

Places on the Colorado Prairie

RAMAH (platted town) was named in reference to a name in a book by the wife of a Rock Island railroad official. The Rock Island railroad was built to the site of Ramah in 1888, and a town plat was filed on December 12, 1888, by Lemuel Gammon. Ramah was preceded in the area by the O. Z. post office which was in operation from 1877 to 1889. O.Z. was named after "Old Zounds," who applied for the post office.

RUSH (rural post office) is located about seven miles east of Yoder, and the Rush post office has been in operation since 1908.

SECURITY (unincorporated metropolitan area) is located just southeast of Colorado Springs and is shown on a 1975 map. Security was preceded by Widefield which is shown on 1873 through 1920 maps. Security's post office opened in 1958.

STRATMOOR HILLS AND STRATMOOR VALLEY (unincorporated metropolitan area) are shown just west of Security on a 1975 map.

STRATTON MEADOWS (unincorporated metropolitan area) is located just northeast of Broadmoor and is shown on a 1975 map.

TRUCKTON (place name) is shown about eight miles southeast of Yoder on 1956 and 1968 maps.

UNITED STATES AIR FORCE ACADEMY (military installation) was authorized by Congress in 1954. The first class of cadets in the academy began their training at Lowry Air Force Base in Denver in July 1955, while the academy was being constructed eight miles north of Colorado Springs. The cadets began formal occupation of the academy in 1957.

WIGWAM (railroad post office) is located on the Denver and Rio Grande railroad and about four miles southeast of Buttes. The Wigwam post office was in operation from 1882 to 1922.

YODER (rural post office) is located about seven miles west of Rush, and the Yoder post office began operation in 1904.

El Paso County

Places in the Past

AIR FORCE BASE (military installation) was established east of Colorado Springs in 1942. After World War II, the air base was renamed "Ent," and the airfield was named "Paterson Field."

ALBANO (rural post office) was located about four miles northwest of Rush, and the Albano post office was in operation from 1904 to 1912.

ALLAN RANCH (stage station) was located on the Cherokee Trail stage route and about four miles northwest from the site of Black Forest. The Allan Ranch station was operated in conjunction with a tavern, and both were located on the north bank of Squirrel Creek.

AMO (rural post office) was located about fifteen miles northeast of Colorado Springs, and the Amo post office was in operation from 1899 to 1916.

BASSETTS MILL (rural post office) was located about eight miles southeast of Monument, and the Bassetts Mill post office was in operation from 1869 to 1872.

BIG SANDY (rural post office) was located about thirty miles southeast of Elbert, and the Big Sandy post office was in operation from 1876 to 1877 and from 1882 to 1888. The Big Sandy post office was named after the nearby Big Sandy Creek.

BROOKSIDE (platted town) has been absorbed by Colorado Springs; however, the town plat for Brookside was filed on July 31, 1891, by James Curtis. Brookside was not shown on maps.

BURT (rural post office) was located about ten miles south of Calhan, and the Burt post office was in operation from 1910 to 1916.

CHICO BASIN (place name) is shown about nine miles east of Wigwam on 1909 through 1920 maps.

Places on the Colorado Prairie

COLORADO CITY (platted town) was established by a town company from Denver which was headed by R. E. Cable and Melancthon Beach. Colorado City was established in 1859, and the Colorado City post office opened in the same year. Colorado City was made county seat of El Paso County; however, it lost that position to nearby Colorado Springs in 1873. Colorado Springs dominated the area at the base of Ute Pass, and Colorado City was eventually annexed in 1917.

CROW'S ROOST (rural post office) was located about five miles south of Ellicott, and the Crow's Roost post office was in operation from 1913 to 1916.

DRENNAN (rural post office) was located about seven miles southwest of Ellicott, and the Drennan post office was in operation from the 1930s to 1951.

EDGERTON (railroad post office) was located on the Denver and Rio Grande railroad and about eight miles north of Colorado Springs. The Edgerton post office was in operation from 1870 to 1902.

EDISON (place name) is shown about eight miles south of the site of Truckton on a 1956 map.

EL PASO (early settlement) was located at the base of Ute Pass and preceded Colorado City and Colorado Springs in the area. El Paso City was established in 1858 by the Lawrence party of gold-seekers; however, the community was short-lived and gave way to Colorado City.

ELSMERE (railroad post office) was located on the Rock Island railroad and about seven miles east of Colorado Springs. The Elsmere post office was in operation from 1889 to 1890.

FRANCEVILLE (railroad post office) was located on the Colorado and Southern railroad and about twelve miles east of Colorado Springs. The Franceville post office was in operation from 1881 to 1894.

El Paso County

FRANCEVILLE JUNCTION (railroad post office) was located about six miles southwest of Franceville and next to the Colorado and Southern railroad. The Franceville Junction post office was in operation from 1892 to 1899.

GLENEATH (rural post office) was located about thirteen miles northeast of Fountain, and the Gleneath post office was in operation from 1910 to 1916.

GLENN (rural post office) was located about ten miles southeast of Ramah, and the Glenn post office was in operation from 1896 to 1901 and again in 1903.

GRANGER (railroad post office) was located about six miles southwest of Peyton and next to the Colorado and Southern Railroad. The Granger post office was in operation from 1883 to 1888.

GWILLIAMSVILLE (rural post office) was located about six miles east of Monument, and the Gwilliamsville post office was in operation from 1878 to 1898.

HANOVER (rural post office) was located about twenty-six miles southeast of Colorado Springs, and the Hanover post office was in operation from 1913 to 1921. Hanover was named after Hanover, Iowa, which was the hometown of a Mr. Fankell who established the post office.

HOLTWOLD (rural post office) was located in Elbert County in the 1890s and is shown in El Paso County on 1916 and 1920 maps. The Holtwold post office was in operation from 1889 to 1902 and from 1910 to 1917.

HUSTED (railroad post office) was located next to the Denver and Rio Grande railroad, and the Husted post office was in operation from 1878 to 1920. Husted was named after Calvin Husted, an early-day sawmill operator in the area.

Places on the Colorado Prairie

JIMMY CAMP (cabin site) was named after Jimmy Daugherty, who built his cabin either in the 1820s or 1830s about eight miles east of the site of Colorado Springs. Daugherty was a member of Major Long's expedition into Colorado during the 1820s, and he returned to the Pike's Peak area shortly after the expedition. Daugherty was a friend of the Ute Indians, and, when he was killed by several Mexicans in 1833, the Utes tracked down and killed the murderers. The road from Fountain to Russellville became known as the Jimmy Camp Road, and Jimmy Camp Creek carries the name of Jimmy Daugherty. There was a Jimmy Camp post office near the site of Jimmy Camp in the late 1870s, and a railroad siding on the Colorado and Southern railroad through the area was called "Jimmy Camp."

KELKER (railroad post office) was located next to the Denver and Rio Grande Railroad and about two miles northwest of Skinners. The Kelker post office was in operation from 1912 to 1914.

LA VERGNE (platted town) was platted just northwest of Colorado Springs, and the plat was filed on March 8, 1887, by William Swift. La Vergne was not shown on the map, and it did not obtain a post office. The land description on the La Vergne plat has been absorbed by Colorado Springs.

LITTLE BUTTES (stage station) was located about one-fourth mile south of the Buttes railroad station and on the Cherokee Trail stage route.

LORAINE (platted town) was platted just north of the Broadmoor Hotel; the plat was filed on July 18, 1888, by a person whose name is not discernible on the plat. Loraine did not obtain a post office, and it was not on the map.

LOVE (rural post office) was located about twenty-two miles east of Fountain. The Love post office was in operation from 1894 to 1902.

LYTLE (rural post office) was first called "Turkey Creek," and the Turkey Creek post office was in operation from 1877 to 1881.

El Paso County

The Lytle post office was in operation from 1885 to 1920 and was located about twelve miles southwest of Fountain.

MAJORS (rural post office) was located about fourteen miles southwest of Rush, and the Majors post office was in operation from 1911 to 1912.

MOSBY (rural post office) was located about eight miles northeast of Ellicott, and the Mosby post office was in operation from 1910 to 1913.

NEWFIELD (rural post office) was located about one mile south of Franceville, and the Newfield post office was in operation from 1896 to 1898. Newfield was first called "McFerran," and the McFerran post office was in operation from 1889 to 1896.

PAPETON (platted town) was established when the Curtis coal mine which was one-half mile from the site of Papeton had labor disputes. The white strikers at the Curtis mine became enraged at the use of black strikebreakers and moved from the mine to the site of Papeton. A town plat was filed for Papeton May 13, 1901, by Page and Kent. The site of Papeton was just north of Colorado Springs.

PIEDMONT (platted town) was platted just northeast of the Broadmoor, and the plat was filed on May 19, 1891, by James Newton. Piedmont did not obtain a post office. It was not shown on any maps.

ROSWELL (railroad post office) was located next to the Denver and Rio Grande railroad and just north of Colorado Springs. The Roswell post office was in operation from 1889 to 1908.

SOUTHWATER (railroad post office) was located next to the Denver and Rio Grande railroad and about four miles southeast of Monument, and the Southwater post office was in operation from 1872 to 1878. Southwater was called "Borsts" after the post office was discontinued.

Places on the Colorado Prairie

SQUIRREL CREEK (rural post office) was located about sixteen miles east of Fountain and was named after a nearby creek. The Squirrel Creek post office was in operation from 1911 to 1916.

SUFFOLK (rural post office) was located about twenty miles southeast of Fountain, and the Suffolk post office was in operation from 1879 to 1886.

SURBER (rural post office) was located about six miles northwest of Ellicott. The Surber post office was in operation from 1895 to 1916.

TABLE ROCK (rural post office) was named after a nearby rock formation, and the Table Rock post office was in operation from 1873 to 1893.

TEACHOUTS (stage station) was located near the site of Edgerton and was named after Leafy Teachout, who ran the station. The Teachout station was in operation in the late 1860s.

UNION HILL (place name) is shown about six miles northwest of Yoder on 1909 and 1916 maps.

WAYNE (rural post office) was located about eight miles northwest of Rush, and the Wayne post office was in operation from 1909 to 1912.

WEISSPORT (railroad post office) was located about one-half mile south of the site of Palmer Lake and next to the Denver and Rio Grande railroad. The Weissport post office was in operation from 1875 to 1887.

WHEATFIELD (rural post office) was located about four miles southeast of Colorado Springs, and the Wheatfield post office was in operation from 1869 to 1873.

WIDEFIELD (stage station) was located about six miles northwest of the site of Fountain and where Security is now located. The Widefield station was on the Cherokee stage route.

El Paso County

WILLOW SPRINGS (stage station) was located about eight miles southwest of the site of Black Forest and was on the Cherokee stage route.

WOODBURN (platted town) was platted about one mile northeast of the Broadmoor, and the plat was filed on July 29, 1889, by Edgar Ensign; however, Woodburn did not obtain a post office, and it was not shown on the maps.

Some Railroad Tracks

ATCHISON, TOPEKA & SANTA FE from Douglas County to Pueblo County:

    1887–1900 Denver & Santa Fe RR

    1900–   Atchison, Topeka & Santa Fe Ry.

CHICAGO, ROCK ISLAND & PACIFIC from Elbert County to Colorado Springs:

    1888–1891 Chicago, Kansas & Nebraska Ry.

    1891– Chicago, Rock Island & Pacific Ry.

COLORADO & SOUTHERN from Elbert County to Pueblo County:

    1881–1886 Denver & New Orleans RR

    1886–1888 Denver, Texas & Gulf RR

    1888–1890 Denver, Texas & Fort Worth RR

    1890–1898 Union Pacific, Denver & Gulf Ry.

    1898–1936 Colorado & Southern Ry.

CRIPPLE CREEK & COLORADO SPRINGS from Colorado Springs to Cripple Creek:

    1901–1904 Colorado Springs & Cripple Creek Dist. Ry.

    1904–1911 Colorado & Southern Ry.

    1911–1915 Florence & Cripple Creek Ry.

    1915–1920 Cripple Creek & Colorado Springs RR

DENVER & RIO GRANDE WESTERN from Douglas County to Colorado Springs:

    1871–1886 Denver & Rio Grande Ry.

    1886–1921 Denver & Rio Grande RR

    1921–   Denver & Rio Grande Western RR

DENVER & RIO GRANDE WESTERN from Colorado Springs to Pueblo County:

    1872–1886 Denver & Rio Grande Ry.

    1886–1921 Denver & Rio Grande RR

    1921–   Denver & Rio Grande Western RR

MIDLAND TERMINAL from Colorado Springs into the mountains:

    1888–1890 Colorado Midland Ry.

    1890–1900 Atchison, Topeka & Santa Fe Ry.

    1900–1917 Colorado & Southern Ry. and Rio Grande Western Ry.

    1917–1921 Carlton Interests

    1921–1934 Midland Terminal Ry.

    1934–1949 Golden Cycle Mining and Milling Co.

Some Whistlestops

AETNA (D&RGW) is shown about eight miles southeast of Monument on a 1913 map.

BIERSTADT (C&S) is shown about three miles southwest of Falcon on 1892 through 1902 maps.

BREED (AT&SF) is shown about eight miles north of Colorado Springs on 1909 through 1968 maps.

El Paso County

CARLTON (AT&SF) is shown about one mile south of Breed on a 1920 map.

CREWS (AT&SF) is shown about three miles northwest of Fountain on 1909 through 1968 maps.

HALL (AT&SF) is shown about two miles south of Fountain on 1902 and 1909 maps.

HENKEL (D&RGW) is shown about two miles northwest of Buttes on 1909 through 1956 maps.

HOLMES (AT&SF) is shown about four miles south of Fountain on 1916 and 1920 maps.

JIMMY CAMP (C&S) is shown about eight miles east of Colorado Springs on 1882 and 1892 maps.

MCCONNELISVILLE (C&S) is shown about twelve miles southwest of Elbert on an 1887 map.

PRING (AT&SF) is shown about four miles southeast of Monument on 1902 through 1968 maps.

SKINNERS (D&RGW) is shown about seven miles southeast of Colorado Springs on 1909 through 1968 maps.

SOMMERS (AT&SF) is shown about four miles northwest of Breed on 1909 through 1920 maps.

TIP TOP (CRI&P) is shown about eight miles northwest of Calhan on 1892 and 1902 maps.

WIDEFIELD (D&RGW) is shown about five miles northwest of Fountain on 1873 through 1920 maps.

WOODMEN (D&RGW) is shown about one mile north of Pikeview on a 1916 map.

Places to Live

Dearfield, Weld County

Southwest of Fort Morgan, Morgan County

Chapter 14

Huerfano County

Still on the Map

Carbonado
Delcarbon
Lascar
Mustang

Pictou
Pryor
Ravenwood
Walsenburg

Places in the Past

Apache
Caddel
Camp Shumway
Cucharas
Farr
Gordon

Ideal
Larimer
Lester
Loma Park
Maitland

Huerfano County

Mayne
McGuire
Muriel
Pauley
Rattlesnake Butte
Raybal

Rosedale
Round Oak
Rouse
Tioga
Walsen

Some Railroad Tracks

Colorado & Southern Railway (two parts)
Denver & Rio Grande Western (seven parts)

Some Whistlestops

Black Cañon
Breen
Cameron
Champion
Consul
Dresden
Globe
Hezron
Hezron Junction
Monson

Nichols
Orlando
Roof
Rouse Junction
Sandy
Santa Clara Junction
Sunshine
Toltec
Tuna
Winchell

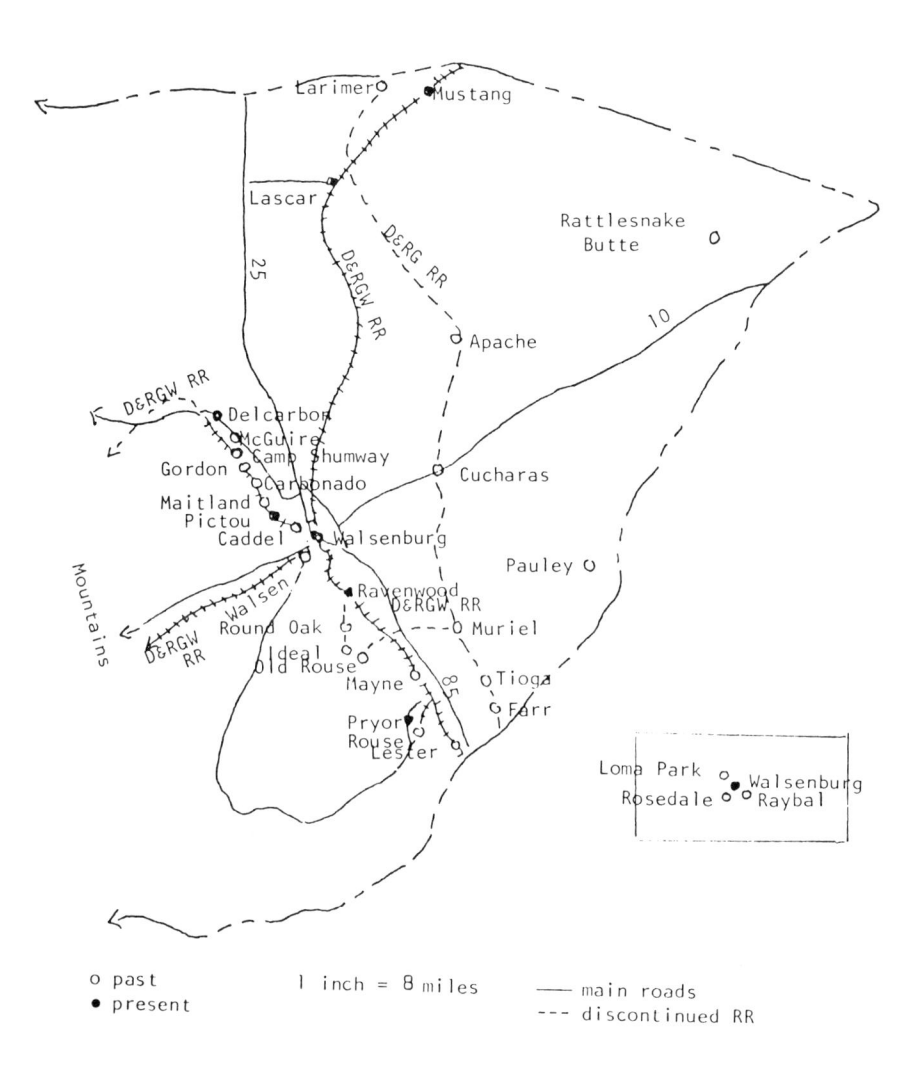

HUERFANO COUNTY

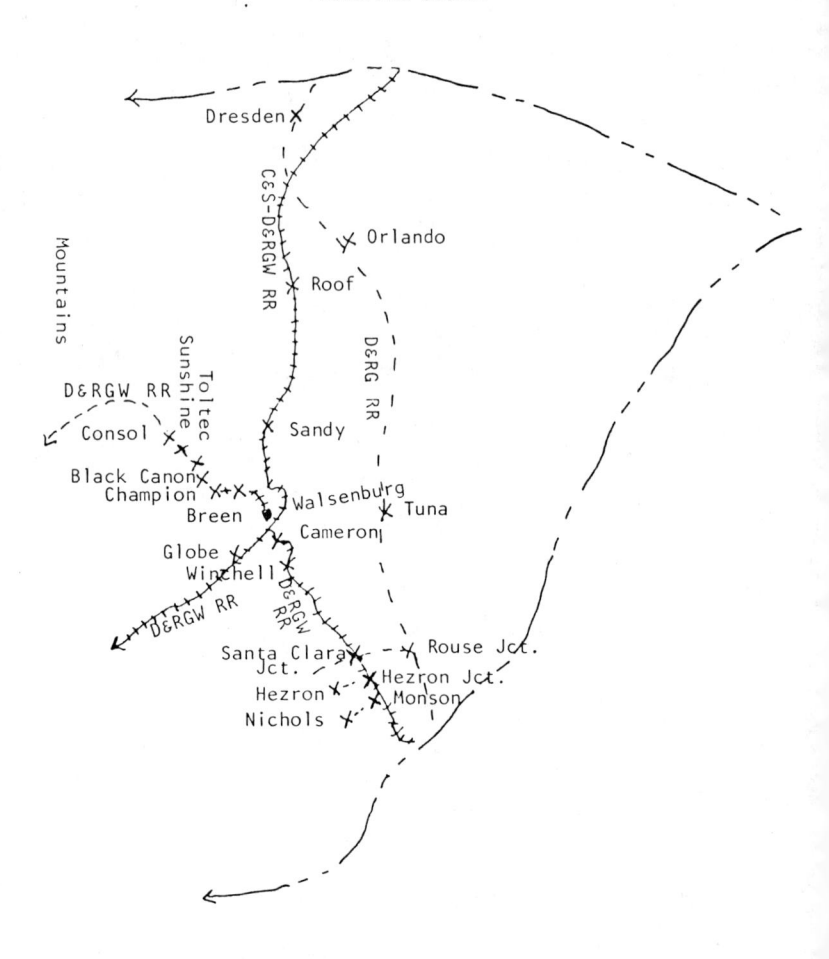

x whistlestops   1 inch = 8 miles   ---- discontinued RR

Still on the Map

CARBONADO (place name) is shown in the same approximate location as Gordon on a 1974 map; however, Carbonado is not listed in the postal guide, nor is it shown on a survey map. Carbonado probably serves as a way-stop.

DELCARBON (railroad post office) is located about nine miles northwest of Walsenburg on the Denver and Rio Grande Railroad to Alamo. The Delcarbon post office was in operation from 1915 to 1953.

LASCAR (railroad post office) is located about thirteen miles north of Walsenburg on the Colorado and Southern and Rio Grande double-track line. Lascar was first called "Concord," and the Lascar post office was in operation from 1916 to 1947.

MUSTANG (railroad post office) is located about four miles northeast of Lascar on the Colorado and Southern and Rio Grande double-track line. The Mustang post office was in operation from 1914 to 1940.

PICTOU (railroad post office) is located about three miles northwest of Walsenburg on the Rio Grande railroad into the coal field northwest of Walsenburg. The Pictou post office was in operation from 1889 to 1932.

PRYOR (railroad post office) is located about ten miles southeast of Walsenburg. Pryor was the terminus of a spur line from the branch line to Santa Clara, which was built by the Denver and Rio Grande Railroad in 1888. The branch and spur line to Pryor were removed in 1941; however, the Pryor post office has maintained operation since 1898.

RAVENWOOD (railroad post office) is located about two miles south of Walsenburg on the Colorado and Southern Railroad. The Ravenwood post office was in operation from 1910 to 1939.

Huerfano County

WALSENBURG (platted town) is the focal point and dominating community of Huerfano County—all roads lead to Walsenburg. Walsenburg was named after its founder, Fred Walsen. The site of Walsenburg was the location of the Mexican settlement, La Plaza de las Leones, in the 1840s; however, it was another thirty years before Walsen started his town on the Cucharos River. A town plat was filed for Walsenburg on October 20, 1873, but the Walsenburg post office started three years earlier. After the arrival of the railroad, Walsenburg became the center of coal development in southern Colorado.

Places in the Past

APACHE (railroad post office) was one of two places in Huerfano County which were named "Apache"; however, this Apache was located on the Denver and Rio Grande railroad from Cucharas to Pueblo County. The Apache post office was in operation from 1894 to 1925.

CADDEL (platted town) was named after its founder, Edward Caddel, who filed a plat for the town in 1908. Caddel was platted next to Walsenburg, but it never obtained a post office. Caddel was located on the Denver and Rio Grande Railroad, which ran to the coal fields northwest of Walsenburg.

CAMP SHUMWAY (railroad post office) was located about a mile southeast of Delcarbon on the Denver and Rio Grande railroad northwest from Walsenburg. Camp Shumway handled the postal services for Gordon from 1911 until the Gordon post office opened in 1924.

CUCHARAS (platted town) once competed with Walsenburg as a rail center in Huerfano County. A town plat was filed for Cucharas on August 1, 1874, by the Southern Colorado Improvement Company, and Cucharas was named after the nearby Cucharas

Places on the Colorado Prairie

River. Cucharas became a vitally important junction for the Denver and Rio Grande Railroad; however, when a direct line was built from Pueblo to Walsenburg in 1911, the line through Cucharas steadily deteriorated until all track had been removed by 1936.

FARR (railroad post office) was located south of Rouse Junction on the Denver and Rio Grande railroad. The Farr post office was in operation from 1907 to 1946.

GORDON (platted town) was located northwest of Walsenburg on the Denver and Rio Grande railroad. A town plat was filed for Gordon by John Jones on May 29, 1908, but Camp Shumway was the designated post office for the area until the Gordon post office opened in 1924.

IDEAL (railroad post office) was located at the terminus of a short spur from Round Oak on the Colorado and Southern railroad. The Ideal post office serviced the Ideal Mine area from 1910 to 1929.

LARIMER (platted town) was established on the Denver and Rio Grande railroad to Cucharas. A town plat for Larimer was filed by C. Vallentin on December 21, 1906, but Larimer soon surrendered its post office to Mustang on the nearby double-track line to Walsenburg.

LESTER (railroad post office) was located just south of Monson on the Colorado and Southern railroad south of Walsenburg; however, the station at Lester was called "Bunker Hill." The Lester post office was in operation from 1910 to 1929.

LOMA PARK (platted town) was platted next to Walsenburg, and the plat was filed on June 17, 1908, by Tom Sproull. Loma Park did not obtain a post office, and it is not shown on the maps. Most of the communities which were platted near Walsenburg were expansions of Walsenburg because of the increased activity in coal mining in the area.

MAITLAND (railroad post office) was one of many post office communities that sprang up along the Rio Grande's line from

151

Huerfano County

Walsenburg to Alamo in the coal field. Maitland's post office opened in 1898 and continued service until 1935.

MAYNE (railroad post office) was the terminus of a spur from the Rio Grande's railroad to "new" Rouse. Mayne was one of many coal communities which were reached by spur lines off the Colorado and Southern and Rio Grande railroads south of Walsenburg. The Mayne post office was in operation only from 1905 to 1907, but Mayne stayed on the map for a number of years afterward.

McGUIRE (railroad post office) was located on the Denver and Rio Grande railroad northwest of Walsenburg. McGuire was the forerunner to the Camp Shumway post office and was in operation from 1905 to 1911.

MURIEL (railroad post office) was located at Rouse Junction on the Denver and Rio Grande railroad south of Cucharas. The Muriel post office operated in the early 1900s.

PAULEY (rural post office) was located about thirteen miles southeast of Walsenburg, and the Pauley post office was in operation during the 1920s.

RATTLESNAKE BUTTE (rural post office) was located in the northeastern part of Huerfano County. The Rattlesnake post office was in operation from 1918 to 1938.

RAYBAL (platted town) was platted just northwest of Walsenburg, and the plat was filed on July 19, 1940, by Clestina Guerrero. Raybal did not obtain a post office.

ROSEDALE (platted town) was platted just southwest of Walsenburg, and the plat was filed on June 4, 1887, by several persons; however, Rosedale did not obtain a post office, and it did not "make" the maps.

ROUND OAK (railroad post office) was located on the line to the Ideal Mine. The Round Oak post office was in operation from 1908 to 1910.

Places on the Colorado Prairie

ROUSE (railroad post office) was first located about five miles south of Walsenburg, and then it was moved to the Santa Clara post office on the Denver and Rio Grande line through Pryor. The Santa Clara post office operated off and on from 1873 to 1894, and the Rouse post office operated from 1889 to 1929.

TIOGA (railroad post office) was located south of Cucharas on the Denver and Rio Grande railroad. The Tioga post office operated from 1907 to 1954.

WALSEN (railroad post office) was located just southwest of Walsenburg on the Denver and Rio Grande line to LaVeta. The Walsen post office operated from 1902 to 1932.

Some Railroad Tracks

COLORADO AND SOUTHERN from Walsenburg to Las Animas County:
    1895–1898 Union Pacific, Denver & Gulf Ry.
    1898–   Colorado & Southern Ry.

COLORADO AND SOUTHERN from Pueblo County to Walsenburg:
    1911–1930 Colorado RR
    1930–   Colorado & Southern Ry. (jointly with D&RGW)

DENVER AND RIO GRANDE WESTERN from Pueblo County to Walsenburg (double track with C&S):
    1911–1921 Denver & Rio Grande RR
    1921–   Denver & Rio Grande Western RR

DENVER AND RIO GRANDE WESTERN from Pueblo County through Cucharas to Las Animas County:
    1876–1886 Denver & Rio Grande Ry.
    1886–1921 Denver & Rio Grande RR
    1921–1936 Denver & Rio Grande Western RR.
        1924 discontinued from Lascar to Larimer

Huerfano County

    1932 Discontinued from Cucharas to Lascar
    1936 Discontinued from Cucharas to Las Animas County

DENVER AND RIO GRANDE WESTERN from Mustang to Larimer:
    1924–1955 Denver & Rio Grande Western RR

DENVER AND RIO GRANDE WESTERN from Cucharas to LaVeta:
    1876–1886 Denver & Rio Grande Ry.
    1886–1921 Denver & Rio Grande RR
    1921–   Denver & Rio Grande Western RR
    1937   Discontinued from Cucharas to Walsenburg

DENVER AND RIO GRANDE WESTERN from Rouse to Rouse Junction:
    1888–1921 Denver & Rio Grande RR
    1921–1949 Denver & Rio Grande Western RR
        1936 Discontinued from Rouse Junction to Mayne
        1947 Discontinued from Pryor to Mayne
        1949 Discontinued from Rouse to Pryor

DENVER AND RIO GRANDE WESTERN from Pictou to the New Pacific Mine:
    1927–1937 Denver & Rio Grande Western RR

DENVER AND RIO GRANDE WESTERN from Walsenburg to Alamo:
  Walsenburg to Pictou:
    1888–1921 Denver & Rio Grande RR
    1921–   Denver & Rio Grande Western RR

  Pictou to Maitland:
    1896–1921 Denver & Rio Grande RR
    1921–   Denver & Rio Grande Western RR
  Maitland to Strong:
    1904–1921 Denver & Rio Grande RR

Places on the Colorado Prairie

    1921–   Denver & Rio Grande Western RR
            1942 Discontinued from Strong to Calumet
            1959 Discontinued from Calumet to Kebler
Strong to Big Four:
    1908–1921 Denver & Rio Grande RR
    1921–1942 Denver & Rio Grande Western RR
Big Four to Alamo:
    1923–1942 Denver & Rio Grande Western RR

Some Whistlestops

BLACK CAÑON (D&RGW) is shown about five miles northwest of Walsenburg on a railroad map.

BREEN (D&RGW) is shown about one mile west of Walsenburg on a railroad map.

CAMERON (C&S) is shown about one mile south of Walsenburg on a 1969 map.

CHAMPION (D&RGW) is shown about three miles northwest of Walsenburg on a railroad map.

CONSUL (D&RGW) is shown about seven miles northwest of Walsenburg on a railroad map.

DRESDEN (D&RGW) is shown about three miles northeast of Lascar on 1909 through 1916 maps.

GLOBE (C&S) is shown about two miles southwest of Walsenburg on a 1969 map.

HEZRON (D&RGW) is shown about seven miles southeast of Walsenburg on 1909 through 1920 maps.

HEZRON JUNCTION (D&RGW) is shown about seven miles southwest of Walsenburg on a railroad map.

155

Huerfano County

Monson (C&S) is shown about eight miles southeast of Walsenburg on 1916 through 1959 maps.

Nichols (D&RGW) is shown just south of Pryor on a railroad map.

Orlando (D&RGW) is shown about seven miles north of Cucharas on 1902 through 1920 maps.

Roof (C&S) is shown about five miles south of Lascar on 1916 and 1920 maps.

Rouse Junction (D&RGW) is shown about eight miles southeast of Walsenburg on 1892 through 1920 maps.

Sandy (C&S—D&RGW) is shown about five miles north of Walsenburg on 1916 through 1968 maps.

Santa Clara Junction is shown about six miles southeast of Walsenburg on a 1902 map.

Sunshine (D&RGW) is shown about three miles northwest of Walsenburg on a railroad map.

Toltec (D&RGW) is shown about one mile west of Walsenburg on 1916 and 1920 maps.

Tuna (D&RGW) is shown about six miles east of Walsenburg on 1892 through 1920 maps.

Winchell (D&RGW) is shown about three miles southeast of Walsenburg on 1902 through 1920 maps.

Places To Stop

Haxtun, Phillips County

Grover, Weld County

Chapter 15

Jefferson County

Still on the Map

Applewood
Arvada
Camp George West
Edgewater
Golden
Kassler
Lakewood

Leyden
Morrison
Mountain View
Plainview
Pleasant View
Wheatridge

Places in the Past

Arapahoe City
Archers
Berkeley
Church's
Fisk Orchard Place
Gate City
Gilman

Morningside
Mount Vernon
Norwood
Ralston
Semper
Strouseville
Waterton

Jefferson County

Some Railroad Tracks

Associated Railroads
Burlington Northern Railroad
Colorado Central Railroad (two parts)
Colorado & Southern Railway (four parts)
Denver & Interurban Railroad
Denver Tramway Corporation (four parts)
Denver & Rio Grande Western Railroad
Denver, Utah & Pacific Railroad
Union Pacific, Denver & Gulf Ry. (two parts)

Some Whistlestops

Arena	Juchem
Church's	Lees Siding
Church's	Mount Carbon
Church's	Mount Olivet
Clear Creek Junction	Ralston
Coal Creek	Ridge
College Hill	Rifle Range
Cowan	Standley Lake
Glencoe	Thomas
Hallack Junction	Wyman
Jones	

Still on the Map

APPLEWOOD (unincorporated metropolitan area) is located just southwest of Wheatridge and is shown on a 1975 map.

JEFFERSON COUNTY

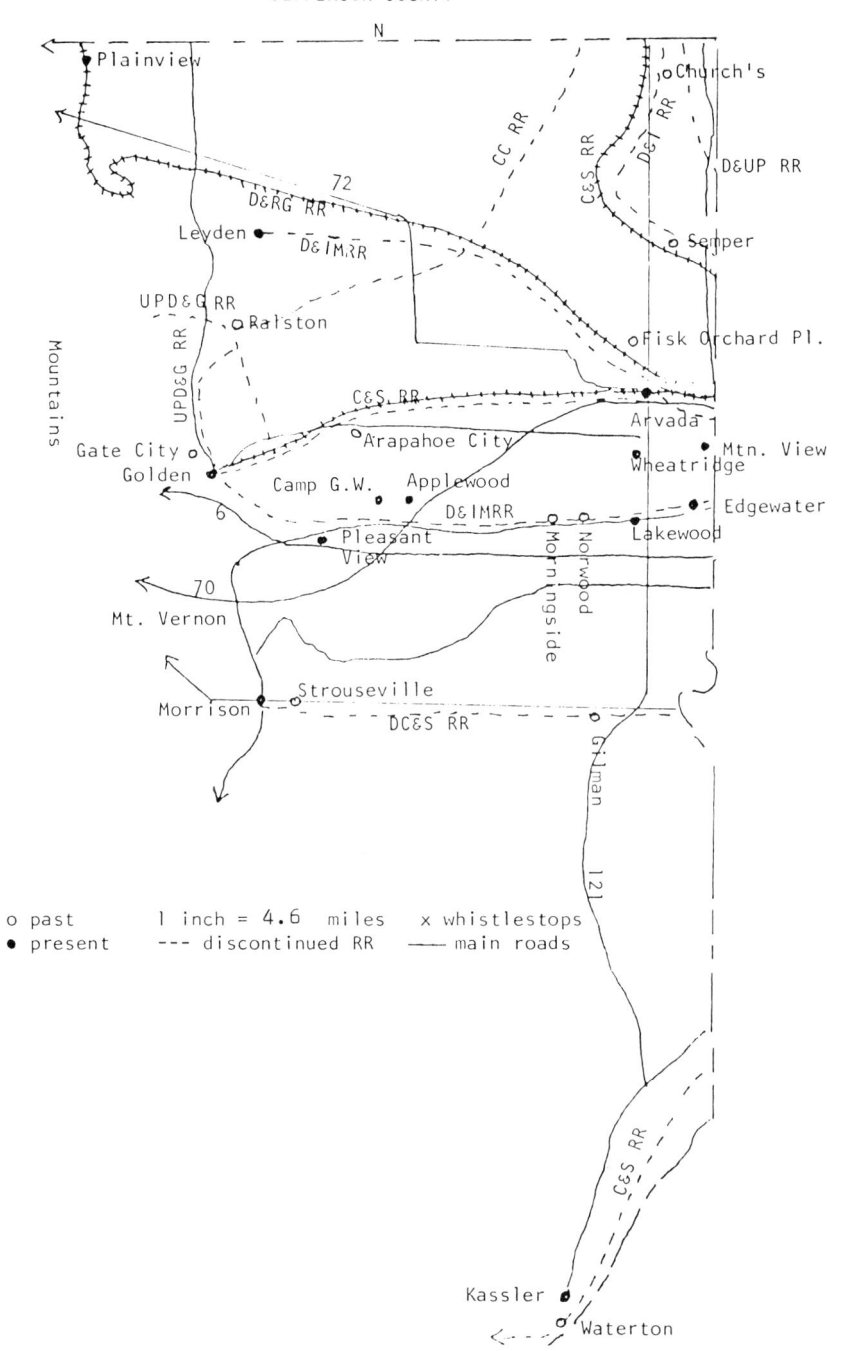

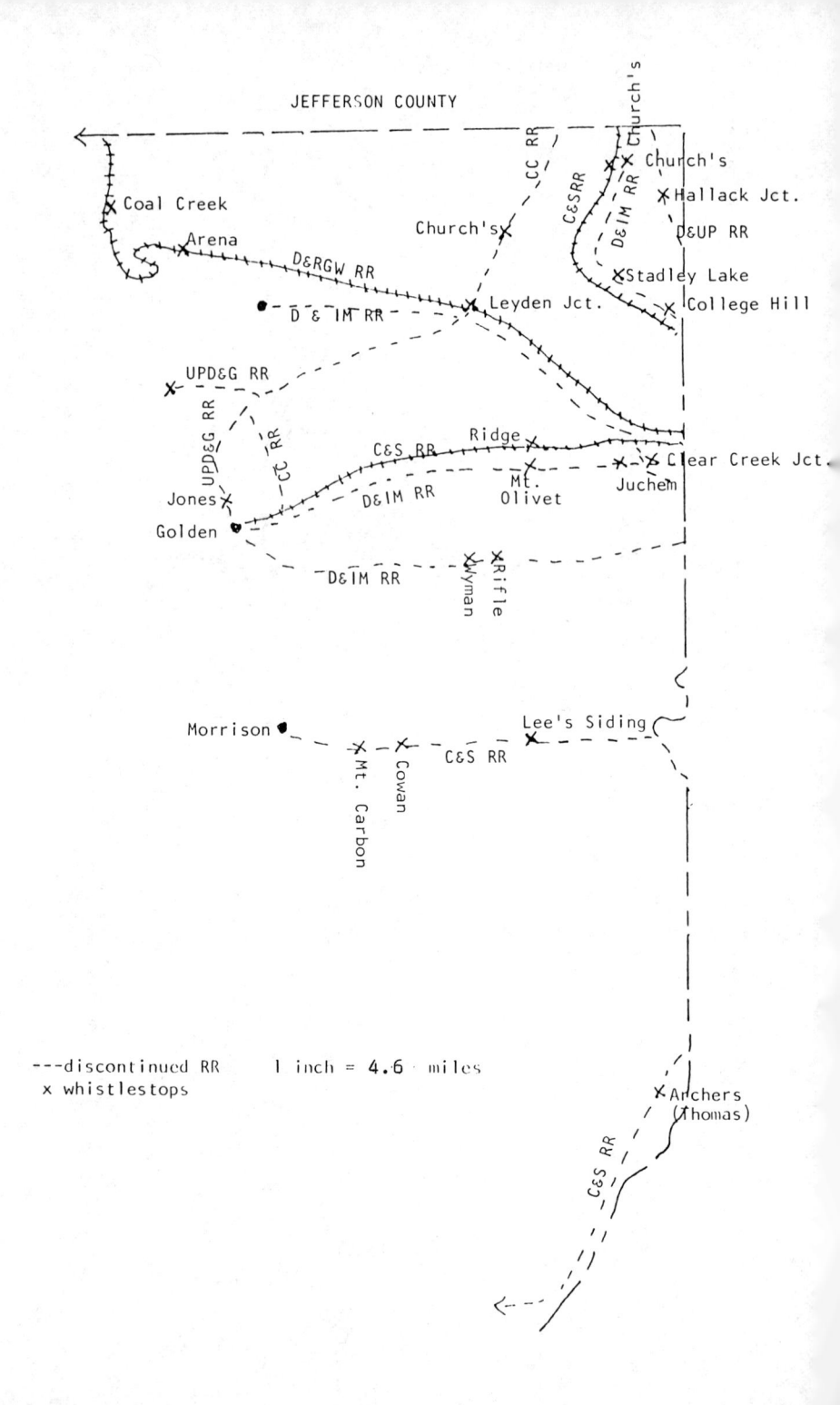

Places on the Colorado Prairie

ARVADA (platted town) was platted when the Colorado Central railroad was built through the area in 1870, and the plat was filed by Lewis A. Reno and B. F. Wadsworth on November 28, 1870. Arvada was named after Hiram Arvada Hoskins who was the brother-in-law of B. F. Wadsworth. Arvada was first known as "Ralston Creek" after Lewis Ralston who was a member of a California-bound party of Cherokee Indians from Georgia. The Cherokees found some "color" in Ralston Creek, and their find eventually led to the famous find of another Cherokee, William Green Russell, in 1858; thus, it can be said that the discovery of gold near the site of Arvada was the forerunner of the Colorado gold rush.

CAMP GEORGE WEST (military installation) was established on 675 acres just southeast of Golden as headquarters for the Colorado National Guard.

EDGEWATER (platted town) was named in reference to its location next to Sloan's Lake. A town plat was filed for Edgewater on May 13, 1889, by Carleton Ellis, Al Townsend, and others. The Manhattan Beach Amusement Park, which was later called "Luna Park," was constructed next to Sloan's Lake in 1890 and served as a constant irritant to Edgewater until the Park burned down in 1912.

GOLDEN (platted town) was named after Tom Golden, who was a co-founder of the town. A town plat was filed for Golden in 1863 and included part of an 1859 plat. Golden was first called "Golden City" and was established by the Boston Company. Golden was the capital of the Colorado Territory from 1862 to 1867. The Colorado School of Mines was established in Golden as part of Randal's University in 1871 and was deeded to the Territory in 1874.

KASSLER (water treatment plant) is shown on 1956 and 1968 maps. Kassler is located near the site of Waterton, a railroad station on the Denver, South Park and Pacific Railroad.

LAKEWOOD (platted town) was named after Lakewood, New Jersey, and a town plat for the first Lakewood was filed on July 26,

Jefferson County

1889, by Charles Welch, Miranda Loveland, and William A. Loveland, president of the Colorado Central Railroad. The Denver, Lakewood and Golden Railroad, which was operated by William Loveland, was built through the Lakewood area in 1892, and the line later became known as the "Loop" of the Denver Tramway Corporation. The plat for the first Lakewood was vacated in 1927; however, the site of the first Lakewood and the surrounding area continued to be called "Lakewood". The area which was known as "Lakewood" expanded rapidly after World War II and was finally incorporated as "Lakewood" in 1969.

LEYDEN (platted town) was named after the Leyden brothers who were residents in the area. Coal-mining activity commenced in the Leyden area during the 1870s; however, a town plat was not filed for Leyden until Paul Pattridge filed one on July 31, 1950.

MORRISON (platted town) is located at the base of the foothills and near the Red Rocks amphitheater. Morrison was named after George Morrison who founded the town. A town plat was filed for Morrison on November 28, 1874, by the Morrison Stone, Lime, and Town Company. Morrison was once billed as a resort town, but declined in that respect as metropolitan Denver expanded toward the foothills.

MOUNTAIN VIEW (platted town) was named after its location and was established in 1904. The site of Mountain View was first platted as "Berkeley" by Ellis and John McDonough in 1888; however, the plat was vacated, and Berkeley was replatted north of its original site. Mountain View has gained some distinction as one of the few conclaves in the Denver area which has resisted annexation.

PLAINVIEW (rural post office) was named after its location which is at the base of the foothills. The Plainview post office was in operation from 1909 to 1952. It is located about four miles south of Eldorado Springs.

PLEASANT VIEW (unincorporated metropolitan area) is located just southeast of Golden and is shown on a 1975 map.

Places on the Colorado Prairie

WHEATRIDGE (platted town) was named after the famed wheat farms in the area which were owned by Henry Lee, a state senator from 1885 to 1889. The area just northwest of Denver was called "Wheatridge" and the Wheatridge post office was established in 1913; however, Wheatridge was not incorporated until 1969.

Places in the Past

ARAPAHOE CITY (mining camp) was located about three miles east of Golden and is shown on an 1866 map. Arapahoe City emerged as a gold camp in 1858, but the gold strikes in the mountains led to its demise a few years later. George Jackson and John Gregory, who made famous gold discoveries at Idaho Springs and Central City, respectively, stopped at Arapahoe City en route to the "diggin's" in the mountains.

ARCHERS (railroad post office) was located about six miles southwest of Littleton and on the Denver, South Park and Pacific railroad. The Archers post office was in operation from 1888 to 1893.

BERKELEY (platted town) was platted in approximately the same location as Mountain View, and the plat was filed on December 28, 1888, by Ellis and John McDonough. The first Berkeley plat was vacated, and another plat was filed for Berkeley in 1894 by A. C. Fisk. The 1894 plat placed Berkeley just north of "Inspiration Point."

CHURCH'S (stage station) was located on the Overland stage route and about three miles south of the site of Broomfield. Church's Station was also known as "Childs" and "Twelve-Mile House." Church's was a large twenty-room house.

FISK ORCHARD PLACE (platted town) was platted just north of Arvada, and the plat was filed by A. C. Fisk on March 22, 1892. Fisk Orchard Place did not obtain a post office, and it was not shown on the map. Fisk also founded "Fisk's Gardens,"

Jefferson County

forerunner to Englewood, and he filed a plat for the second Berkeley.

GATE CITY (toll station) was located just north of Golden and was named in reference to its function as a toll station on the road to Central City. Gate City was established by Tom Golden, co-founder of Golden; thus, Golden Gate Canyon was named in reference to Golden's Gate City at the mouth of the canyon. After the main supply route was moved to Clear Creek Canyon, Gate City lost its importance.

GILMAN (railroad post office) was located about three miles west from the site of Englewood and next to the Denver, South Park and Pacific railroad. The Gilman post office was in operation from 1874 to 1876.

MORNINGSIDE (platted town) was platted between Golden and Denver and next to the Denver and Intermountain electric railway. A town plat was filed for Morningside on May 17, 1911, by Ettie Reynolds; however, Morningside never obtained a post office, nor was it shown on the map.

MOUNT VERNON (platted town) was not a "prairie town" in the strictest sense; however, it was near the base of the foothills and similar to Morrison in location. Mount Vernon was named after its location, which was at the mouth of Mount Vernon Canyon. Mount Vernon was established by the Denver, Auraria, and Colorado Wagon Road Company in 1860, and the company was organized by such notables as Robert Steele, a territorial governor, and George Morrison, founder of Morrison. Mount Vernon served as a toll gate to Mount Vernon Canyon, and a town plat was filed on March 6, 1866, by George W. Charles. The Mount Vernon post office was in operation off and on from 1860 to 1885.

NORWOOD (platted town) was platted just north of the original Lakewood, and the town plat was filed on February 4, 1888, by George C. Hummel. Norwood did not obtain a post office, and it was not shown on the map.

Places on the Colorado Prairie

RALSTON (railroad post office) was named after nearby Ralston Creek and was located next to the Colorado Central railroad from Golden to Cheyenne. The Ralston post office was in operation from 1863 to 1870 and in 1887. The track that was north of Ralston was removed in 1888, and the track that was south of Ralston was removed in 1898.

SEMPER (platted town) was platted next to the Denver, Utah and Pacific railroad, and the plat was filed on March 4, 1886, by John Witler and Ben Brewer. Semper was named after Charles Semper, who was an early resident in the area. The Semper post office was established in 1882 and discontinued in 1900. Semper was also served by the Denver, Marshall and Boulder railroad and the Denver and Intermountain railway.

STROUSEVILLE (platted town) was platted just east of Morrison, and the plat was filed on April 1, 1874, by John Strouse. Strouseville was platted in the same year that the Denver, South Park and Pacific railroad was built to Morrison. Strouseville did not obtain a post office.

WATERTON (railroad post office) was located at the mouth of the South Platte Canyon and next to the Denver, South Park and Pacific railroad. Waterton was first called "Enterprise," and the Enterprise post office was in operation from 1879 to 1881. Waterton was next called "Platte Cañon," and the Platte Cañon post office operated from 1881 to 1893. Waterton and the railroad was discontinued in 1942.

Some Railroad Tracks

ASSOCIATED RAILROADS from Denver to the Federal Center:
   1890–1904 Denver, Lakewood & Golden RR
   1904–1907 Denver & Intermountain Ry.
   1907–1909 Intermountain Ry.
   1909–1913 Denver & Intermountain RR.
   1913–1914 Denver City Tramway (used Denver & Intermountain name)

Jefferson County

  1914–1925 Denver Tramway Co.
  1925–1953 Denver Tramway Corp.
  1953– Associated Railroads

BURLINGTON NORTHERN from Boulder County to Adams County (joint line with C&S):
  1889–1908 Denver, Utah & Pacific RR
  1908–1970 Chicago, Burlington & Quincy RR
  1970– Burlington Northern RR

COLORADO CENTRAL from Boulder County to Ralston:
  1872–1888 Colorado Central RR

COLORADO CENTRAL from Ralston to Boulder Junction:
  1872–1878 Colorado Central RR (on east side of Table Mountain)

COLORADO & SOUTHERN from Boulder County to Adams County (joint line with BN):
  1886–1890 Denver, Marshall & Boulder Ry.
  1890–1898 Union Pacific, Denver & Gulf Ry.

COLORADO & SOUTHERN from Adams County to Golden:
  1870–1890 Colorado Central RR
  1890–1898 Union Pacific, Denver & Gulf Ry.
  1898– Colorado & Southern Ry.

COLORADO & SOUTHERN from Arapahoe County to Waterton:
  1873–1889 Denver, South Park & Pacific Ry.
  1889–1898 Denver, Leadville & Gunnison Ry.
  1898–1942 Colorado & Southern Ry.

COLORADO & SOUTHERN from Arapahoe County to Morrison:
  1874–1889 Denver, South Park & Pacific RR
  1889–1898 Denver, Leadville & Gunnison RR
  1898–1938 Colorado & Southern Ry.
    1919 abandoned one-half mile
    1934 abandoned six miles

DENVER & INTERURBAN from Boulder County to Adams County (electric):
  1908–1926 Denver & Interurban RR

Places on the Colorado Prairie

DENVER TRAMWAY CORP. from Denver Federal Center Spur to Golden (standard and electric):
    1890–1904 Denver, Lakewood & Golden RR
    1904–1907 Denver & Intermountain Ry.
    1907–1909 Intermountain Ry.
    1909–1913 Denver & Intermountain RR
    1913–1914 Denver City Tramway (used Denver & Intermountain name)
    1914–1925 Denver Tramway Co.
    1925–1953 Denver Tramway Corp.

DENVER TRAMWAY CORP. from Clear Creek Junction to Golden (electric):
    1903–1913 Denver & Northwestern Ry.
    1913–1914 Denver City Tramway
    1914–1925 Denver Tramway Co.
    1925–1953 Denver Tramway Corp.

DENVER TRAMWAY CORP. from Denver to Leyden (standard and electric):
    1901–1913 Denver & Northwestern Ry.
    1913–1914 Denver City Tramway
    1914–1925 Denver Tramway Co.
    1925–1953 Denver Tramway Corp.

DENVER TRAMWAY CORP. from Wyman to the clay pits:
    1909–1920 Denver, Golden & Morrison RR
    1920–1925 Denver Tramway Co.
    1925–1953 Denver Tramway Corp.

DENVER & RIO GRANDE WESTERN from Adams County to Boulder County:
    1902–1912 Denver, Northwestern & Pacific RR
    1912–1947 Denver & Salt Lake RR
    1947–   Denver & Rio Grande Western RR

DENVER, UTAH & PACIFIC from Adams County to Boulder County:
    1881–1889 Denver, Utah & Pacific RR

Jefferson County

UNION PACIFIC, DENVER & GULF from Golden to Ralston:
   1877–1890 Colorado Central RR
   1890–1898 Union Pacific, Denver & Gulf Ry. (tracks on west side of Table Mountain)

UNION PACIFIC, DENVER & GULF from Ralston to Glencoe:
   1884–1890 Denver & Middle Park RR
   1890–1898 Union Pacific, Denver & Gulf Ry.

Some Whistlestops

ARENA (D&RG) is shown about nine miles northwest of Golden on a railroad map.

CHURCH'S (CC) is shown about three miles southwest of Broomfield on 1882 to 1897 maps.

CHURCH'S (C&S) is shown about three miles south of Broomfield on 1909 to 1920 maps.

CHURCH'S (D&I) is shown about three miles south of Broomfield on a 1920 map. (Church's was a whistlestop for three railroads.)

CLEAR CREEK JUNCTION (D&IM) is shown about one mile southeast of Arvada on a railroad map.

COAL CREEK (D&RG) is shown about one mile south of Plainview on a 1909 map.

COLLEGE HILL (D&I) is shown about two miles east of Semper on a 1920 map.

COWAN (C&S) is shown about three miles east of Morrison on a 1920 map.

GLENCOE (UPD&G) is shown about seven miles northwest of Golden on 1892 through 1902 maps.

Places on the Colorado Prairie

HALLACK JUNCTION (DU&P) is shown about four miles southeast of Broomfield on a 1909 map.

JONES (UPD&G) is shown about one mile north of Golden on 1882 through 1892 maps.

JUCHEM (D&IM) is shown about one mile west of Clear Creek Junction on a railroad map.

LEES SIDING (C&S) is shown about six miles east of Morrison on 1882 through 1892 maps.

MOUNT CARBON (C&S) is shown about three miles east of Morrison on a 1920 map.

MOUNT OLIVET (D&IM) is shown about four miles west of Clear Creek Junction on a 1920 map.

RALSTON (D&RG) is shown about one mile east of Arvada on a 1909 map.

RIDGE (C&S) is shown about three miles southwest of Arvada on 1916 through 1940 maps.

RIFLE RANGE (D&IM) is shown about four miles west of Lakewood on a 1920 map.

STANDLEY LAKE (D&I) is shown about one mile northwest of Semper on a 1920 map.

THOMAS (C&S) is shown about six miles southwest of Littleton on a 1920 map.

WYMAN (D&IM) is shown about five miles west of Lakewood on a railroad map.

Chapter 16

Kiowa County

Still on the Map

Arlington
Brandon
Chivington
Eads
Galatea

Haswell
Hawkins
Sheridan Lake
Stuart
Towner

Places in the Past

Arden
Coon Valley
Dayton
Kilburn
Queen Beach

Salt Springs
Sand Creek
Segreganset
Sweetwater
Water Valley

Some Railroad Tracks

Arkansas Valley Railway
Missouri Pacific Railroad

Kiowa County

Some Whistlestops

Diston

Inman

Still on the Map

ARLINGTON (railroad post office) was first named "Joliet" and was the "J" in Jessie Thayer's alphabetical naming of places along the Pueblo and State Line railroad. The Arlington post office has been in operation since 1887.

BRANDON (platted town) was the "B" in Jessie Thayer's alphabetical naming of places along the railroad. Jessie Thayer was the daughter of S. H. Mallory, who headed the Pueblo and State Line Railroad which built from Kansas to Pueblo in 1887. A town plat was filed for Brandon on March 25, 1910, by I. S. Ritchey; the Brandon post office opened in 1888, closed in 1893, and reopened in 1908.

CHIVINGTON (platted town) was the "C" in Thayer's alphabetical naming of towns along the railroad and was named in reference to the ill-fated Colonel John Chivington of the Sand Creek Massacre. The town of Chivington was a railroad "boom town" for a while, with a Missouri Pacific railroad roundhouse located in the town. A town plat was filed for Chivington on April 14, 1920, by someone whose name was not stated on the plat. Chivington was incorporated in 1888; thus, it was probably platted in 1887, but the earlier plat is not on file.

EADS (platted town) was platted, but the plat on file has neither a date of filing nor the name of the filer of the plat. Eads was established by S. H. Mallory, who was the head of the Pueblo and State Line Railroad which built to Eads in 1887. Eads was preceded in the area by Dayton, which was established on a proposed route of the railroad; however, the railroad was built on a

Places on the Colorado Prairie

different route, and Mallory's Eads was made the railroad station for the area. Eads obtained the county seat from Sheridan Lake in 1902.

GALATEA (railroad post office) was the "G" in Jessie Thayer's alphabetical naming of places along her father's railroad. The Galatea post office was in operation from 1887 to 1948.

HASWELL (railroad post office) was the "H" in Jessie Thayer's alphabetical naming of places along her father's railroad. The Haswell post office has been in operation next to the Missouri Pacific railroad since 1903.

HAWKINS (railroad post office) was first called "Fergus," the "F" in Thayer's naming of places. The Fergus post office operated from 1888 to 1890, and a post office is not listed for Hawkins.

SHERIDAN LAKE (platted town) was named in reference to Colonel Phil Sheridan of Civil War fame. A town plat is not on file for Sheridan Lake; however, it is likely that a plat was filed for Sheridan Lake in 1888, because Sheridan Lake was made the seat of Kiowa County when the county was formed in 1889. The Pueblo and State Line railroad first used the Arden station until Sheridan Lake enticed the railroad to use its independently built station. The county seat was moved to Eads in 1902.

STUART (railroad post office) is located about four miles west of Towner, and the Stuart post office was in operation from 1888 to 1889 and from 1911 to 1912.

TOWNER (railroad post office) was first called "Memphis," and the Towner post office opened in 1888. Towner gained national attention in 1931 when several children and the driver froze to death on a stalled school bus in a winter storm. The rest of the students on the bus were saved by a student, Bryan Unteidt, who kept them active until they were rescued.

175

Kiowa County

Places in the Past

ARDEN (railroad post office) was the "A" of Thayer's alphabetical naming of towns along the railroad. The Arden post office was in operation only in 1888 because Sheridan Lake won the railroad's favor over nearby Arden; however, Arden is shown on a 1902 map.

COON VALLEY (place name) is shown about twelve miles southwest of Sheridan Lake on 1892 and 1902 maps.

DAYTON (proposed railroad station) was located about three miles south of Eads and was a proposed station on the Pueblo and State Line railroad; however, the railroad was routed through Eads, and Dayton ceased to exist.

KILBURN (railroad post office) was located about six miles southwest of Arlington, and the Kilburn post office was in operation in 1890 and 1891.

QUEEN BEACH (platted town) was named after its location, which was next to King Reservoir. Queen Beach was a planned recreational community, and a town plat was filed for Queen Beach on August 26, 1908, by the Queen Beach Resort and Amusement Company. The town of Queen Beach was short-lived, and the Queen Beach post office closed in 1911.

SALT SPRINGS (place name) is shown about seven miles south of the site of Galatea on an 1882 map.

SAND CREEK (battleground) was the site of the infamous Sand Creek Massacre. On November 29, 1864, Colonel John Chivington and a force of 750 soldiers attacked an encampment of Indians (Cheyenne and Arapahoe) near Sandy Creek. The Indians, who were led by Chief Black Kettle, were mostly women and children. Colonel Chivington gave orders for no survivors, and, of the 650 Indians in the village, only about 150 survived the massacre. Although the massacre aroused nationwide indignation,

Places on the Colorado Prairie

Colonel Chivington was never court martialed for his part in the attack.

SEGREGANSET (rural post office) was located about twelve miles north of Hasty. The Segreganset post office was in operation from 1914 to 1917.

SWEETWATER (rural post office) was located about thirteen miles south of Eads, and the Sweetwater post office was in operation from 1908 to 1918. Sweetwater was located next to one of the Great Plains Reservoirs and was named after its location.

WATER VALLEY (rural post office) was located next to Big Sandy Creek and about twelve miles northwest of Sheridan Lake. The Water Valley post office was in operation from 1887 to 1894.

Some Railroad Tracks

ARKANSAS VALLEY from Cheyenne County to Otero County:
    1873–1877 Arkansas Valley Ry.

MISSOURI PACIFIC from Kansas to Crowley County:
    1887–1917 Missouri Pacific Ry.
    1917–   Missouri Pacific RR.

Some Whistlestops

DISTON (MP) is shown about seven miles east of Eads on 1882 through 1956 maps.

INMAN (MP) is shown about six miles northeast of Arlington on 1892 through 1956 maps. Inman was the "I" in Thayer's alphabetical naming of places along her father's railroad, and Inman was named in reference to Colonel Henry Inman, author of *The Santa Fe Trail*.

NOTE: The earlier of many town plats for towns in Kiowa County were not on file in 1973.

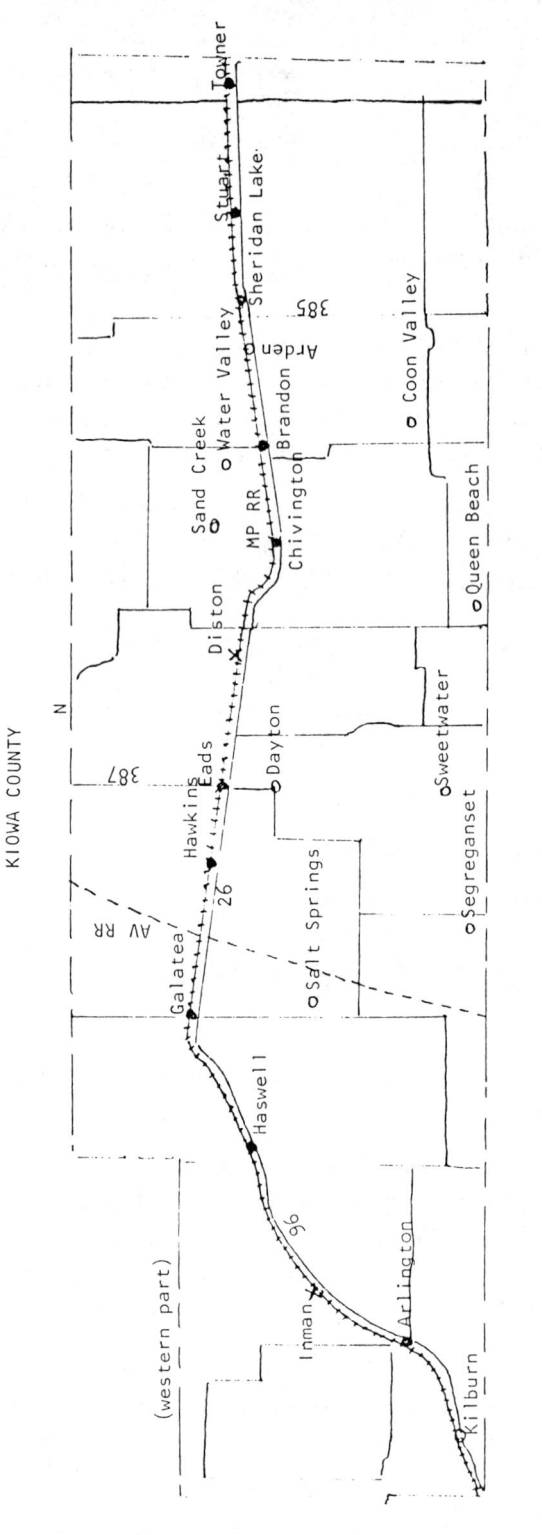

Chapter 17
Kit Carson County

Still on the Map

Bethune
Burlington
Flagler

Seibert
Stratton
Vona

Places in the Past

Ashland
Avendale
Beaverton
Beloit
Bonny
Carey
Carlisle
Chapin
Cole
Columbia
Crystal Springs
Elphis
Goff
Hoyt

Landsman
Loco
Morris
Old Burlington
Oriska
Perry's Corner
Station 21
Station 22
Station 23
Tuttle
Valley
Van's Point
Wallett
Yale

Kit Carson County

Some Railroad Tracks

Chicago, Rock Island & Pacific Railway

Some Whistlestops

Muskoka
Peconic

Still on the Map

BETHUNE (platted town) began as a post office station on the Rock Island railroad in 1889. A town plat was filed for Bethune on May 17, 1918. Bethune was incorporated in 1926.

BURLINGTON (platted town) was platted about two miles west of "Old Burlington" when the Rock Island railroad was built through the county in 1888. The town plat for Burlington was filed on June 23, 1888, by R. S. and Anna Newell. Burlington and Old Burlington were named after Burlington, Kansas, which was the hometown of an early settler in the area. Burlington was designated the seat of Kit Carson County when the county was formed in 1889.

FLAGLER (platted town) was first called "Malowe," then "Bowser." A town plat was filed for Flagler on October 18, 1888, by J. B. McGonigal, and the town was named in reference to Henry Flagler, a Rock Island Railroad official. The town of Flagler was incorporated in 1916.

SEIBERT (platted town) was named in reference to Henry Seibert, who was an official of the Rock Island Railroad which built through the area in 1888. A town plat was filed for Seibert on August 29, 1888, by the Rock Island townmaker, C. F. Jilson.

KIT CARSON COUNTY

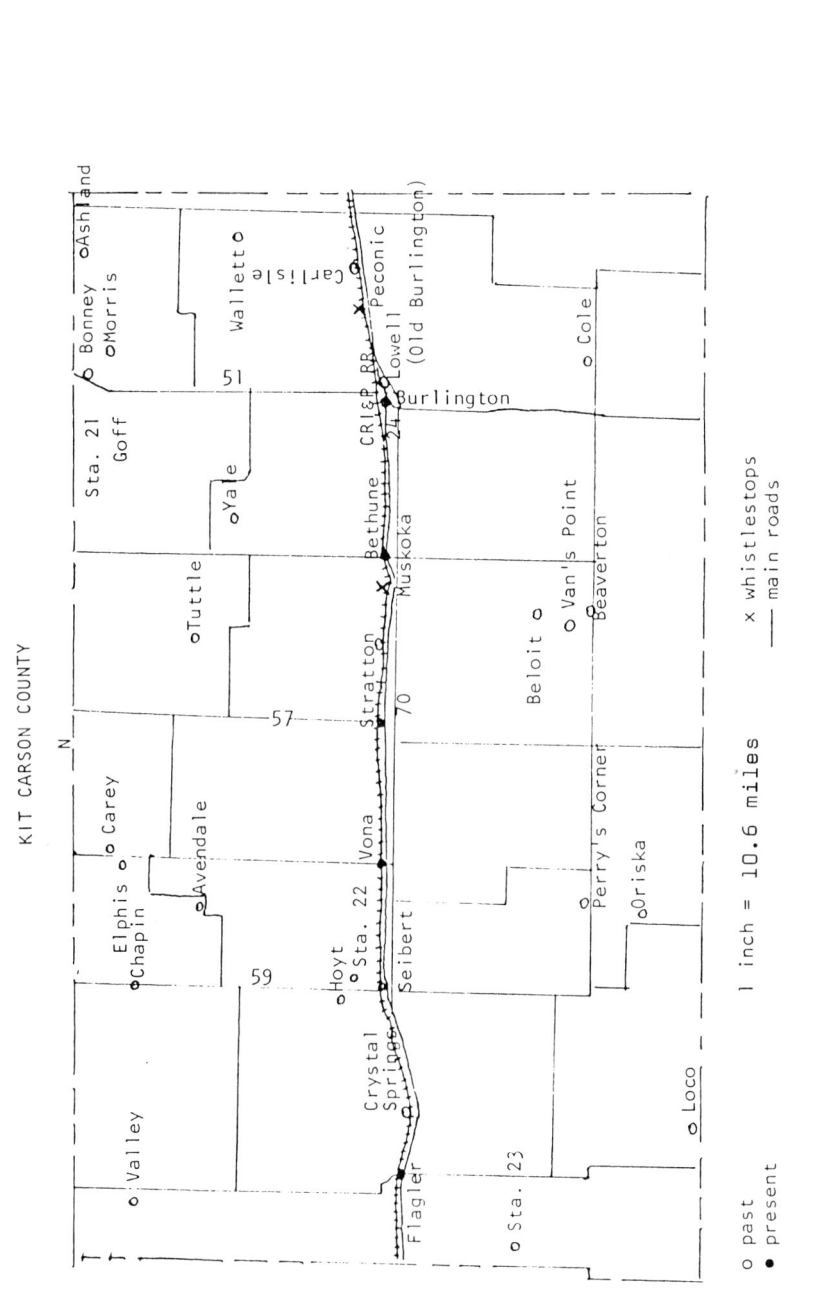

(Map of Kit Carson County showing towns and railroad line)

Towns and locations shown:
- Valley, Elphis, Chapin, Carey, Avendale, Hoyt, Sta. 22, Vona, Seibert, Crystal Springs, Flagler, Sta. 23
- Bonney, Ashland, Morris, Sta. 21, Goff, Wallett, Carlisle, Yale, Tuttle
- Bethune, Lowell, Peconic (Old Burlington), Burlington, CRI&P RR
- Stratton, Muskoka, Beloit, Van's Point, Beaverton, Cole
- Perry's Corner, Oriska, Loco

Route markers: 59, 57, 51, 70, 24

N ↑

1 inch = 10.6 miles

o past
● present

x whistlestops
— main roads

Kit Carson County

STRATTON (platted town) was platted as "Claremont" by C. F. Jilson and R. S. Newell in July 1888. Newell was instrumental in the platting of "Old Burlington," and Jilson, as has been suggested, was involved with the platting of many towns along the Rock Island railroad. Claremont was renamed "Stratton" in 1906.

VONA (platted town) was named after a niece of Pearl King who filed the plat for Vona on March 20, 1889. Vona and most of the platted towns along the Rock Island railroad in Kit Carson County were platted within a year of the railroad's arrival in 1888. Vona was incorporated in 1919.

Places in the Past

ASHLAND (rural post office) was located about twenty miles northeast of Burlington, and the Ashland post office was in operation from 1890 to 1909.

AVENDALE (rural post office) was located about ten miles northeast of Seibert. The Avendale post office was in operation from 1889 to 1890.

BEAVERTON (rural post office) was located about twelve miles southwest of Bethune, and the Beaverton post office was in operation from 1910 to 1915.

BELOIT (rural post office) was located about nine miles southwest of Bethune; the Beloit post office was in operation from 1888 to 1893.

BONNY (rural post office) was located about eighteen miles north of Burlington, and the Bonny post office was in operation from 1915 to 1924.

CAREY (rural post office) was located about fifteen miles north of Vona. The Carey post office was in operation from 1910 to 1916.

Places on the Colorado Prairie

CARLISLE (railroad post office) was located about eight miles northeast of Burlington, and the Carlisle post office was in operation from 1887 to 1890.

CHAPIN (rural post office) was located about six miles northwest of Avendale, and the Chapin post office was in operation from 1890 to 1894.

COLE (rural post office) was located about fifteen miles south of Burlington, and the Cole post office was in operation from 1907 to 1919.

COLUMBIA (platted town) was platted next to the Rock Island railroad, and the plat was filed on May 28, 1888; however, Columbia never obtained a post office and was little more than a plat.

CRYSTALSPRINGS (platted town) is shown on an 1892 map, and the plat for Crystal Springs was filed on July 7, 1888, by S. S. Strode; however, Crystal Springs never obtained a post office.

ELPHIS (rural post office) was located near the site of Carey; the Elphis post office operated from 1916 to 1923.

GOFF (rural post office) was located about eighteen miles northwest of Bethune. The post office at Goff was in operation from 1888 to 1910.

HOYT (rural post office) was located about five miles north of Seibert, and the Hoyt post office operated in 1888.

LANDSMAN (rural post office) was located near Landsman Creek and about twenty miles northwest of Burlington. The Landsman post office was in operation from 1883 to 1918 (also shown in Yuma County).

LOCO (rural post office) was located about fifteen miles northeast of Wildhorse. The Loco post office was in operation from 1903 to 1922. Loco remained on the map into the 1940s.

Kit Carson County

MORRIS (rural post office) was located about sixteen miles northeast of Burlington, and the Morris post office was in operation from 1907 to 1914. Morris was also called "Cottage House."

OLD BURLINGTON (platted town) was located about two miles east from the present site of Burlington. Old Burlington was preceded on the site by Lowell, which was platted one month earlier by the Lowell Townsite Company. A town plat was filed for Old Burlington on June 3, 1887, by the Lowell Townsite Company, which had platted Lowell on the same site. Old Burlington and Burlington were named after Burlington, Kansas, which was the hometown of an earlier settler in the area.

ORISKA (rural post office) was located about twenty-two miles north of Kit Carson, and the Oriska post office was in operation from 1910 to 1917.

PERRY'S CORNER (place name) is shown about fourteen miles southeast of Seibert on a 1916 map.

STATION 21 (stage station) was located on the Leavenworth and Pikes Peak stage route and near the Yuma and Kit Carson County line.

STATION 22 (stage station) was located on the Leavenworth and Pikes Peak stage route and about two miles north from the site of Seibert.

STATION 23 (stage station) was located on the Leavenworth and Pikes Peak stage route and somewhere within ten miles southwest of Flagler.

TUTTLE (rural post office) was located about twenty miles northeast of Stratton, and the Tuttle post office was in operation from 1883 to 1918.

VALLEY (rural post office) was located about seventeen miles north of Genoa, and the Valley post office was in operation from 1898 to 1901.

Places on the Colorado Prairie

VAN'S POINT (place name) is shown about eleven miles southwest of Bethune on a 1916 map.

WALLETT (rural post office) was located about fourteen miles northeast of Burlington, and the Wallett post office was in operation from 1890 to 1907.

YALE (rural post office) was located about twelve miles northeast of Bethune, and the Yale post office was in operation from 1891 to 1905.

Some Railroad Tracks

CHICAGO, ROCK ISLAND & PACIFIC from Kansas to Lincoln County:

  1888–1891 Chicago, Kansas and Nebraska Ry.

  1891–   Chicago, Rock Island & Pacific Ry.

Some Whistlestops

MUSKOKA (MP) is shown about sixteen miles west of Bethune on 1916 and 1920 maps.

PECONIC (CRI&P) is shown about six miles northeast of Burlington on a 1968 map.

Places to Pray

Elbert, Elbert County

Ramah, El Paso County

Chapter 18

Larimer County

Still on the Map

Bellvue
Berthoud
Buckeye
Bulger
Drake
Forks
Fort Collins
Kenyon Corner

Laporte
Loveland
Timnath
Virginia Dale
Waverly
Wellington
Wilds

Places in the Past

Arkins
Boner Spring
Box Elder
Bristol
Fort Collins
Little Thompson
Namaqua
Park Creek
Petra
Pollack

Saint Louis
Scott
Spring Canyon
Stonewall
Stout
Virginia Dale
Washburn
Wheatland
Winona

Larimer County

Some Railroad Tracks

Colorado & Southern Railway (eight parts)
Great Western Railway (three parts)
Union Pacific Railroad (two parts)
Union Pacific, Denver and Gulf Railway

Some Whistlestops

Alfalfa	Marion
Barnett	McClellands
Benson	Miner
Boettcher	Norfolk
Boyd	Officer
Braidwood	Omega
Campion	Orcutt
Crouse	Owl Canyon
Cuthbertson	Plummers
Dixon	Portner
Fife	Poudre
Fossil Creek	Redmond
Frys	Remmington
Giddings	Rex
Greys	Ripple
Harmony	Roberts
Heston	Sinnard
Ingleside	Taylor
Kerns	Ted's Place
Kluver	Trilby
Lords	Valentines
Lowery	Woods
Malabys	

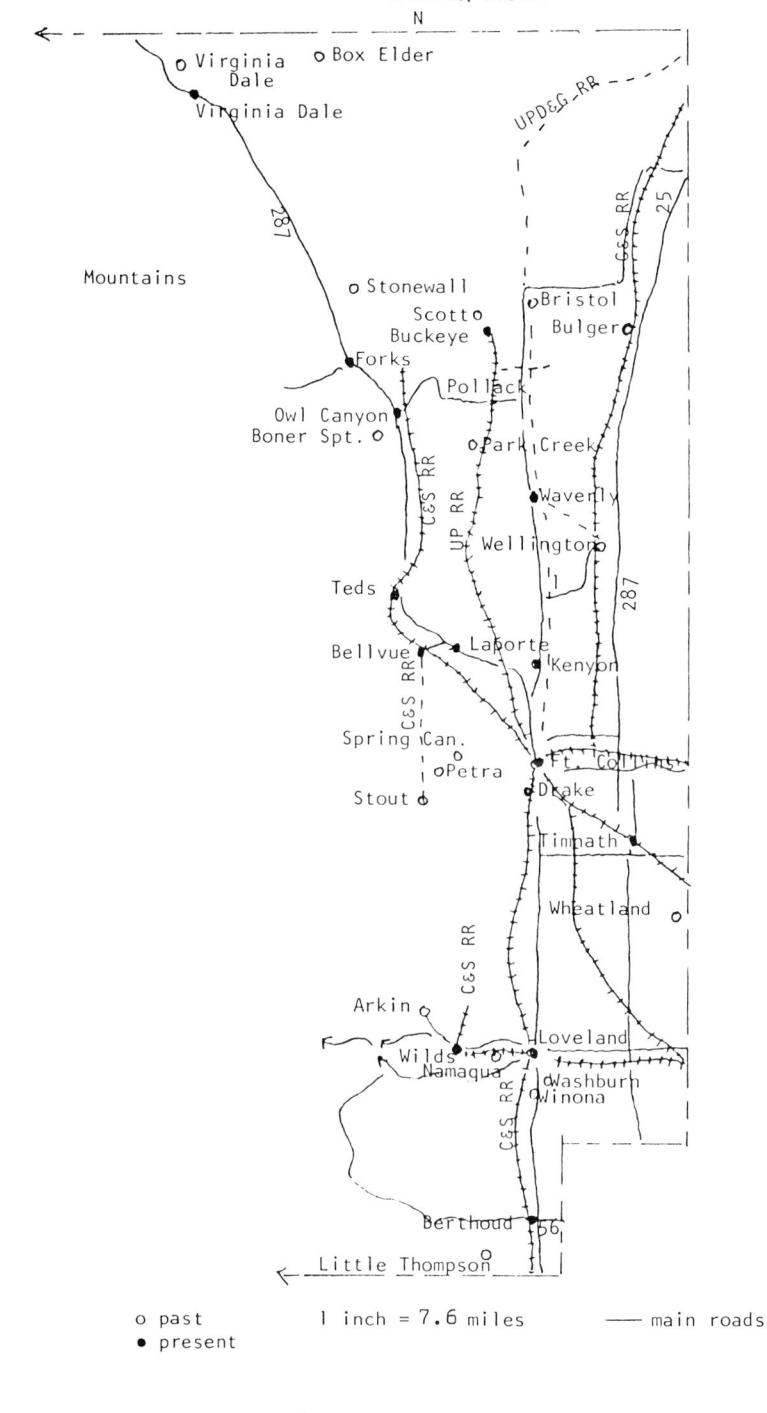

LARIMER COUNTY

N

- ○ past
- ● present

1 inch = 7.6 miles

—— main roads

Locations shown on map:
- Virginia Dale
- Box Elder
- Stonewall
- Scotto
- Buckeye
- Bristol
- Bulger
- Forks
- Pollack
- Owl Canyon
- Boner Spt.
- Park Creek
- Waverly
- Wellington
- Teds
- Bellvue
- Laporte
- Kenyon
- Spring Can.
- Petra
- Stout
- Ft. Collins
- Drake
- Timnath
- Wheatland
- Arkin
- Loveland
- Wilds
- Namaqua
- Washburn
- Winona
- Berthoud
- Little Thompson

Railroads: UPD&G RR, C&S RR, UP RR

Highways: 287, 25

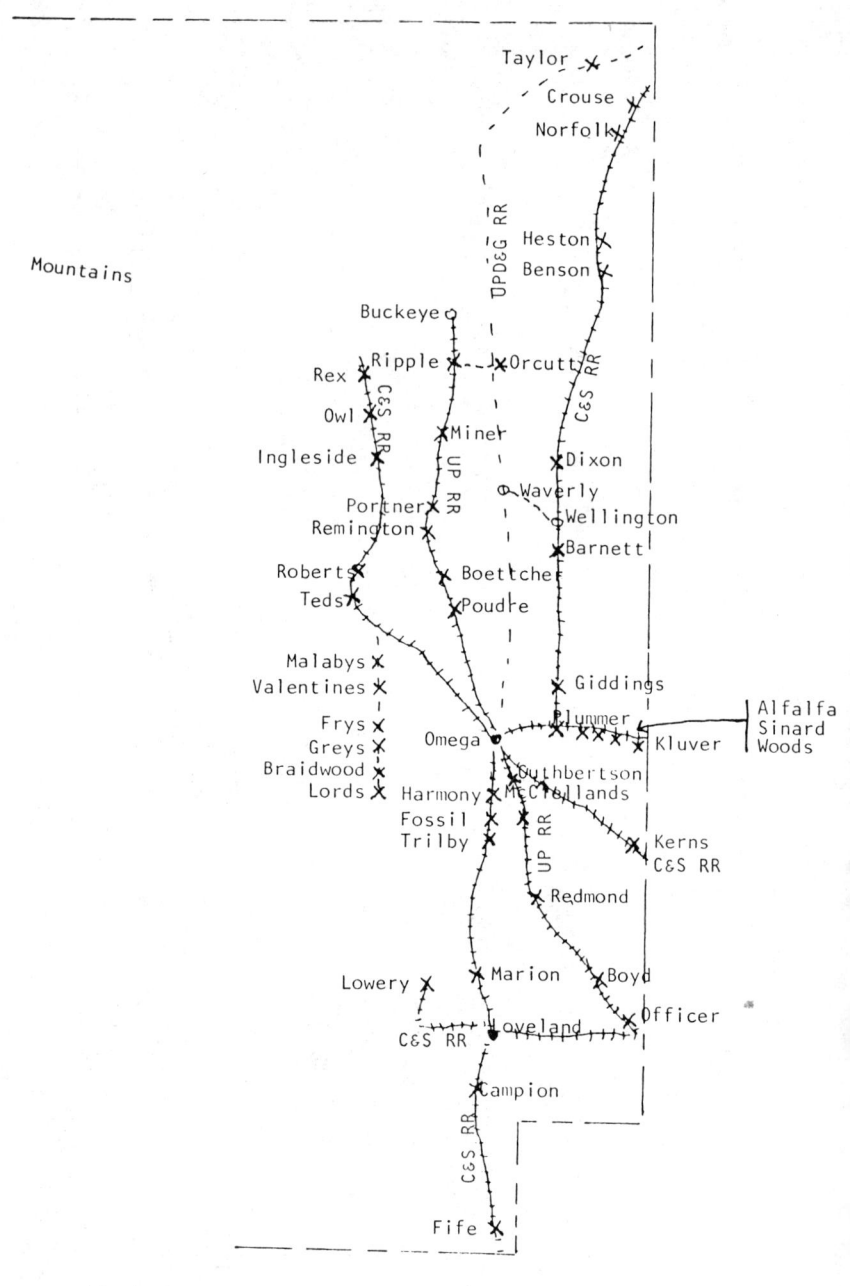

Still on the Map

BELLVUE (platted town) was established by Jacob Flowers, who brought a small colony of settlers from Wyandotte, Kansas, to northern Colorado. The Bellvue post office was established in 1884, and the town plat was filed on July 30, 1887. Jacob Flowers became noted for demonstrating that it was feasible to grow fruit in northern Colorado, and the Flowers Wagon Road to North Park became a landmark in Larimer County.

BERTHOUD (platted town) was established when the Colorado Central Railroad extended a line into northern Colorado in 1877, and the town was named after Captain Edward Berthoud, a civil engineer for the railroad, who was also honored in the naming of Berthoud Pass, which he surveyed for the railroad. A town plat was filed for Berthoud on November 12, 1883, by Peter Turner, and the town became noted as a center for Seventh Day Adventists.

BUCKEYE (platted town) was the terminus of the Union Pacific railroad which was built north of Fort Collins in 1924 and discontinued in 1967. A town plat was filed for Buckeye on May 1, 1925, by E. F. Munroe, and the town was named after the Buckeye Ranch Company which owned the property.

BULGER (platted town) was named after James Bulger, who first filed a plat for a Bulger City in 1909 and then filed the plat for Bulger in 1912. Bulger is about four miles south of the Bulger City site. Later, James Bulger was committed to a mental institution after he killed a man.

DRAKE (railroad post office) is located about two miles south of downtown Fort Collins on the Colorado and Southern railroad. The post office has been operating since 1905.

FORKS (rural post office and hotel) originated in 1874 as a hotel to accommodate workers from nearby lumbering operations. The Forks post office operated from 1898 to 1905 and was named after its location on two wagon roads. Forks is now a way-stop.

Larimer County

FORT COLLINS (platted town) was named after the military fort which served the area from 1863 to 1867. The town of Fort Collins began as an agricultural colony, and a town plat was filed for the town in 1873 by R. A. Cameron, who was also honored in the naming of Cameron Pass at the head of the Poudre River. Fort Collins became the seat of the county in 1868, and replaced Laporte as the leading community in northern Colorado. The state established an agricultural college at Fort Collins in 1870; however, the first students in the college were not enrolled until 1879. The Great Western Sugar Company built a refinery at Fort Collins in 1903, but Fort Collins has remained basically a "college town."

KENYON CORNER (place name) is shown on a 1968 map and is a way-stop on the road from Fort Collins to Wellington.

LAPORTE (stage station and post office) was one of the earliest settlements in Colorado. Laporte was first settled by Antoine Janis in 1844 and was a well-established trading post when the Mormons came through the area in 1847. Laporte was an important station on the Overland stage route in the early 1860s and was made county seat when Larimer County was formed in 1861. Laporte, which was named after its position as "gateway" to the Cache La Poudre River, was of such stature in early Colorado that it was seriously considered as a possible capital of Colorado. Laporte lost much of its importance when the "military" Fort Collins was established downstream from Laporte in 1864. The town of Fort Collins was quick to assume a role of importance when the military fort was abandoned in 1867. Thus, Laporte, like Auraria and Colorado City, relinquished its leadership to the neighboring "greenhorns" who had more permanence in their approach to settlement.

LOVELAND (platted town) was named after W.A.H. Loveland, who was president of the Colorado Central Railroad when it built to the site in 1877. The first buildings in Loveland were moved from nearby St. Louis, and many of the early residents in Loveland were former gold-seekers from the Colorado gold rush. A town plat was filed for Loveland on October 18, 1877, by Sarah and David Barnes. The Great Western Sugar Company built a refinery at Loveland in 1901, and Loveland became known as the "Sweetheart City" (because of its name, not the sugar).

TIMNATH (platted town) was named after Timnath in the 14th Chapter of Judges in the Holy Bible and was named by the Reverend Charles A. Taylor, who was the first minister in the town. A town plat was filed for Timnath on January 7, 1905, by F. P. Kearn and Ed Miller; however, the Timnath post office began shortly after the Greeley, Salt Lake and Pacific Railroad built to the site in 1882.

VIRGINIA DALE (rural post office) was named in reference to the Virginia Dale Stage Station which was located about one and one-half miles northeast of the present post office. The Virginia Dale post office was in operation in 1868 and again since 1874; however, the post office was located at the stage station for some time.

WAVERLY (platted town) began as the terminus of a spur line which was built to Waverly in 1905. A town plat was filed on October 17, 1908, by L. C. Moore. The Waverly post office was discontinued in 1912, and the spur line was discontinued in 1954.

WELLINGTON (platted town) was named after a Mr. Wellington who was a traffic manager for the Colorado and Southern Railway which built to the site in 1903. A plat was filed for Wellington on July 15, 1903, by the North Poudre Irrigation Company. Wellington was the hometown of United States Supreme Court Justice Byron ("Whizzer") White.

WILDS (railroad post office) was the junction of short lines to Lowery and Arkins. The Wilds post office was in operation from 1926 to 1934.

Places in the Past

ARKINS (railroad post office) was the terminus of the Colorado and Southern line from Loveland. The Arkins post office was in operation from 1887 to 1906.

Larimer County

BONER SPRING (stage station) was located about one mile south of the Owl Canyon way-stop. It serviced the Overland Stage Route. A grave at Boner Spring is marked with the name "L. E. Hale—1864." Hale was a small boy who died while traveling with an immigrant wagon train.

BOX ELDER (rural post office) was named after nearby Box Elder Creek and was located about seventeen miles northwest of Fort Collins. The Box Elder post office, landmark in Larimer County, was in operation during the 1870s and from 1884 to 1924.

BRISTOL (rural post office) was located about eighteen miles north of Fort Collins and was named after Noah Bristol who started ranching on nearby Box Elder Creek in 1874. The Bristol post office was in operation from 1877 to 1890.

FORT COLLINS (military fort) was first established as a military camp near Laporte in 1863. The military Fort Collins was established downstream from the camp in 1864 and was named after Lieutenant Colonel W. O. Collins, the commanding officer at Fort Laramie, who established the site for Fort Collins. Fort Collins was abandoned as a military post in 1867.

LITTLE THOMPSON (stage station) was located about seven miles north of Longmont on the Overland stage route from Denver. The Little Thompson station was named after the nearby Little Thompson River.

NAMAQUA (stage station) was located on the Overland stage route from Denver and about three miles west of Loveland. Namaqua was the fort-like home of Mariano Modena, who was a trapper, scout, and pioneer. Namaqua, which means "by the water," was located next to the Big Thompson River.

PARK CREEK (stage station) was named after nearby Park Creek and was located about two miles southeast of the Owl Canyon store site and on the Overland stage route from Laporte.

PETRA (rural post office) was located near the Greeley, Salt Lake and Pacific railroad from Bellvue to Stout. The Petra post office

Places on the Colorado Prairie

was in operation for a short time in 1884 and then was moved to Stout.

POLLACK (place name) was located about eleven miles northwest of Fort Collins at the junction of wagon roads south of Bristol and Virginia Dale. Pollack is shown on 1882 through 1902 maps.

SAINT LOUIS (early community) preceded Loveland in the area, and the buildings from Saint Louis were moved to Loveland in 1877.

SCOTT (platted town) was established by the Denver and Laramie Realty Company when it filed a plat for the town on July 25, 1911. Scott never obtained a post office and was replaced in the area by Buckeye, which was established shortly after the Union Pacific Railroad built to the area in 1924.

SPRING CANYON (stage station) was located near Spring Canyon, which is about ten miles northwest of Loveland. The Spring Canyon Station served the Overland Route from Namaqua.

STONEWALL (stage station) was located about six miles north of the Forks site and just southeast of the Stonewall Creek confluence with Ten-Mile Creek. The Stonewall Station was also called "Cherokee" and "Ten Mile" and served the Overland route from Laporte to Wyoming.

STOUT (railroad post office) was the terminus of the Colorado and Southern line south of Bellvue. The Stout post office was in operation from 1882 to 1908.

VIRGINIA DALE (stage station) was first operated by the notorious Jack Slade who named the station after his wife, Virginia. The Virginia Dale stage station was in operation from 1862 to 1867 and was located about two miles northwest of the present-day Virginia Dale gas station.

WASHBURN (stage station) was one of the later stations on the Overland route to Cheyenne from Denver and was located about

195

Larimer County

three miles south of Namaqua, which had been discontinued when the stage route was moved to the east in 1867.

WHEATLAND (rural post office) was located about twelve miles southeast of Fort Collins on the wagon road from Greeley to Fort Collins. The Wheatland post office was in operation from 1878 to 1881.

WINONA (platted town) was located about one mile south of Loveland. A town plat for Winona was prepared by Sylvester Douty and others and notarized in September of 1874. The Winona post office was in operation from 1889 to 1891.

Some Railroad Tracks

COLORADO & SOUTHERN from Plummer to Weld County:
    1906–1930 Colorado RR Co.
    1930–   Colorado & Southern Ry.

COLORADO & SOUTHERN from Bellvue to Rex:

  Bellvue to Ingleside:
    1906–1930 Colorado RR Co.
    1930–   Colorado & Southern Ry.
  Ingleside to Rex:
    1938–   Colorado & Southern Ry.

COLORADO & SOUTHERN from Bellvue to Stout:
    1883–1890 Greeley, Salt Lake & Pacific Ry.
    1890–1898 Union Pacific, Denver & Gulf Ry.
    1898–1938 Colorado & Southern Ry.
        1894 Removal started
        1938 Removal started

COLORADO & SOUTHERN from Fort Collins through Wellington to Weld County:
  Fort Collins to Wellington:
    1903–1907 Fort Collins Development Ry.
    1907–1930 Colorado RR Co.
    1930–   Colorado & Southern Ry.

Places on the Colorado Prairie

Wellington to Dixon:
  1906–1907 Fort Collins Development Ry.
  1907–1930 Colorado RR Co.
  1930–   Colorado & Southern Ry.
Dixon to Weld County:
  1911–1930 Colorado RR Co.
  1930–   Colorado & Southern Ry.

COLORADO & SOUTHERN from main line through Wellington to Waverly:
  1905–1907 Fort Collins Development Ry.
  1907–1930 Colorado RR Co.
  1930–1954 Colorado & Southern Ry.

COLORADO & SOUTHERN from Loveland to Arkins:
  1886–1890 Greeley, Salt Lake & Pacific Ry.
  1890–1898 Union Pacific, Denver & Gulf Ry.
  1898–1937 Colorado & Southern Ry.

COLORADO & SOUTHERN from Wilds to Lowery:
  1886–1890 Greeley, Salt Lake & Pacific Ry.
  1890–1898 Union Pacific, Denver & Gulf Ry.
  1898–1914 Colorado & Southern Ry.

COLORADO & SOUTHERN from Fort Collins to Boulder County:
  1877–1890 Colorado Central RR
  1890–1898 Union Pacific, Denver & Gulf Ry.
  1898–   Colorado & Southern Ry.

GREAT WESTERN from Loveland to Officer:
  1901–   Great Western Ry.

GREAT WESTERN from Officer to Weld County (Johnstown):
  1901–   Great Western Ry.

GREAT WESTERN from Weld County (Windsor) to Officer:
  1907–   Great Western Ry.

UNION PACIFIC from Fort Collins to Weld County:
  1914–   Union Pacific RR

197

Larimer County

UNION PACIFIC from Fort Collins to Buckeye:
    Fort Collins to Buckeye:
        1924–1967 Union Pacific RR
    Spur Line to Orcutt:
        1924–1946 Union Pacific RR

UNION PACIFIC, DENVER & GULF from Fort Collins to Wyoming:
    1877–1890 Colorado Central RR
    1890–1890 Union Pacific, Denver & Gulf Ry.
        1888 Removed from Bristol to Taylors
        1890 Removed rest of the line

Some Whistlestops

ALFALFA (C&S) is shown about five miles east of Fort Collins on a 1916 map.

BARNETT (C&S) is shown about two miles south of Wellington on 1906 through 1920 maps. Barnett is shown as "Barnes" on a 1907 map.

BENSON (C&S) is shown about nine miles north of Wellington on a 1934 map.

BOETTCHER (UP) is shown about six miles northwest of Fort Collins on a railroad map. Boettcher was named after Charles Boettcher, who was responsible for the development of the nearby Ideal Cement Plant.

BOYD (UP) is shown about five miles northeast of Loveland on 1909 through 1920 maps. Boyd was named after nearby Boyd Lake.

BRAIDWOOD (C&S) is shown about five miles south of Bellvue on a 1906 map.

CAMPION (C&S) is shown about three miles north of Berthoud on 1909 through 1970 maps. Campion was named in reference to a

Places on the Colorado Prairie

Mr. Campion, and is a well-established community. Campion became the site of the Seventh Day Adventist Church.

CROUSE (C&S) is shown about four miles south of the Wyoming state line on 1916 and 1920 maps.

CUTHBERTSON (C&S) is shown about three miles northwest of Timnath on 1909 through 1920 maps.

DIXON (C&S) is shown about three miles north of Wellington on 1909 through 1927 maps.

FIFE (C&S) is shown about three miles south of Berthoud on a 1910 map.

FOSSIL CREEK (C&S) is shown about four miles south of Fort Collins on 1882 through 1902 maps. Fossil Creek was named after nearby Fossil Creek in which many fossilized fish from the prehistoric era have been found in recent times.

FRYS (C&S) is shown about seven miles south of Bellvue on a 1916 map. Frys and most of the Stout Branch of the railroad is now covered by Horsetooth Reservoir.

GIDDINGS (C&S) is shown about four miles northeast of Fort Collins on 1909 through 1920 maps.

GREYS (C&S) is shown about four miles southwest of Fort Collins on 1909 through 1916 maps and was another of the sites eventually covered by Horsetooth Reservoir.

HARMONY (UP) is shown about four miles southeast of Fort Collins on 1916 through 1968 maps.

HESTON (C&S) is shown about ten miles north of Wellington on a 1920 map.

INGLESIDE (C&S) is shown about five miles north of Ted's Place on 1906 through 1940 maps. Ingleside was the temporary terminus of the Colorado and Southern railroad to Rex from Bellvue.

Larimer County

KERNS (C&S) is shown about nine miles southeast of Fort Collins on a 1920 map.

KLUVER (C&S) is shown about seven miles east of Fort Collins on 1916 through 1968 maps; it is also shown in Weld County.

LORDS (C&S) is shown about five miles southwest of Fort Collins on 1909 through 1916 maps.

LOWERY is shown about seven miles northwest of Loveland on 1909 through 1924 maps.

MALABYS (C&S) is shown about two miles south of Bellvue on a 1906 map.

MARION (C&S) is shown about three miles north of Loveland on 1909 through 1920 maps.

MCCLELLANDS (C&S) is shown about four miles south of Fort Collins on 1906 through 1957 maps.

MINER (UPD&G) is shown about eleven miles north of Fort Collins on 1892 through 1902 maps.

NORFOLK (C&S) is shown about six miles south of the Wyoming state line on 1916 through 1968 maps.

OFFICER (UP) is shown about six miles east of Loveland on 1909 through 1968 maps.

OMEGA (C&S) is shown about one mile south of Fort Collins on a 1968 map.

ORCUTT (UP) is shown about eight miles northwest of Wellington on 1954 and 1968 maps.

OWL CANYON (C&S) is shown about seven miles north of Ted's Place on a railroad map.

200

Places on the Colorado Prairie

PLUMMERS (C&S) is shown about three miles east of Fort Collins on 1906 and 1909 maps.

PORTNER (UP) is shown about six miles north of Fort Collins on a railroad map.

POUDRE (UP) is shown about five miles north of Fort Collins on a railroad map.

REDMOND (UP) is shown about six miles northeast of Loveland on 1916 through 1968 maps.

REMMINGTON (UP) is shown about eight miles north of Fort Collins on a railroad map.

REX (C&S) is shown about ten miles north of Ted's Place on a railroad map.

RIPPLE (UP) is shown about twelve miles north of Fort Collins on a railroad map.

ROBERTS (C&S) is shown about three miles north of Ted's Place on a 1954 map.

SINNARD (C&S) is shown about four miles east of Fort Collins on a 1916 map.

TAYLOR (UPD&G) is shown about four miles south of the Wyoming state line on 1882 through 1902 maps.

TED'S PLACE (C&S) is shown about five miles northwest of Laporte on a 1954 map. The siding at Ted's Place was first called "Graves." Ted's Place is also a way-stop on the highways to Laramie and the Poudre River.

TRILBY (C&S) is shown about seven miles north of Loveland on 1909 through 1920 maps.

VALENTINES (C&S) is shown about four miles south of Bellvue on 1909 and 1916 maps.

WOODS (C&S) is shown about seven miles east of Fort Collins on a 1916 map.

Chapter 19

Las Animas County

Still on the Map

Aguilar	Ludlow
Andrix	Model
Barela	Sopris
Beshoar	Thatcher
Bowen	Tobe
Branson	Trinchera
Dalerose	Trinchera Plaza
Delhi	Trinidad
Earl	Troy
El Moro	Tyrone
Hoehne	Villegreen
Jansen	Watervale
Kim	

Las Animas County

Places in the Past

- Alcreek
- Alfalfa
- Alkalai Springs
- Apishipa
- Atwell
- Bent Canyon
- Brodhead
- Buster
- Cedarhurst
- Chicosa
- Chilili
- Clanda
- Dillview
- Downing
- Druce
- Engle
- Flues
- Gillette
- Gotera
- Graycreek
- Gray's Landing
- Green Canyon
- Greenfield
- Grinnell
- Hoehne
- Hog Back
- Hole-In-The-Prairie
- Hole-In-The-Rock
- Hoopup
- Indianapolis
- Irwin Canyon
- Kazan
- Laub
- Linwood
- Lockwood
- Marguerite
- McDonald
- Media
- Officer
- Onine
- Patches
- Patt
- Piñon Spring
- Placita
- Plum Valley
- Pulaski
- Rapson
- Red Rock
- Rugby
- San Miguel
- Stage Canyon
- Stage Canyon
- Stockville
- Wormington
- Yachita
- Yeiser

Places on the Colorado Prairie

Some Railroad Tracks

Atchison, Topeka & Santa Fe Railway
Colorado & Southern Railway (five parts)
Colorado & Southeastern Railroad
Colorado & Wyoming Railway
Denver & Rio Grande Western Railroad (four parts)

Some Whistlestops

Abeyta	Houghton
Acme	Lynn
Barnes	Nola
Barnes Junction	Rivera
Boaz	Sherman Spur
Chicosa Junction	Silvia
Forbes Junction	Simpson
Garcia	Suffield
Higgins	

Still on the Map

AGUILAR (platted town) was named after Jose Aguilar, who was a pioneer in the area. The town plat for Aguilar was filed on July 7, 1892, by Jose Aguilar and Casimiro Barela, who had served as a senator in the territorial legislature. Aguilar was first called ''Schulter Plaza''; however, the plat was filed for Aguilar in the same year that the Union Pacific, Denver and Gulf railroad was built through the area.

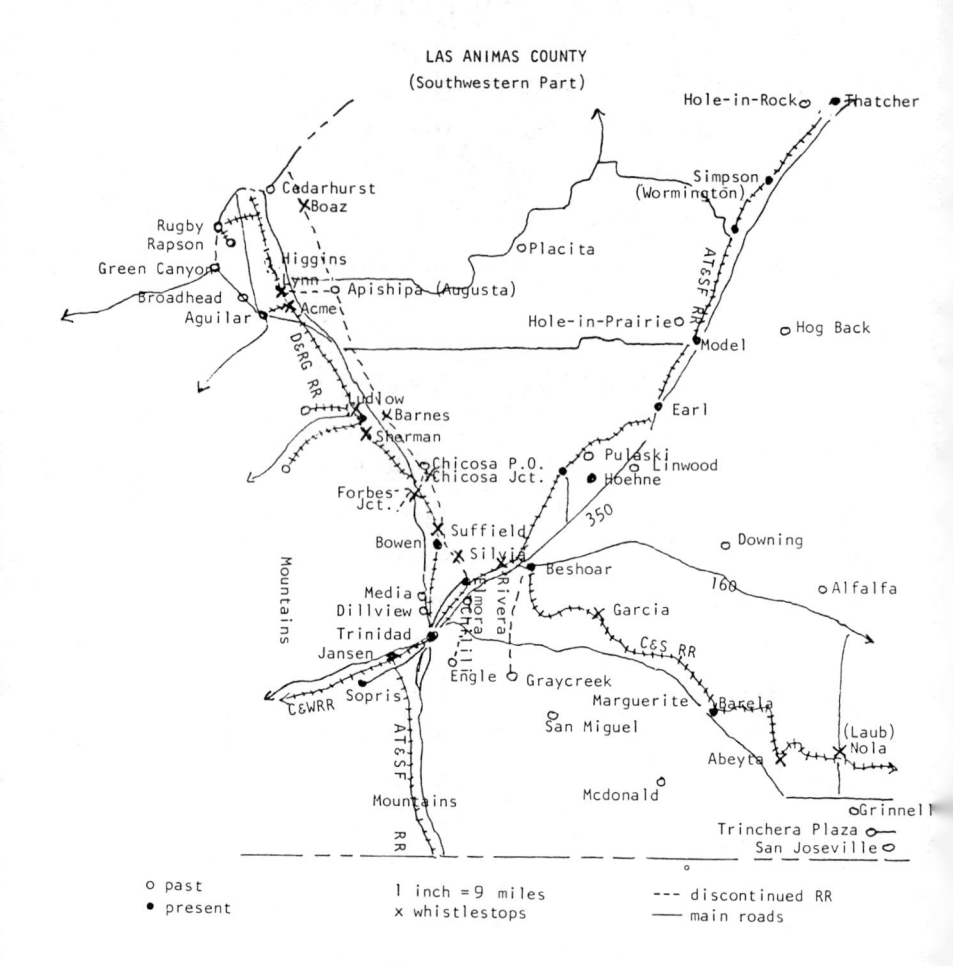

LAS ANIMAS COUNTY
(Southwestern Part)

Hole-in-Rock ○ — ● Thatcher
Simpson (Wormington)
Cedarhurst ○
X Boaz
Rugby ○
Rapson ○
Green Canyon ○
Higgins
Broadhead ○
Aguilar ●
Lynn
X Acme
Apishpa (Augusta)
Placita ○
Hole-in-Prairie ○ ● Model
Hog Back ○
Ludlow ●
X Barnes
X Sharman
Chicosa P.O. ○
Chicosa Jct.
Pulaski ○
Linwood ●
Hoehne ●
Earl ●
Forbes Jct. X
Suffield X
Bowen ●
Silvia X
Rivera
Beshoar ●
Downing ○
Alfalfa ○
Media ○
Dillview ○
Trinidad ●
Jansen ●
Sopris ●
Engle ○
Graycreek ○
Garcia X
Marguerite ●
Barela ●
San Miguel ○
Abeyta X
(Laub) Nola X
Mcdonald ○
Grinnell ○
Trinchera Plaza ○
San Joseville ○

D&RG RR
AT&SF RR
C&S RR
C&WRR
AT&SF RR
Mountains
Mountains
350
160

○ past
● present
1 inch = 9 miles
x whistlestops
--- discontinued RR
— main roads

LAS ANIMAS COUNTY
(Northern Part)

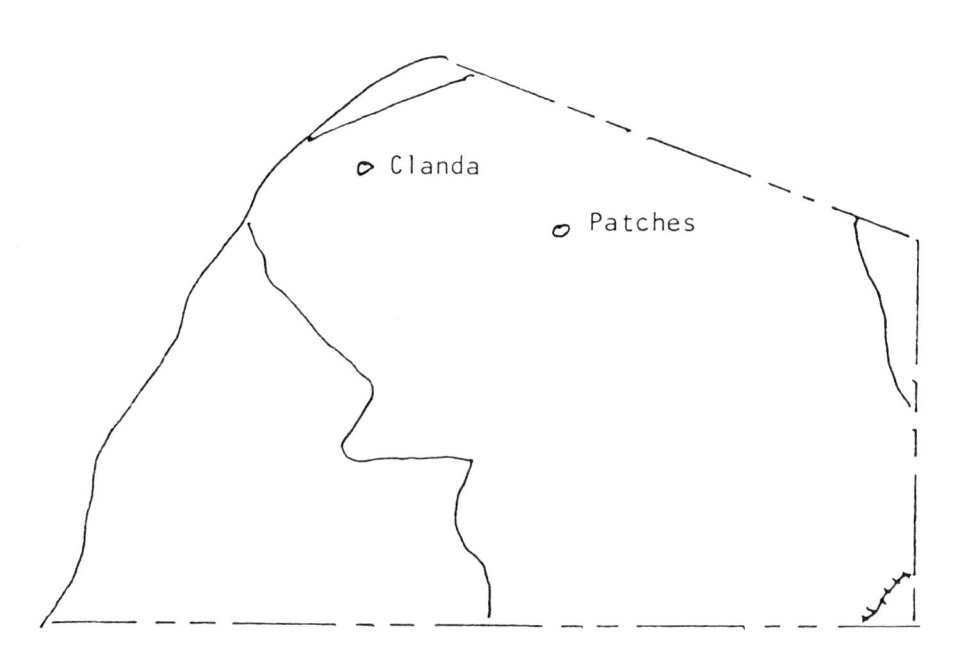

o past   1 inch = 6 miles   —— main roads

LAS ANIMAS COUNTY
(Eastern Part)

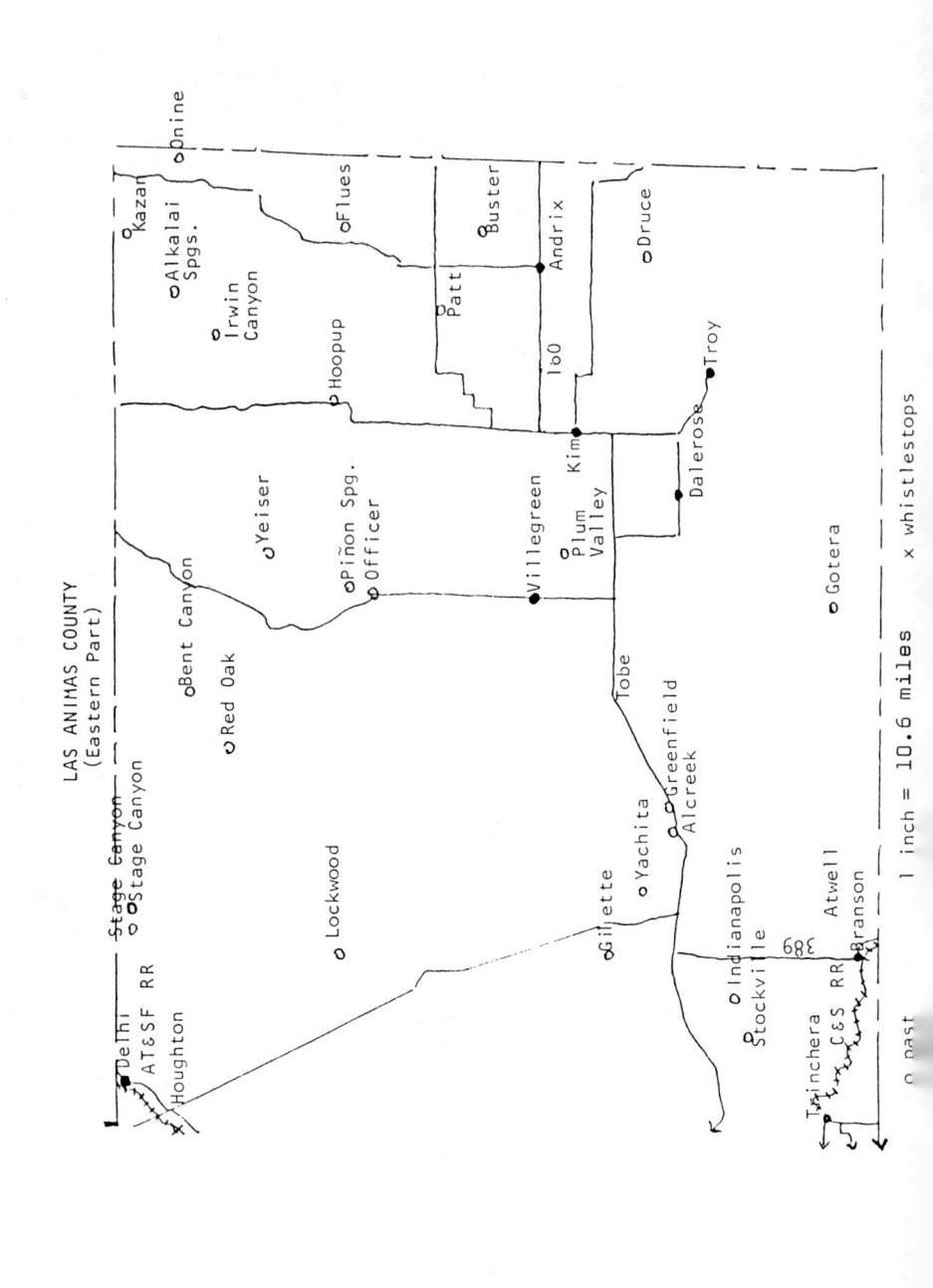

1 inch = 10.6 miles   x whistlestops

Places on the Colorado Prairie

ANDRIX (rural post office) is located about ten miles northeast of Kim, and the Andrix post office was in operation from 1920 to 1953.

BARELA (railroad post office) is located next to the Colorado and Southern railroad and about fifteen miles southeast of Trinidad. The Barela post office was named after Senator Casimiro Barela who lived in nearby Rivera. The Barela post office was in operation from 1874 to 1896 and from 1920 to 1934.

BESHOAR (railroad post office) is located on the Colorado and Southern railroad and about four miles east of El Moro. Beshoar was named after Michael Beshoar, an early resident of Trinidad. The Beshoar post office operated from 1901 to 1903.

BOWEN (railroad post office) is located about three miles northwest of El Moro and next to the Colorado and Southern railroad. The Bowen post office was in operation from 1906 to 1929 and was named after Senator Thomas Bowen. The Bowen post office was preceded in the area by the Aylmer post office, which was in operation from 1899 to 1906. .

BRANSON (platted town) was named after Al Branson, who was a merchant and leading citizen of Trinidad. A town plat was filed for Branson on March 26, 1921, and the town received its impetus from the Colorado and Southern railroad. However, the Branson area had been well traveled for some time because of the Goodnight cattle trail which was routed through nearby Tollgate Canyon.

DALEROSE (rural post office) is located about seven miles southwest of Kim, and the Dalerose post office was in operation from 1916 to 1943.

DELHI (platted town) was established on the Santa Fe Railroad, and the Delhi post office opened in 1908. Except for the land description, there is little information on the town plat for Delhi. However, Delhi is shown on the 1892 map.

Las Animas County

EARL (platted town) was named after a Mr. Earl who was an early resident of the area. A town plat was filed for Earl on June 27, 1921, by M. L. Baker; however, the Earl post office opened in 1895. The Earl post office closed in 1923, just two years after the plat was filed for the town.

EL MORO (platted town) was named after the moor-like appearance of nearby peat fields. The Denver and Rio Grande railroad was built to El Moro in 1876, and a town plat was filed for the town in the same year by the Southern Colorado Coal and Town Company. El Moro became a "coke" camp for the Colorado Fuel and Iron Company; coal was El Moro's main business.

HOEHNE (platted town) was named after William Hoehne, who settled in the area during 1865 and later became county treasurer. A town plat was filed for Hoehne on July 13, 1887, by the Hoehne City Town and Development Company, and the town received its impetus from the Santa Fe railroad which had been built through the area ten years before.

JANSEN (railroad post office) was initiated when the Colorado and Wyoming railroad was built west from Trinidad to Tercio and Stonewall in 1901. The Jansen post office was in operation from 1902 to 1913 and was reopened in 1932.

KIM (platted town) was named after the boy in Rudyard Kipling's famous novel; the town was named by the wife of Olin Simpson, who established the first store and post office in the town. A town plat was filed for Kim on February 20, 1920, by Joseph Terral; however, a plat for "Kim City" had been filed a few days earlier by William Cole, and the land description was two miles northeast of the Kim site. Kim City lost in the bid for a townsite, and Kim has prevailed in a sparsely populated section of Las Animas County.

LUDLOW (railroad post office) is located about fourteen miles northwest of Trinidad and next to the Colorado and Southern railroad. The Ludlow post office was in operation from 1896 to 1954. Ludlow was the site of the famous "Battle of Ludlow," in

Places on the Colorado Prairie

which several miners, women, and children were killed by the militia when the miners went on strike in 1913 and 1914.

MODEL (platted town) was named in hopes that it would become a "model" town. Model was first called "Poso" which means "dry hole" in Spanish. A town plat for "Model City" was filed on June 12, 1911, by the Model Land and Irrigation Company, and a town plat was filed for Model on February 10, 1913, by the Model Townsite and Investment Company. Model was platted about three miles northeast of Model City.

SOPRIS (platted town) was named after general E. R. Sopris, who commanded the Colorado Militia that defended the Santa Fe Trail. A town plat was filed for Sopris on February 26, 1889, by W. H. James, who was president of the Denver Fuel Company. Sopris, like so many places near Trinidad, was initiated because of the coal industry.

THATCHER (platted town) was named in reference to M. D. Thatcher, a prominent banker in southeastern Colorado. The Pueblo and Arkansas Valley railroad was built to the site of Thatcher in 1877, and the Thatcher post office opened five years later; however, a town plat was not filed for the town until 1928. C. W. Taylor and N. W. Bolling filed a town plat for Thatcher on March 22, 1928.

TOBE (platted town) was established as a post office in 1910, and a town plat was filed for Tobe on June 25, 1920, by S. J. Mathews. Tobe is located near Mesa de Maya and has been more post office than town. The Tobe post office closed in 1960.

TRINCHERA (platted town) was named in reference to the Spanish word meaning "ditches," because of the gap in a mesa close to the town. Trinchera was established when the Denver, Texas and Fort Worth railroad reached the area in 1888. A town plat was filed for Trinchera on August 10, 1916, by A. J. Hollenbeck, but the Trinchera post office opened in 1889.

Las Animas County

TRINCHERA PLAZA (place name) is located about four miles southwest of Trinchera and is shown on 1916 through 1968 maps. Trinchera Plaza was preceded by the Brazil post office which was in operation from 1895 to 1899 and from 1911 to 1912.

TRINIDAD (platted town) was named after the Holy Trinity. The first permanent settlement on the Trinidad site was in 1859, when Gabriel and Juan Guiterrez built a cabin on the site, and the ensuing settlement was first called Rio de Las Animas. Later a group of settlers selected "Santisima Trinidad" for the name of their settlement; the name was eventually shortened to "Trinidad." The town of Trinidad was made the seat of Las Animas County when the county was formed in 1866. Frank Bloom initiated the coal mining industry in the Trinidad area during 1867, and Trinidad became noted for this industry. A town plat was filed for Trinidad on July 7, 1877.

TROY (rural post office) is located about twelve miles southeast of Kim, and the Troy post office was in operation from 1887 to 1942. The Troy post office was preceded by the Humbar post office in 1887.

TYRONE (platted town) was platted as "Yetta" and the town plat for Yetta was filed on September 22, 1919, by Fred Schmidt. The name of Yetta as changed to "Tyrone" in 1929. Tyrone was sustained by the Santa Fe Railroad; however, the Tyrone post office closed in 1968.

VILLEGREEN (rural post office) is shown in several locations about twelve miles northwest of Kim on 1920 through 1968 maps. The Villegreen post office opened in 1917.

WATERVALE (railroad post office) is located about five miles west of Branson and next to the Colorado and Southern Railroad. The Watervale post office was in operation from 1888 to 1921.

Places in the Past

ALCREEK (rural post office) was located about eight miles southeast of Tobe, and the Alcreek post office was in operation from 1916 to 1935.

ALFALFA (rural post office) was first called "Raton" and the Raton post office was in operation from 1878 to 1881. The Alfalfa post office was in operation from 1881 to 1882 and from 1885 to 1923.

ALKALAI SPRINGS (place name) is shown about twenty miles north of Andrix on a 1902 map.

APISHIPA (platted town) was named after the nearby Apishipa River. The Apishipa post office was opened in 1867, but the name of the post office was changed to "San Antonia" and then back to "Apishipa" in 1876. A town plat was filed for Apishipa on October 11, 1887. The name of the Apishipa post office was changed to "Augusta" in 1911. The Augusta post office was closed in 1928.

ATWELL (rural post office) was located about eleven miles east of Trinchera, and the Atwell post office was in operation from 1915 to 1920.

BENT CANYON (rural post office) was located about twenty miles southeast of Bloom, and the Bent Canyon post office was in operation from 1872 to 1902.

BRODHEAD (railroad post office) was located on the line from Aguilar to Green Canyon, and the Brodhead post office was in operation from 1902 to 1913 and from 1915 to 1939.

BUSTER (rural post office) is shown about five miles northeast of Andrix on a 1920 map and about nine miles northeast of Andrix on 1924 through 1934 maps. The Buster post office was in operation from 1916 to 1927.

213

Las Animas County

CEDARHURST (railroad post office) was located about six miles north of Aguilar and next to the Colorado and Southern railroad. The Cedarhurst post office was in operation from 1903 to 1913. Cedarhurst was actually a short distance from the railroad.

CHICOSA (railroad post office) was located on the Denver and Rio Grande railroad and about nine miles northwest of Trinidad. The Chicosa post office was in operation fron 1890 to 1894 and from 1896 to 1910. Chicosa was located at the junction of the railroad to Forbes and Trinidad.

CHILILI (platted town) was platted next to the Colorado and Southern railroad to New Mexico, and the town plat for Chilili was filed on June 13, 1887, by Thomas T. Woodruff. Chilili did not obtain a post office and was probably more siding than town. Chilili was spelled "Chilelilla" on an 1892 map.

CLANDA (rural post office) was located about twenty miles west of Delhi, and the Clanda post office was in operation from 1920 to 1926.

DILLVIEW (platted town) was platted just north of Trinidad and close to the Denver and Rio Grande railroad, and the plat for Dillview was filed on April 5, 1890, by Ida Dill. Dillview never obtained a post office.

DOWNING (railroad post office) was located next to the Santa Fe railroad and about thirteen miles northeast of Trinidad. The Downing post office was in operation from 1886 to 1896.

DRUCE (rural post office) was located about eight miles southeast of Andrix, and the Druce post office was in operation from 1916 to 1922; however, Druce is shown on the maps into the 1940s.

ENGLE (platted town) was named after George Engle who was the first superintendent of the nearby Engle coal mine which was first called the El Moro Mine. Engle was first called "Engleville." The Engle post office opened in 1882 and closed in 1913. However, a town plat for Engle wasn't filed until July 27, 1891.

Places on the Colorado Prairie

FLUES (rural post office) was located about thirteen miles north of Andrix, and the Andrix post office was in operation from 1915 to 1933.

GILLETTE (rural post office) was located about sixteen miles northeast of Branson. The Gillette post office was in operation in 1888.

GOTERA (rural post office) was located about fourteen miles east of Branson, and the Gotera post office was in operation from 1916 to 1922. The Gotera post office was preceded in the area by the Duncan post office, which was in operation from 1901 to 1916.

GRAYCREEK (railroad post office) was located on the Colorado and Southern railroad and about six miles southeast of Trinidad. The Graycreek post office was named after nearby Gray Creek and serviced the community near Gray's Mine from 1895 to 1921.

GRAY's LANDING (stage station) was located at the site of El Moro and was a station on the Santa Fe Trail stage route. Gray's Landing was named after the landing established by Jim Gray on the north side of the Purgatoire River.

GREEN CANYON (railroad post office) was the terminus of a short line through Aguilar to the Brodhead Mine. The Green Canyon post office operated in 1909 and 1910.

GREENFIELD (platted town) was platted about nine miles southwest of Tobe; the town plat for Greenfield was filed on June 2, 1922, by Samuel Lucero. However, Greenfield did not obtain a post office, and it was not shown on the map.

GRINNELL (rural post office) was located about thirteen miles northwest of Branson and was named after the maternal family name of Jerome Abbott, who raised livestock in the area. The Grinnell post office was in operation from 1878 to 1883 and was preceded in the area by the San Jose post office, which operated from 1873 to 1878.

215

Las Animas County

HOEHNE (stage station) was located about a mile and a half east of the town of Hoehne and was named after William Hoehne, who settled in the area during 1865. The Hoehne station was the Purgatoire branch of the Santa Fe Trail stage route.

HOG BACK (stage station) was located on the Purgatoire branch of the Santa Fe Trail stage route. The Hog back station was named after the local terrain on that portion of Van Bremer Creek.

HOLE-IN-THE-PRAIRIE (stage station) was the fourth station on the Santa Fe Trail up Timpas Creek. Years after it started, the Goodnight Cattle Trail included the Hole-In-The-Prairie site.

HOLE-IN-THE-ROCK (stage station) was the third station on the Timpas Creek stage route which preceded the Purgatoire route of the Santa Fe Trail. Hole-In-The-Rock was named after the holes in nearby walls of the Timpas Canyon. There was a fortification just north of the corrals near the Hole-In-The-Rock station.

HOOPUP (rural post office) was located about eight miles northwest of Andrix, and the Hoopup post office was in operation from 1919 to 1937. There has been considerable conjecture about the source of Hoopup's name, but research has produced no information.

INDIANAPOLIS (rural post office) was named after Indianapolis, Indiana, which was the hometown of many residents in the area. Indianapolis resulted from the land boom which prevailed in southeastern Colorado during the late 1880s. The Indianapolis post office was in operation from 1887 to 1889.

IRWIN CANYON (rural post office) was located about ten miles northeast of Kim, and the Irwin Canyon post office was in operation from 1920 to 1924.

KAZAN (rural post office) was located about four miles southeast of Ninaview; the Kazan post office was in operation from 1920 to 1931.

Places on the Colorado Prairie

LAUB (railroad post office) was located at the Nola Siding on the Colorado and Southern railroad. The Laub post office was in operation from 1916 to 1923.

LINWOOD (rural post office) was located about five miles east of the site of Hoehne; the Linwood post office was in operation from 1876 to 1886. Linwood was preceded in the area by the Dodsonville post office from 1873 to 1876.

LOCKWOOD (stage station) was on the Purgatoire branch of the Santa Fe Trail stage route and was located on the north bank of Lockwood Creek.

MARGUERITE (platted town) was platted about one mile west of Barela; the town plat for Marguerite was filed on March 22, 1927 by Florence Davey. However, Marguerite did not obtain a post office, nor was it shown on the map.

MCDONALD (place name) is shown about ten miles southwest of Barela on a 1905 map.

MEDIA (platted town) was platted just north of Trinidad, and the plat was filed by The Media Town Company on December 30, 1887; however, Media neither obtained a post office, nor was it shown on the map.

OFFICER (rural post office) was located about twenty miles northwest of Kim. The Officer post office was named after its first postmaster, Charles Officer, and was in operation from 1917 to 1938.

ONINE (rural post office) was located about twenty-four miles northeast of Andrix, and its post office was in operation from 1918 to 1921.

PATCHES (rural post office) was located about twenty-four miles northeast of Cucharas, and the Patches post office was in operation from 1917 to 1928.

Las Animas County

PATT (rural post office) was located about six miles north of Andrix. The Patt post office was in operation from 1919 to 1944.

PIÑON SPRING (place name) is shown about ten miles north of Villegreen on 1882 through 1902 maps.

PLACITA (place name) is shown about eleven miles west of Tyrone on 1884 and 1897 maps.

PLUM VALLEY (rural post office) was located about ten miles northwest of Kim, and the Plum Valley post office was in operation from 1917 to 1935.

PULASKI (rural post office) was located about two miles northeast of Hoehne; the Pulaski post office was in operation from 1874 to 1886.

RAPSON (railroad post office) was located on the Colorado and Southern railroad and about five miles north of Aguilar. The Rapson post office was in operation from 1911 to 1917 and from 1920 to 1934, and served the Rapson Coal Mine.

RED ROCK (place name) is shown about six miles southwest of Bent Canyon on an 1882 map.

RUGBY (railroad post office) was located on the Colorado and Southern railroad and was named in reference to Rugby, England, by an English mine owner in the area. The Rugby post office was in operation from 1900 to 1947, and served the Rugby Coal Mine.

SAN MIGUEL (place name) is shown about eight miles southeast of Trinidad on 1916 through 1924 maps. San Miguel was preceded by the Maldanado post office which was in operation from 1901 to 1905.

STAGE CANYON (stage station) was located on the Purgatoire branch of the Santa Fe Trail stage route and at the head of Bent Canyon.

Places on the Colorado Prairie

STAGE CANYON (rural post office) was located about one mile west of the site of the Stage Canyon stage station. The Stage Canyon post office was in operation from 1919 to 1920.

STOCKVILLE (rural post office) was located bout five miles northeast of Trinchera. The Stockville post office was in operation only from 1873 to 1875; however, Stockville is shown on an 1897 map.

WORMINGTON (railroad post office) was located on the Simpson Siding of the Santa Fe railroad. The Wormington site was called "Simpson" before the Wormington post office was in operation and is shown as "Simpson" after the Wormington post office was closed. The Wormington post office was in operation from 1919 to 1934.

YACHITA (rural post office) was located about twelve miles southwest of Tobe, and the Yachita post office was in operation from 1916 to 1918.

YEISER (rural post office) is shown about twenty-eight miles northwest of Kim, and the Yeiser post office was in operation from 1904 to 1929.

Some Railroad Tracks

ATCHISON, TOPEKA & SANTA FE from Otero County to New Mexico:
    1877–1900 Pueblo & Arkansas Valley RR
    1900–   Atchison, Topeka & Santa Fe Ry.

COLORADO & SOUTHERN from Huerfano County to Trinidad:
  Huerfano County to Acme:
    1895–1898 Union Pacific, Denver & Gulf Ry.
    1898–   Colorado & Southern Ry.

Las Animas County

Aguilar to Ludlow:
- 1892–1898 Union Pacific, Denver & Gulf Ry.
- 1898– Colorado & Southern Ry.

Ludlow to Forbes Junction:
- 1889–1890 Denver, Texas & Ft. Worth RR
- 1890–1898 Union Pacific, Denver & Gulf Ry.
- 1898– Colorado & Southern Ry.

Forbes Junction to Trinidad:
- 1895–1898 Union Pacific, Denver & Gulf Ry.
- 1898– Colorado & Southern Ry.

COLORADO & SOUTHERN from Trinidad to New Mexico:

Trinidad to Martinsen:
- 1888–1890 Denver, Texas & Ft. Worth RR
- 1890–1898 Union Pacific, Denver & Gulf Ry.
- 1898–1940 Colorado & Southern Ry.
  - 1908 Abandoned from Martinsen to Long's
  - 1940 Abandoned from Long's to Trinidad

Martinsen to New Mexico:
- 1890–1898 Union Pacific, Denver & Gulf Ry.
- 1898–1908 Colorado & Southern Ry.

COLORADO & SOUTHERN from Ludlow to Bear Canyon Mine:

Ludlow to Berwind:
- 1889–1890 Road Canon RR (grading)
- 1890–1898 Union Pacific, Denver & Gulf Ry.
- 1898–1955 Colorado & Southern Ry.

Berwind to Bear Canyon:
- 1898–1898 Union Pacific, Denver & Gulf Ry.
- 1898–1955 Colorado & Southern Ry.

Places on the Colorado Prairie

Bear Canyon to Bear Canyon Mine:
1898–1913 Bear Canyon RR
1913–1955 Colorado & Southern Ry.

COLORADO & SOUTHERN from Trinidad through Barela to New Mexico:
1888–1890 Denver, Texas & Ft. Worth RR
1890–1898 Union Pacific, Denver & Gulf Ry.
1898– Colorado & Southern Ry.

COLORADO & SOUTHERN from Beshoar to Graycreek:
1888–1890 Denver, Texas & Ft. Worth RR
1890–1898 Union Pacific, Denver & Gulf Ry.
1898– Colorado & Southern Ry.

COLORADO & SOUTHEASTERN from Barnes to Delagua:
Barnes to Barnes Junction:
1903–1909 Colorado & South Eastern Ry.
1909–1951 Colorado & Southeastern RR
Ludlow to Barnes Junction and Hastings:
1889–1890 Cañon de Agua RR
1890–1898 Union Pacific, Denver & Gulf Ry.
1898–1904 Colorado & Southern Ry.
1904–1909 Colorado & South Eastern Ry.
1909–1951 Colorado & Southeastern RR
    1904 Discontinued from Ludlow to Barnes Junction
Hastings to Delagua:
1903–1903 Victor Fuel Co.
1903–1909 Colorado & South Eastern Ry.
1909–1951 Colorado & Southeastern RR

COLORADO & WYOMING from Jansen to Tercio:

221

Las Animas County

Jansen to Weston:
1901– Colorado & Wyoming Ry.

Weston to Tercio:
1902–1952 Colorado & Wyoming Ry.

DENVER & RIO GRANDE WESTERN from Chicosa Junction to Forbes Junction:
1889–1890 Chicosa Cañon Ry.
1890–1897 Union Pacific, Denver & Gulf Ry.
1897–1921 Denver & Rio Grande RR
1921–1936 Denver & Rio Grande Western RR

DENVER & RIO GRANDE WESTERN from El Moro to Engleville:
1877–1886 Denver & Rio Grande Ry.
1886–1921 Denver & Rio Grande RR
1921–1930 Denver & Rio Grande Western RR

DENVER & RIO GRANDE WESTERN from Huerfano County to Trinidad:

Huerfano County to El Moro:
1876–1886 Denver & Rio Grande Ry.
1886–1921 Denver & Rio Grande RR
1921–1936 Denver & Rio Grande Western RR

Engleville Junction to Trinidad:
1887–1888 Trinidad & Denver RR
1888–1921 Denver & Rio Grande RR
1921–1936 Denver & Rio Grande Western RR

DENVER & RIO GRANDE WESTERN from Longsdale to Bon Carbo:

Longsdale to Cokedale:
1906–1921 Denver & Rio Grande RR

Places on the Colorado Prairie

    1921–1950 Denver & Rio Grande Western RR
Cokedale to Bon Carbo:
    1917–1917 American Smelting & Refining Co.
    1917–1921 Denver & Rio Grande RR
    1921–1950 Denver & Rio Grande Western RR

Some Whistlestops

ABEYTA (C&S) is shown about six miles southeast of Barela on a 1909 map. Abeyta was preceded by San Isidro which is shown on 1882 through 1902 maps.

ACME (C&S) is shown about two miles northeast of Aguilar on 1902 through 1920 maps.

BARNES (D&RGW) is shown about five miles northeast of Berwind on 1892 through 1927 maps.

BARNES JUNCTION (C&S) is shown about three miles west of Ludlow on 1892 through 1920 maps.

BOAZ (D&RGW) is shown about three miles south of Huerfano County on 1902 through 1920 maps.

CHICOSA JUNCTION (D&RGW) is shown about one mile northeast of Forbes Junction on 1882 through 1920 maps.

FORBES JUNCTION (C&S) is shown about six miles northwest of El Moro on 1902 through 1920 maps.

GARCIA (C&S) is shown about nine miles northwest of Barela on 1909 through 1956 maps.

HIGGINS (C&S) is shown about two miles north of Acme on a 1916 map.

Las Animas County

HOUGHTON (AT&SF) is shown about seven miles northeast of Thatcher on 1956 and 1968 maps.

LYNN (C&S) is shown about two miles northeast of Aguilar on 1902 through 1920 maps.

NOLA (C&S) is shown about five miles northwest of Trinchera on 1909 through 1968 maps.

RIVERA (C&S) is shown about three miles northeast of El Moro on a 1916 map.

SHERMAN SPUR (C&S) is shown about three miles northeast of Berwind on railroad map.

SILVIA (D&RG) is shown about three miles north of El Moro on 1902 through 1920 maps.

SIMPSON (AT&SF) is shown about six miles southwest of Thatcher on 1909 through 1920 and on 1956 through 1968 maps.

SUFFIELD (C&S) is shown about four miles northwest of El Moro on a 1902 map.

Places to Stop

Fleming, Logan County

Willard, Logan County

Chapter 20

Lincoln County

Still on the Map

Arriba
Bovina
Boyero
Genoa
Hugo

Karval
Limon
Punkin Center
Saugus
Shaw

Places in the Past

Amy
Carr Crossing
Connell Creek
Coon Creek
Cowans
Damascus
Forder
Frontier City
Girard
Green Knoll
Hall Station

Hedinger Lake
Hogan
Hugo Springs
Kendrick
Sanborn
Station 24
Swift
Wellons
Wezel
Willow Springs

Lincoln County

Some Railroad Tracks

Chicago, Rock Island & Pacific Railway
Union Pacific Railroad

Some Whistlestops

Bagdad
Clifford
Lake

Still on the Map

ARRIBA (platted town) was established when the Chicago, Rock Island, and Pacific Railroad built a line to Colorado Springs through a subsidiary, the Chicago, Kansas, and Nebraska Railway, in 1888. A town plat was filed for Arriba on September 17, 1888, by Charles A. Creel. The town takes its name from the Spanish word meaning "above," because Arriba's altitude is higher than that of nearby towns.

BOVINA (platted town) was platted in cattle country, and Bovina means "cattle" in Spanish. A town plat was filed for Bovina on October 20, 1888, by J. F. Jilson, who also filed plats for Claremont, Mattison, Resolis, and Seibert. Since Bovina and the other towns that were platted by Jilson were all located on the Rock Island railroad, it is likely that Jilson was the Rock Island's "Lincoln Land Company" in Colorado.

BOYERO (platted town) was a late arrival on the Union Pacific Railroad. The town was built by the Kansas Pacific Railroad in 1870. The Boyero post office began in 1902, and the town plat was notarized in 1908. Boyero means "bull pen" in Spanish, and the

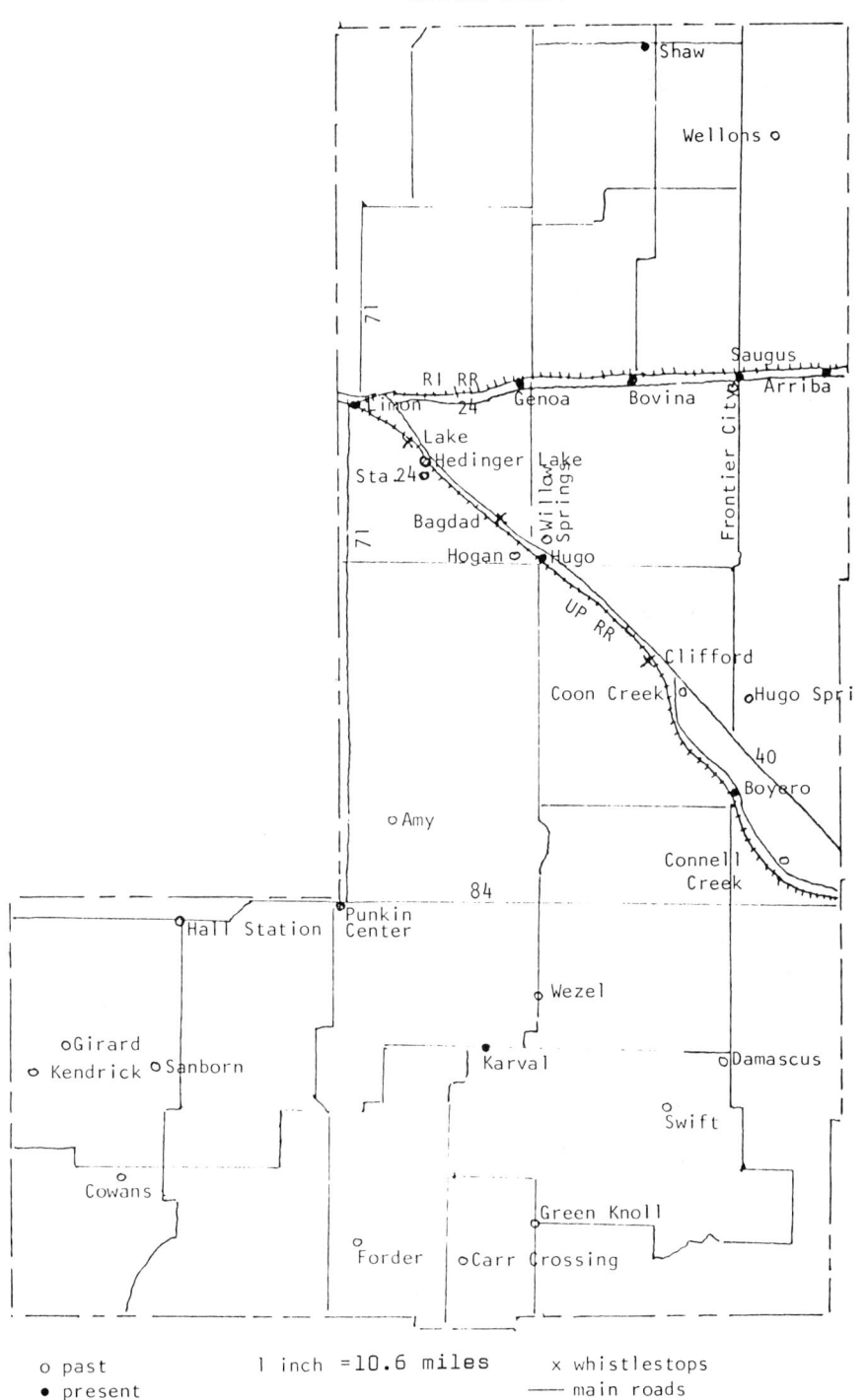

LINCOLN COUNTY

- Shaw
- Wellons
- Saugus
- RI RR
- Limon / 24 / Genoa / Bovina / Arriba
- Lake
- Hedinger Lake
- Sta 24
- Willow Springs
- Bagdad
- Hogan / Hugo
- Frontier City
- UP RR
- Clifford
- Coon Creek
- Hugo Spri
- 40
- Boyero
- Amy
- Connell Creek
- 84
- Hall Station / Punkin Center
- Wezel
- Girard
- Kendrick / Sanborn
- Karval
- Damascus
- Swift
- Cowans
- Forder / Carr Crossing / Green Knoll

o past
• present
1 inch = 10.6 miles
x whistlestops
—— main roads

Lincoln County

town was named after the nearby stockyards. Boyero and nearby Aroya were left stranded when Highway 40 was straightened between Wild Horse and Hugo, and little remains of either community.

GENOA (platted town) was first called "Creech" and was a siding on the Rock Island railroad. The Genoa post office was first established in 1895, but was discontinued in the same year; however, the post office reopened in 1903. A town plat was filed for Genoa on May 19, 1906, by John Nolan and W. H. Echternacht. Genoa was named after Genoa, Italy.

HUGO (platted town) began as a stop on the Smoky Hill stage route and was called "Willow Springs"; however, after the Kansas Pacific Railroad built through the area in 1870, the Hugo post office was established in 1871 and was named after an early pioneer in the area, Hugo Richards. A town plat was filed for Hugo on February 27, 1877, by Clifford J. Rogers, and Hugo was made the county seat of Lincoln County when the county was formed in 1889. Probably the most noted event in the history of Hugo was when President "Teddy" Roosevelt stepped off the train in Hugo for a "cowboy breakfast" on May 7, 1903.

KARVAL (platted town) was first called "Kravig"; however, the name was changed to "Karval" by the postal department when a post office was opened in the area during 1911. A town plat was filed for Karval on February 11, 1920, by Lloyd L. Page. G. K. Kravig was the first postmaster of Karval. Despite the lack of a railroad and its isolated location, Karval has managed to cling to the map and to Mr. Kravig's post office.

LIMON (platted town) was named after a foreman on the Rock Island Railroad, which built through the area in 1888. A town plat was filed for Limon on April 29, 1889, by the Union Land Company, and Limon became an important junction for the Rock Island and Union Pacific railroads. The Kansas Pacific railroad reached the site of Limon in 1870; however, the Kansas Pacific utilized nearby Lake siding, and Limon wasn't established until the Rock Island Railroad built through the area.

Places on the Colorado Prairie

PUNKIN CENTER (place name) is located about eleven miles northwest of Karval and at the junction of Colorado Highways 71 and 94. Punkin Center has a fascinating name, but there's not much there—just a center for "punkins."

SAUGUS (railroad post office) is located about six miles east of Arriba on the Rock Island Railroad. The Saugus post office was in operation from 1908 to 1914.

SHAW (rural post office) was named after Charles Shaw who established a store and the post office in Shaw. The Shaw post office was in operation from 1908 to 1955.

Places in the Past

AMY (rural post office) was named in reference to Amy Collins who was the niece of the postmistress in Amy. The Amy post office was in operation from 1909 to 1937.

CARR CROSSING (rural post office) maintained postal operations from 1915 to 1930 and was located about eleven miles southwest of Karval; however, Carr Crossing stayed on the map into the 1940s.

CONNELL CREEK (stage station) was also shown as Cornett Creek, Conell, and Cornell, and was located on the Smoky Hill South stage route. Connell Creek station was named after a nearby creek.

COON CREEK (stage station) was located on the Smoky Hill South stage route and was named after a nearby creek. The living springs in the area of the Coon Creek station never froze and provided an inducement for locating a stage station.

COWANS (rural post office) was located about twelve or thirteen miles northwest of Forder, and the Cowans post office was in operation from 1915 to 1929. Cowans was on the map into the 1940s.

231

Lincoln County

DAMASCUS (rural post office) was located about thirteen miles east of Karval, and the Damascus post office was in operation from 1914 to 1917.

FORDER (rural post office) was named after a local rancher, Adolph Forder. The Forder post office was in operation from 1901 to 1944, and was located about twelve miles southwest of Karval.

FRONTIER CITY (platted town) was platted next to the location of Arriba; the plat was filed on March 16, 1906, by Charles C. Coleman. Frontier City did not obtain a post office, nor was it shown on the map; thus, it can be assumed that Frontier City was an unsuccessful adventure to either replace or suburbanize Arriba.

GIRARD (rural post office) was located about ten miles southwest of Kutch, and the Girard post office was in operation from 1912 to 1917.

GREEN KNOLL (rural post office) was named in reference to a nearby knoll, and the Green Knoll post office was in operation from 1913 to 1917.

HALL STATION (place name) is shown about six miles southwest of Punkin Center on a 1954 map.

HEDINGER LAKE (stage station) was located at the junction of the Smoky Hill South and Smoky Hill North stage lines. Hedinger Lake Station was in the same vicinity as Station 24, on the Leavenworth and Pikes Peak stage road.

HOGAN (stage station) was located near "Cap Barron" Spring on the Smoky Hill North stage route.

HUGO SPRINGS (stage station) was located about seven miles north of Boyero and was on the Smoky Hill North stage route.

KENDRICK (rural post office) was named after a Dr. Kendrick who settled in the area. The Kendrick post office was in operation from

Places on the Colorado Prairie

1906 to 1955. Kendrick was located about twenty-four miles west of Karval.

SANBORN (rural post office) was located almost in the center of the southwest portion of Lincoln County. The Sanborn post office was in operation from 1878 to 1905. Sanborn was an isolated citadel on the prairie; there was little else other than Sanborn east of Colorado Springs around the turn of the century.

STATION 24 (stage station) was located on the Leavenworth and Pike's Peak Express road and was one of seventeen stations on the 1859 stage line in Colorado. The L.&P.P. stage line was the first line to accommodate the gold rush to Colorado.

SWIFT (rural post office) was located about eight miles southeast of Karval, and the Swift post office was in operation from 1910 to 1919.

WELLONS (rural post office) was located about fifteen miles northeast of Arriba, and the Wellons post office was in operation from 1908 to 1916.

WEZEL (rural post office) was located about four miles northeast of Karval. The Wezel post office was in operation from 1911 to 1919.

WILLOW SPRINGS (stage station) was located on the site of the fairgrounds in Hugo and serviced the Smoky Hill South stage route. Willow Springs was named in reference to nearby Willow Creek.

Some Railroad Tracks

CHICAGO, ROCK ISLAND AND PACIFIC from Kit Carson County to Elbert County:
  1888–1891 Chicago, Kansas & Nebraska Ry.
  1891–   Chicago, Rock Island & Pacific Ry.

Lincoln County

UNION PACIFIC from Cheyenne County to Elbert County:
- 1870–1880 Kansas Pacific Ry.
- 1880–1898 Union Pacific Ry.
- 1898– Union Pacific RR

Some Whistlestops

BAGDAD (UP) is shown about five or six miles northwest of Hugo on 1909 through 1959 maps.

CLIFFORD (UP) is shown about eight miles southeast of Hugo on 1916 through 1970 maps. Clifford was first called "Mirage," which is shown on 1873 through 1909 maps.

LAKE (UP) is shown about three miles southeast of Limon on 1873 through 1920 maps. Lake was named after the Hedinger Lake stage station, which was located in the same vicinity.

Chapter 21

Logan County

Still on the Map

Atwood
Beetland
Crook
Dailey
Fleming
Iliff
Merino
Padroni

Peetz
Proctor
Red Lion
Saint Petersburg
Sterling
Westplains
Willard
Winston

Places in the Past

American Ranch
Armstrong
Chenoa
Dennison's
Godfrey's

Graylin
Hadfield's Island
Kelley
Laura

235

Logan County

Leroy	South Platte
Lillian Springs	Spring Hill
New Haven	Valley
Rockland	
Sarinda	

Some Railroad Tracks

Burlington Northern Railroad (three parts)
Union Pacific Railroad

Some Whistlestops

Ackerman	Jessica
Beta	Logan
Brownard	Marcott
Buchanan	Minto
Chelsea	Powell
Ford	Selma
Galien	Sherwin
Hall	Stein
Hayford	Toben

LOGAN COUNTY

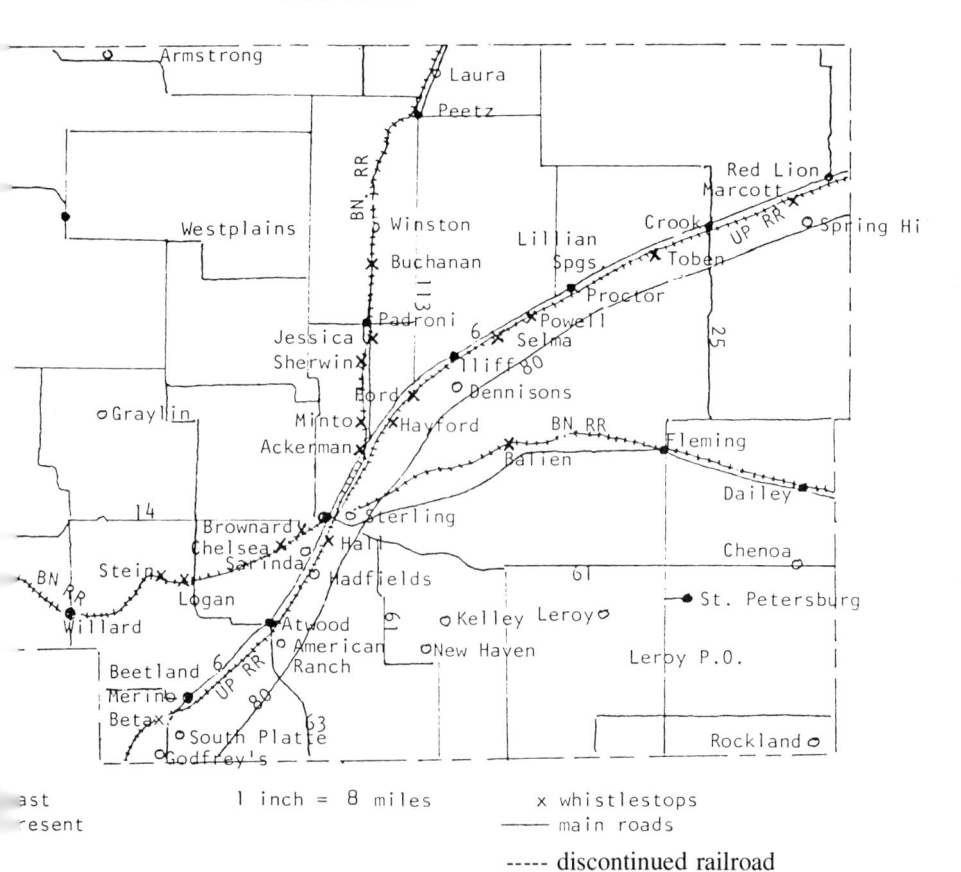

1 inch = 8 miles
x whistlestops
——— main roads
----- discontinued railroad

Logan County

Still on the Map

ATWOOD (platted town) was named after Reverend John Atwood of the Unitarian Church. Vear Wilson, who founded the town, was a Unitarian. A town plat was filed for Atwood on July 29, 1885, by Vear Wilson. Atwood began as a shipping point for cattlemen in the area, and much of the town's early growth was resultant upon the Union Pacific railroad, which had been built through the area in 1880.

BEETLAND (platted town) was named after the sugar beet which is one of the leading crops in the area. A town plat was filed for Beetland, but the date of filing and the name of the filer are not shown on the plat. The Great Western Sugar Company established many loading stations along the Union Pacific railroad, and Beetland was probably an attempt to develop the Beetland station into a town.

CROOK (platted town) was established next to the Union Pacific railroad in the early 1880s and was named after General George Crook, who commanded the Department of the Platte from 1875 to 1882. The Holland Colony attempted to establish a community at the site of Crook in 1893; however, the colony was unsuccessful, and it wasn't until the 1900s that Crook became an established town. A town plat was filed for Crook on February 20, 1909, by the Cedar Valley Land and Irrigation Company. Crook was incorporated in 1918.

DAILEY (platted town) was one of the few towns on the Burlington railroad from Sterling to Nebraska which wasn't initiated by the Lincoln Land Company. A town plat was filed for Dailey on December 17, 1914, by W. B. Ford. Dailey was named after James Dailey, who was a trainmaster for the Burlington Railroad. The Dailey post office was discontinued in 1962.

FLEMING (platted town) was first called "Twenty-Nine-Mile Siding" after the distance between the siding and Haxtun on the Burlington Railroad. A town plat was filed for Fleming on

February 26, 1889, by the Lincoln Land Company, and the town was named in reference to H. B. Fleming, who platted the site for the Lincoln Land Company.

ILIFF (platted town) was another of the several cattle towns which were started next to the Union Pacific railroad soon after the line was built through Logan County in 1880. The Iliff post office was established in 1882 and was named after John Iliff who was one of the cattle "kings" of early Colorado. A town plat was filed for Iliff on July 5, 1887, by the State Board of Commissioners.

MERINO (platted town) was first called "Buffalo," referring to the Buffalo Colony which was established in the area during 1874. The Buffalo Colony did not flourish, and the name was changed to "Merino" in 1883. Merino was named after the many merino sheep in the area. A town plat wasn't filed for Merino until 1906, when the Corona Cattle Company filed a plat on August 10. Buffalo, sheep, and cattle—quite a mixture.

PADRONI (platted town) began as a supply depot for the building of the Sterling reservoir in the early 1900s. Padroni was named in reference to the Padroni brothers who were local farmers. A town plat was filed for Padroni on January 22, 1910, by George E. Clayton and A. V. Hunt, and Padroni has been closely associated with the reservoir ever since.

PEETZ (platted town) was first called "Mercer" when it was established next to the Burlington railroad in 1899; however, the name was changed to "Peetz" in 1908. Peetz was named after Peter Peetz who was an early resident of the area. A town plat was filed for Peetz on March 10, 1908, by the Lincoln Land Company.

PROCTOR (platted town) was developed by J. D. Blue, who owned a ranch near the Proctor siding on the Union Pacific's branch line to Denver. A town plat was filed for Proctor on November 1, 1909, by the Logan County Development Company. Proctor was named after a General Proctor who distinguished himself in campaigns against the Indians. The Proctor post office closed in 1964.

Logan County

RED LION (railroad post office) is located on the Union Pacific railroad and next to the Sedgwick County line. The Red Lion post office was in operation from 1910 to 1936; however, Red Lion has been shown on the maps since 1897. Red Lion was named after the Red Lion Land Company of York, Nebraska, which developed the site. There was another place in Logan County called "Red Lion," but that was an addition to Sterling in the 1880s. The Red Lion plat for the Sterling addition was filed in 1886 by Minos King.

SAINT PETERSBURG (place name) is about ten miles southeast of Fleming on 1934 through 1968 maps. A post office is not listed for Saint Petersburg, but this is one of those places that merits much more investigation.

STERLING (platted town) was named after Sterling, Illinois, which was the hometown of David Leavitt on whose ranch the Sterling post office was established in 1874. The first settlement on the original site of Sterling was initiated by a group of southerners in 1873. When the Union Pacific railroad was built into the county in 1880, Minos King persuaded the Union Pacific Railroad to make Sterling a division point, and King platted Sterling in keeping with the route of the railroad. King had the Sterling plat notarized in 1881, but the plat was not filed until 1888. In 1887, Logan County was formed with Sterling the designated county seat. The Burlington Railroad built a line to Sterling in 1887, and the Great Western Sugar Company built a refinery at Sterling in 1905. The Northeastern Junior College was established at Sterling in 1941.

WESTPLAINS (rural post office) is located about eighteen miles northwest of Sterling. The Westplains post office, which was named after its location, was in operation from 1910 to 1949.

WILLARD (platted town) was named after Dan Willard who was president of the Burlington Railroad when it built into Logan County in 1887. A town plat was filed for Willard on December 7, 1888, by the Lincoln Land Company. In 1910, William House replatted Willard, which had been slow to develop. The Willard post office (called "Arnold" from 1892 to 1900) opened and closed several times and was last closed in 1968.

WINSTON (railroad post office) was located next to the Burlington railroad and about six miles southwest of Peetz. The Winston post office was in operation during 1902 and from 1908 to 1918.

Places in the Past

AMERICAN RANCH (stage station) was located on the Overland route and about one mile south of the site of Atwood. American Ranch, which was also known as "Kelleys," operated a post office from 1863 to 1867.

ARMSTRONG (rural post office) was located about sixteen miles west of Peetz, and the Armstrong post office was in operation from 1911 to 1917. Armstrong was just east of Chimney Canyons, which provided many of the early settlers in the area with red cedar wood.

CHENOA (rural post office) was located on the wagon road from Haxtun to Leroy and on to Fleming. The Chenoa post office, named in reference to Chenoa, Illinois, was in operation from 1886 to 1895.

DENNISON'S (stage stop) was located on the Central Overland route and about two miles south from the site of Iliff. Dennison's must have had some permanence, because it was shown on an 1882 map.

GODFREY'S (stage stop) was located on the Central Overland route and about two miles south of the site of Merino. Godfrey's station became known as "Fort Wicked" because of the bitter defense staged by Holon Godfrey at the station during the Indian uprising of 1864.

GRAYLIN (rural post office) was located about twelve miles northwest of Sterling, and the Graylin post office was in operation from 1910 to 1916..

Logan County

HADFIELD'S ISLAND (place name) was located at the confluence of the South Platte River and Pawnee Creek and was the site on which William Shaw Hadfield settled in 1871. "Billy" Hadfield was the first permanent white settler in what is now Logan County.

KELLEY (rural post office) was located about eight miles southwest of Leroy; the Kelley post office was in operation from 1909 to 1916.

LAURA (railroad post office) was located just north of Peetz on the Burlington railroad, and the Laura post office was in operation from 1910 to 1916. Laura was founded by a Mr. McKibben and was a fierce competitor to Peetz for a while.

LEROY (platted town) was spelled "LeRoy" on an 1892 map, and the town plat for Leroy was filed on February 14, 1889, by Michael Thinigan. Leroy survived the drouth of the 1890s, but its post office closed in 1916.

LILLIAN SPRINGS (stage station) was located on the Central Overland stage route and about four miles northeast of the site of Proctor.

NEW HAVEN (rural post office) was located about seven miles southeast of Leroy. The New Haven post office was in operation from 1910 to 1916. New Haven was named after its founders' goal of finding a haven in which to live.

ROCKLAND (platted town), named after the local topography, was one of several communities which were established along a proposed route of the Burlington Railroad. A town plat was filed for Rockland on November 27, 1888, by Charles E. McPherson; however, the railroad was not built through the area, and the Rockland post office closed in 1891. Rockland did stay on the map for some time after the post office closed.

SARINDA (rural post office) was located about two miles southwest of the site of Sterling, and the Sarinda post office was in operation from 1875 to 1882. Sarinda served the area around Hadfield's Island, on which William Shaw Hadfield settled in 1871.

Places on the Colorado Prairie

SOUTH PLATTE (rural post office) was located about three miles southwest of the site of Merino, and the South Platte post office was in operation from 1873 to 1883. South Platte was preceded by Godfrey's stage station in the area.

SPRING HILL (stage station) was located on the Central Overland stage route and about four miles southeast of the site of Crook. Spring Hill remained on the map past the turn of the century.

VALLEY (stage station) was located on the Central Overland stage route and about one mile southeast of the site of Sterling. Valley was one of the main fortifications during the Indian uprising along the Platte in the 1860s.

Some Railroad Tracks

BURLINGTON NORTHERN from Phillips County to Weld County:
- 1887–1908 Colorado & Wyoming RR
- 1908–1970 Chicago, Burlington & Quincy RR
- 1970– Burlington Northern RR
- 1975 Removed East to Willard

BURLINGTON NORTHERN from Nebraska to Sterling:
- 1899–1970 Chicago, Burlington & Quincy RR
- 1970– Burlington Northern RR

BURLINGTON NORTHERN from Sterling to Morgan County:
- When the C.B.&Q. constructed its line north from Sterling in 1899, it connected with the Wray-to-Denver line by obtaining the usage of the Union Pacific line from Union in Morgan County to Sterling.

UNION PACIFIC from Sedgwick County to Morgan County:
- 1880–1890 Colorado Central RR
- 1890–1898 Union Pacific, Denver & Gulf Ry.
- 1898– Union Pacific RR

243

Logan County

Some Whistlestops

ACKERMAN (BN) is shown about two miles southeast of Sterling on 1916 through 1954 maps.

BETA (BN) is shown about four miles southwest of Sterling on 1916 through 1968 maps.

BROWNARD (BN) is shown about four miles southwest of Sterling on a 1920 map.

BUCHANAN (BN) is shown about fifteen miles northeast of Sterling on 1956 and 1968 maps.

CHELSEA (BN) is shown about eight miles southwest of Sterling on 1892 through 1902 maps.

FORD (UP) is shown about eight miles northeast of Sterling on 1916 through 1968 maps.

GALIEN (BN) is shown about eight miles northeast of Sterling on 1892 through 1968 maps.

HALL (BN) is shown about two miles northeast of Atwood on 1916 and 1920 maps.

HAYFORD (UP) is shown about four miles northeast of Sterling on 1909 through 1920 maps.

JESSICA (BN) is shown about one mile south of Padroni on 1924 through 1968 maps.

LOGAN (BN) is shown about nine miles southwest of Sterling on 1956 through 1968 maps.

MARCOTT (UP) is shown about four miles northeast of Crook on a railroad map.

Places on the Colorado Prairie

MINTO (BN) is shown about five miles northeast of Sterling on 1902 through 1920 maps.

POWELL (UP) is shown about five miles northeast of Iliff on 1911 through 1934 maps.

SELMA (UP) is shown about three miles northeast of Iliff on 1902 through 1916 maps.

SHERWIN (BN) is shown about three miles south of Padroni on a 1924 map.

STEIN (BN) is shown about nine miles southwest of Sterling on a 1920 map. Stein and Logan are shown in the same location.

TOBEN (UP) is shown about four miles southwest of Crook on a railroad map.

Places to Remember

Franktown, Douglas County

Cornish, Weld County

Chapter 22

Morgan County

Still on the Map

Adena
Brush
Fort Morgan
Gary
Goodrich
Hillrose

Hoyt
Log Lane Village
Orchard
Snyder
Weldona
Wiggins

Places in the Past

Antelope Springs
Beaver
Bijou
Bijouview
Cotsworth
Deuel
Dodd
Fort Morgan

Fremont
Grahame Ranch
Glider Training School
Junction House
Littleville
Pawnee
Rock Creek
Vallery

Morgan County

Some Railroad Tracks

Burlington Northern Railroad (three parts)
Union Pacific Railroad

Some Whistlestops

Balzac	Manchester
Bijou	Maudru
Bronco	Moseley
Camden	Narrows
Cooper	Nelson
Giese	North Fort Morgan
Griffin	Story
Hurley	Trowell Ranch
Lamb	White
Lodi	

Still on the Map

ADENA (rural post office) is located about sixteen miles southwest of Fort Morgan, and the Adena post office was in operation from 1910 to 1947. Adena was named after Edna Adena, who was the sweetheart of an early settler in the area. Most of the first settlers in the Adena area were from Illinois and Nebraska.

BRUSH (platted town) was named after Jared Brush, who was one of the most prominent cattlemen in the state at one time. Jared Brush became Lieutenant Governor of Colorado in 1895. The Burlington Railroad built to the site of Brush in 1881, and the Lincoln Land Company filed a town plat for Brush on June 4, 1881. The area around Brush was predominantly cattle country until the Great Western Sugar Company built a sugar factory at Brush in 1906.

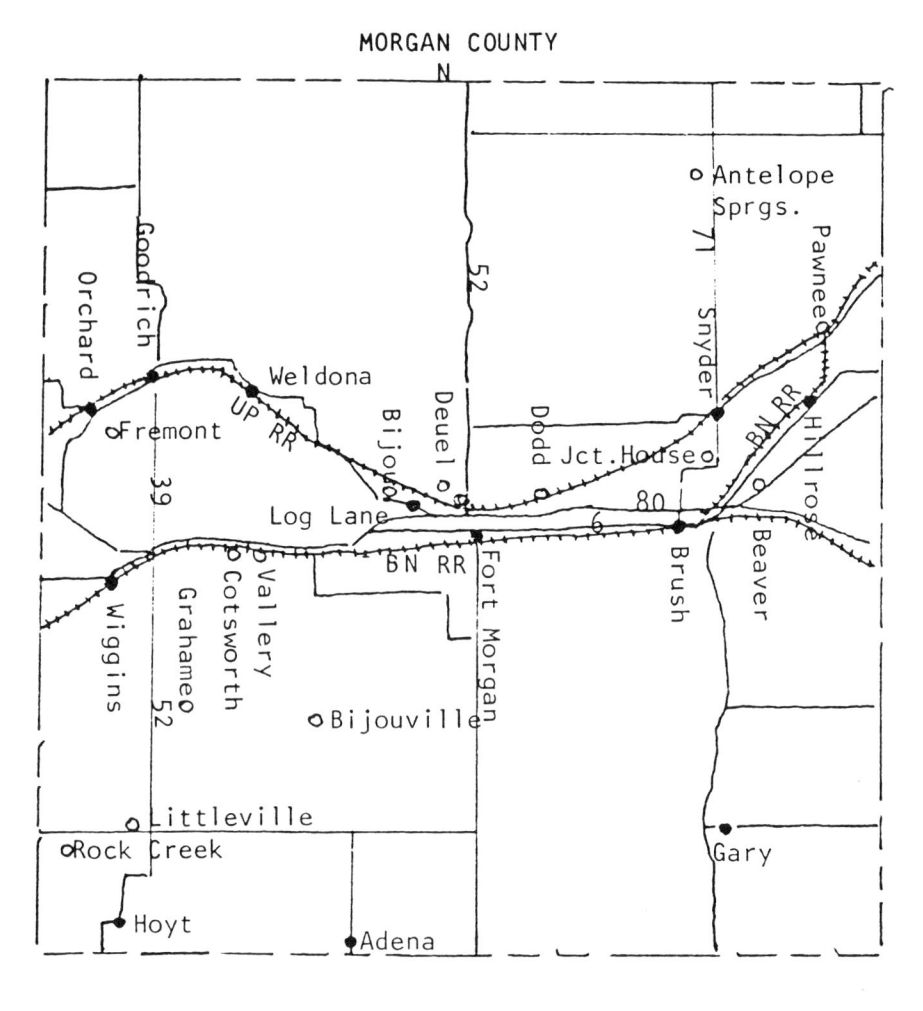

MORGAN COUNTY

MORGAN COUNTY

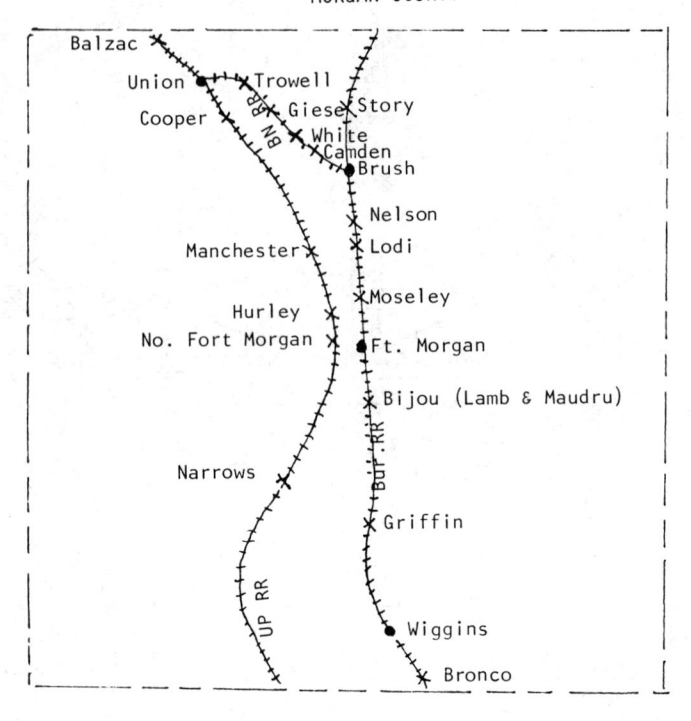

1 inch = 10.6 miles   x whistlestops

Places on the Colorado Prairie

FORT MORGAN (platted town) was named in reference to the military fort which served the area from 1865 to 1868. The Union Pacific and Burlington Railroads built to the site of Fort Morgan in 1880 and 1881, respectively; however, a town plat wasn't filed for several years after the arrival of the railroads. Abner and Sarah Baker filed a plat for Fort Morgan on May 1, 1884. Fort Morgan grew rapidly and was made the seat of Morgan County when the county was formed in 1889. Fort Morgan became an agricultural center after the Great Western Sugar Company built a factory just north of the town in 1907.

GARY (rural post office) is located about thirteen miles south of Brush, and the Gary post office was in operation from 1899 to 1954.

GOODRICH (platted town) was named after a Morgan County pioneer, G. T. Goodrich. The Goodrich post office was established in 1908, but a town plat wasn't filed for Goodrich until October 25, 1916, by the Riverside Lumber Company. Goodrich is located in the heart of the noted Weldon Valley.

HILLROSE (platted town) was named after Rose Hill Emerson, who was a sister of the site's owner, Kate Emerson. Hillrose was established when a connecting railroad was built between the Burlington Railroad's main line and north-south line, and the town plat was filed by the Lincoln Land Company on October 8, 1900.

HOYT (rural post office) was named after Dr. James Hoyt, whose mother settled in the area in the 1880s. The Hoyt post office has been in operation since 1906.

LOG LANE VILLAGE (platted town) is located next to Fort Morgan. It was established during the oil boom around Fort Morgan in the 1950s. A town plat was filed for Log Lane village on August 16, 1955, by Dorothy Hages. Log Lane Village was named after the style of many houses in the community.

ORCHARD (platted town) was named after Fremont's Orchard, which was located across the river southeast of the townsite. Colonel John Fremont journeyed into Colorado several times, and,

Morgan County

during his 1842 expedition, he camped near a group of trees which became known as "Fremont's Orchard." The WeldonValley post office was established at the site of Orchard when the Union Pacific Railroad was being built from Julesburg in 1880. However, the post office was discontinued in the same year, and the Orchard post office was opened on the site in 1882. A town plat was filed for Orchard on July 21, 1890, by George West, who was a co-founder of Golden.

SNYDER (platted town) was named after J. W. Snyder and D. H. Snyder, local cattlemen, who had purchased a portion of the noted John Iliff's vast herds. A post office was established near the Snyder corrals in 1882; however, a town plat wasn't filed for Snyder until H. N. Claney and H. B. Davis filed a plat for Snyder on September 22, 1897.

WELDONA (platted town) was named after the Weldon Valley in which the town is located, and the Weldon Valley was named after General Weldon. The "a" was added to Weldon because of the similarity between the names, Weldon and Walden. A town plat was filed for Weldon on February 24, 1893, by Prucius Putnam, who also filed the plat for the nearby town of Orchard. A post office wasn't established in Weldona until 1907, some fourteen years after the plat was filed by Putnam.

WIGGINS (platted town) was first called "Corona," and a town plat was filed for Corona on September 10, 1888; however, the Corona post office was opened in 1874 and operated until 1878. The Corona post office reopened in 1882 and ran until 1896. A town plat was filed for Wiggins on May 12, 1908, by Frank McCartney and Everett Owens, and the Wiggins post office began in the same year. Wiggins was named after Oliver Wiggins, who was a frontier scout. Thomas McCartney established Corona, and Frank McCartney established Wiggins.

Places in the Past

ANTELOPE SPRINGS (rural post office) was located about eight miles north of Snyder and was named after nearby Antelope Creek.

Places on the Colorado Prairie

The Antelope Springs post office was in operation from 1911 to 1917.

BEAVER (stage station) was located about six miles northeast of Brush and was on the Overland stage route. The Beaver Creek station was named after nearby Beaver Creek. Beaver station stayed on the map into the 1890s.

BIJOU (stage station) served the Overland stages between the Beaver and Fremont Orchard stations. Bijou station was named after nearby Bijou Creek which entered the South Platte River a short distance from the station.

BIJOUVIEW (rural post office) was located about eight miles south of Vallery, and the Bijouview post office was in operation from 1914 to 1921. Bijouview was one of several places which took their names from Bijou Creek which was a dominating force in Morgan County before irrigation controls. One of the most devastating floods in Colorado history was caused by an overflowing Bijou Creek in the 1930s.

COTSWORTH (railroad post office) was located about eleven miles west of Fort Morgan on the Burlington railroad. The Cotsworth post office operated in 1882 and 1883.

DEUEL (platted town) was located across the river from Fort Morgan. The Deuel post office was established in 1883, and a town plat was filed for Deuel on April 5, 1886, by J. Lafayette More. The Deuel post office was relocated in Weldona near the turn of the century; however, the name of the post office wasn't changed to "Weldona" until 1907. After the Deuel post office was moved to Weldona, the Union Pacific siding at Deuel's previous location was called "North Fort Morgan."

DODD (railroad post office) was located about eight or nine miles northeast of Fort Morgan on the Union Pacific Railroad; the Dodd post office was in operation from 1904 to 1907.

FORT MORGAN (military fort) began as "Camp Tyler" in 1864, and the name was changed to "Fort Wardell" in 1865, after

Morgan County

temporary barracks were built on the site. Fort Wardell was renamed "Fort Morgan" in 1866 and was named in honor of Colonel Christopher A. Morgan, of the United States Volunteers. Camp Tyler was established to protect a portion of the Overland route from Indian uprisings. The need for military protection along the Platte had diminished by the late 1860s, and Fort Morgan was abandoned on May 18, 1868.

FREMONT (stage station) was named after the nearby site of Fremont Orchard which was the name for a large stand of trees that was noted by the Colonel Fremont expedition in the 1840s. The Fremont station was located on the Overland route between the site of Fort Morgan and the Latham station. The town of Orchard was platted just northwest of Fremont Orchard.

GLIDER TRAINING SCHOOL (military installation) was located north of Fort Morgan during World War II.

GRAHAME RANCH (stage station) was located on the Fort Morgan Cutoff and about seven miles southeast from the site of Wiggins. The first floor of the ranch house was used as the stage station.

JUNCTION HOUSE (stage station) was located about four miles northeast of the site of Brush and at the junction of the Overland route to Latham and a cutoff to Denver. After the cutoff was moved nearer Fort Morgan, the Junction House post office was moved to the fort in 1866.

LITTLEVILLE (place name) was located about ten miles south of Wiggins and is shown on a 1942 map. Littleville was named after John Little, who ran a grocery store on the site.

PAWNEE (railroad post office) was located at Union Junction of the Burlington and Union Pacific Railroads. The Pawnee post office was in operation from 1903 to 1944.

ROCK CREEK (stage station) was located about four miles northwest of Hoyt and served the stages on the Fort Morgan Cutoff of the Overland route.

Places on the Colorado Prairie

VALLERY (platted town) was located about seven miles southwest of Fort Morgan on the Burlington railroad. A town plat was filed for Vallery on March 11, 1908, by the Lincoln Land Company, and the town was named after John Vallery, a general freight agent for the Burlington Railroad. The Vallery post office was in operation from 1907 to 1919.

Some Railroad Tracks

BURLINGTON NORTHERN from Union to Brush:
    1900–1908 Denver & Montana RR
    1908–1970 Chicago, Burlington & Quincy RR
    1970–   Burlington Northern RR

BURLINGTON NORTHERN from Washington County to Union:
    1900–1908 Denver & Montana RR
    1908–1970 Chicago, Burlington & Quincy RR
    1970–   Burlington Northern RR

BURLINGTON NORTHERN from Washington County to Weld County:
    1881–1908 Burlington & Colorado RR
    1908–1970 Chicago, Burlington & Quincy RR
    1970–   Burlington Northern RR

UNION PACIFIC from Washington County to Weld County:
    1880–1890 Colorado Central RR
    1890–1898 Union Pacific, Denver & Gulf Ry.
    1898–   Union Pacific RR

Morgan County

Some Whistlestops

BALZAC (UP) is shown about three miles northeast of Union on 1902 through 1920 maps.

BIJOU (BN) is shown about three miles west of Fort Morgan on a 1916 map. Bijou is shown in the same location as "Ensign," which is shown on 1884 and 1887 maps, and "Carr," which is shown on a 1902 map.

BRONCO (BN) is shown about five miles southwest of Wiggins on 1916 and 1920 maps.

CAMDEN (BN) is shown about six miles northeast of Brush on 1907 through 1920 maps.

COOPER (UP) is shown about six miles northeast of Snyder on 1916 and 1920 maps.

GIESE (BN) is shown about one mile northeast of Hillrose on a 1970 map.

GRIFFIN (BN) is shown about one mile east of Vallery on 1924 and 1970 railroad maps.

HURLEY (UP) is shown about three miles east of Fort Morgan on a railroad map.

LAMB (BN) is shown about three miles west of Fort Morgan on a 1924 map.

LODI (BN) is shown about four miles west of Brush on 1911 through 1934 maps.

MANCHESTER (UP) is shown about six miles northeast of Fort Morgan on an 1882 map.

Places on the Colorado Prairie

MAUDRU (BN) is shown about three miles west of Fort Morgan on a 1970 map. Maudru is shown in the same location as Lamb.

MOSELEY (BN) is shown about two miles east of Fort Morgan on 1916 and 1924 maps.

NARROWS (UP) is shown about eight miles northwest of Fort Morgan on 1916 through 1927 maps.

NELSON (BN) is shown about three miles west of Brush on 1916 through 1970 maps.

NORTH FORT MORGAN (UP) is shown about one mile north of Fort Morgan on 1902 through 1920 maps.

STORY (BN) is shown about six miles east of Brush on 1916 through 1924 maps.

TROWELL RANCH (BN) is shown about two miles north of Hillrose on the 1902 through 1970 maps.

WHITE (BN) is shown about one mile southwest of Hillrose on a 1970 map.

Places to Live

Larkspur, Douglas County

Palmer Lake, El Paso County

Chapter 23

Otero County

Still on the Map

Ayer
Cheraw
Fowler
LaJunta
Manzanola

Mindeman
Rocky Ford
Swink
Timpas
Vroman

Places in the Past

Andersondale
Angora
Bent's Fort
Bloom
Higbee
Home Place
Iron Springs
King's Ferry
LaJunta Air Force Base

Omer
Orchard Place
Rene
San Joseville
South Side
Spring Bottom
Timpas
Uncle Jack Moore's
Vogel

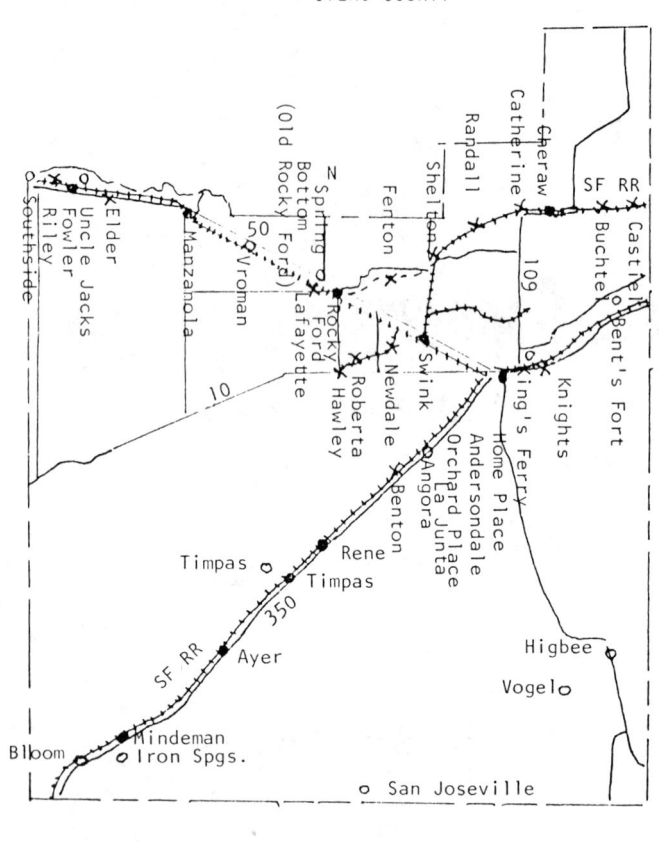

OTERO COUNTY

○ past
● present
1 inch = 8 miles
x whistlestops
—— main roads

Places on the Colorado Prairie

Some Railroad Tracks

Arkansas Valley Railway
Atchison, Topeka & Santa Fe Railway (six parts)
Missouri Pacific Railroad

Some Whistlestops

Benton	Kremis
Buchtel	Lafayette
Case	Newdale
Castiel	Ormega
Catherine	Randall
Elder	Riley
Fenton	Roberta
Hawley	Robinson
Knight's Ferry	Shelton

Still on the Map

AYER (railroad post office) is located about six miles southwest of Timpas and next to the Santa Fe railroad. The Ayer post office was in operation from 1911 to 1941.

CHERAW (platted town) is an Indian word which means "sparkling water." A town plat was filed for Cheraw on November 3, 1906, by Arthur Beymer, and the Santa Fe railroad was built to the townsite in the same year. Cheraw was incorporated in 1917.

FOWLER (platted town) was named after Professor O. S. Fowler, who helped develop the community. Professor Fowler was a phrenologist, one who studies the shape of a skull to determine that person's faculties. A town plat was filed for Fowler on January 29, 1894, by the Fowler Town and Improvement Company, the vice-president of which was George Swink. The Fowler post office was preceded by the Alexander post office, which was preceded by the Oxford post office.

LA JUNTA (platted town) was first named "Otero" after Miguel Otero, who established the town when the Santa Fe railroad was built through the area in 1875. A town plat for Otero, or LaJunta, was not on file; however, a plat was probably filed in 1876 or 1877. Otero was renamed LaJunta, the Spanish word for "junction," when the town became a junction for the Santa Fe Railroad lines to Pueblo and to Trinidad. LaJunta was made the county seat of Otero County when the county was formed in 1889.

MANZANOLA (platted town) was platted as "Catlin," and the plat was filed on August 24, 1891, by James and Joseph Beaty. Catlin, which was named after the nearby Catlin Ditch, was renamed "Manzanola" in 1895. Manzanola is the Spanish word for "red apples" and was named as such after the many apple trees in the area.

MINDEMAN (railroad post office) is located about five miles southwest of Ayer and next to the Santa Fe railroad. The Mindeman post office was in operation from 1917 to 1935. Mindeman was first called "Symons," and Symons is shown on 1909 through 1916 maps.

ROCKY FORD (platted town) was first located about three miles northwest of the present site and was named after a nearby crossing of the Arkansas River. George Swink joined with A. Russell, who operated a trading post at the first site, in opening the first store in Rocky Ford. When the Santa Fe railroad was built through the area in 1875, Rocky Ford moved three miles to the southwest so that it would be next to the railroad. A town plat was filed for Rocky Ford on August 20, 1888, by the Rocky Ford Town and Investment Company.

Places on the Colorado Prairie

SWINK (platted town) was named after George Swink, who was instrumental in the development of the Arkansas Valley. Swink was first called "Fairmount," and the Fairmount post office was in operation from 1900 to 1906. A town plat was filed for Swink by the Swink Town Company on February 20, 1906, which coincided with the building of a short line from Swink to Shelton Junction by the Holly and Swink Railway.

TIMPAS (railroad post office) is located about twenty miles southwest of LaJunta and next to the Santa Fe railroad. The Timpas post office opened in 1891 and was named after nearby Timpas Creek. A Mr. Rounds is credited with being the first settler in the Timpas area; he settled there in 1868.

VROMAN (railroad post office) is located about six miles northwest of Rocky Ford and next to the Santa Fe railroad. Vroman was first called "Weitzer," which is shown on 1909 and 1916 maps. The Vroman post office was in operation from 1918 into the 1950s.

Places in the Past

ANDERSONDALE (platted town) was located next to LaJunta, and the plat for the town was filed on May 10, 1911, by Jay Anderson. Andersondale did not obtain a post office, nor was it shown on the map.

ANGORA (railroad post office) was located next to the Santa Fe Railroad and about six miles southwest of LaJunta. The Angora post office was in operation from 1891 to 1894.

BENT'S FORT (trading post) was established in 1829 by the Bent brothers. The fort-like trading post became a citadel on the Santa Fe Trail and was the "home base" for fur trading in the Rocky Mountain area. The fort was completed in 1832 and was first called "William's Fort." Charles Bent was killed in Taos, New Mexico, during an Indian uprising. In 1853, William Bent set fire to the fort during a dispute with the government, which wanted to buy the

Otero County

fort. Bent's Fort was burned almost to the ground, and William Bent started a new fort about forty miles downstream.

BLOOM (railroad post office) was first called "Iron Springs," which is shown on 1884 through 1902 maps. The Bloom post office was in operation in 1899 and from 1913 to 1938.

HIGBEE (rural post office) was located about seventeen miles southwest of LaJunta. The Higbee post office was in operation from 1872 to 1925. Higbee was named after Uriah Higbee, who had settled in Trinidad in 1860, before moving to the Higbee site. Higbee was first called "Nine-Mile Bottom."

HOME PLACE (platted town) was platted just east of LaJunta, and the plat was filed by Robert Patterson on an unknown date. Home Place did not obtain a post office, and it was not shown on the map.

IRON SPRINGS (stage station) was located on the Timpas Creek stage route of the Santa Fe Trail and about three miles southeast from the site of Mindeman. The Iron Springs station was adjacent to a stockade.

KING'S FERRY (river ford) was located just east of the LaJunta site and on the Santa Fe Trail. King's Ferry was operated by Colonel John Quincy Adams King until the railroad reached the area in 1875.

LAJUNTA AIR FORCE BASE (military installation) was located near LaJunta during World War II.

OMER (rural post office) was located about seventeen miles southwest of Hawley, and the Omer post office was in operation from 1900 to 1909.

ORCHARD PLACE (platted town) was platted just west of LaJunta, and the plat was filed on May 11, 1901, by D. A. Mulvane; however, Orchard Place did not obtain a post office, nor was it shown on the map.

Places on the Colorado Prairie

RENE (railroad post office) was located about four miles northeast of Timpas, and the Rene post office was in operation from 1912 to 1921.

SAN JOSEVILLE (place name) is shown about thirteen miles southeast of Ayer on a 1927 map.

SOUTH SIDE (railroad post office) was located about three miles northwest of Fowler and next to the Atchison, Topeka and Santa Fe railroad. The South Side post office was in operation from 1869 to 1875. South Side was also a stage station on the Santa Fe line.

SPRING BOTTOM (stage station) was located on the stage route from Bent's Old Fort to Pueblo and at or near the Rocky Ford of the Arkansas (three miles northwest of the present town of Rocky Ford).

TIMPAS (stage station) was located about one-half mile northwest of Timpas and was the first station on the Santa Fe Trail up Timpas Creek.

UNCLE JACK MOORE'S (stage station) was located on the stage route from Bent's Fort to Pueblo and across the Arkansas River from the site of Fowler.

VOGEL (stage station) was located on the Purgatoire route of the Santa Fe stage road and about sixteen miles southeast of the site of LaJunta. There are Indian pictographs on the canyon walls above nearby Willow Creek.

Some Railroad Tracks

ARKANSAS VALLEY from Bent County to Rocky Ford:
   1875–1878 Arkansas Valley Ry.

ATCHISON, TOPEKA & SANTA FE from Bent County to Pueblo County:

Otero County

    1875–1900 Pueblo & Arkansas Valley RR
    1900–   Atchison, Topeka & Santa Fe Ry.

ATCHISON, TOPEKA & SANTA FE from LaJunta to Las Animas County:
    1877–1900 Pueblo & Arkansas Valley RR
    1900–   Atchison, Topeka & Santa Fe Ry.

ATCHISON, TOPEKA & SANTA FE from Newdale to Hawley:
    1908–   Atchison, Topeka & Santa Fe Ry.

ATCHISON, TOPEKA & SANTA FE from Bent County to Rocky Ford:
    1908–   Atchison, Topeka & Santa Fe Ry.

ATCHISON, TOPKEA & SANTA FE from Buchtel to Rocky Ford:
    1906–1912 Arkansas Valley Ry.
    1912–   Atchison, Topeka & Santa Fe Ry.

ATCHISON, TOPEKA & SANTA FE from Shelton Junction to Swink:
    1908–1908 Holly & Swink Ry.
    1908–   Atchison, Topeka & Santa Fe Ry.

MISSOURI PACIFIC (just touches northeast corner of Otero County):
    1887–1887 Pueblo & State Line RR
    1887–1917 Missouri Pacific Ry.
    1917–   Missouri Pacific RR

Some Whistlestops

BENTON (AT&SF) is shown about eight miles southwest of LaJunta on 1884 through 1968 maps.

Places on the Colorado Prairie

BUCHTEL (AT&SF) is shown about two miles east of Cheraw on 1909 through 1920 maps.

CASE (AT&SF) is shown about four miles northeast of LaJunta on 1916 and 1920 maps.

CASTIEL (AT&SF) is shown about five miles east of Cheraw on 1916 and 1920 maps.

CATHERINE (AT&SF) is shown about two miles west of Cheraw on 1909 and 1920 maps.

ELDER (AT&SF) is shown about three miles southeast of Fowler on 1916 and 1920 maps.

FENTON (AT&SF) is shown about two miles southwest of Hays on a 1916 map.

HAWLEY (AT&SF) is shown about five miles south of Rocky Ford on 1924 through 1968 maps. Hawley is shown as Hauck on 1909 through 1916 maps.

KNIGHT'S FERRY (AT&SF) is shown about two miles northeast of LaJunta on 1882 through 1897 maps.

KREMIS (AT&SF) is shown about two miles southeast of Rocky Ford on a 1916 map.

LAFAYETTE (AT&SF) is shown about two miles northwest of Rocky Ford on a 1909 map.

NEWDALE (AT&SF) is shown about two miles northwest of Swink on 1909 through 1916 maps.

ORMEGA (AT&SF) is shown about three miles southwest of LaJunta on 1909 through 1927 maps.

RANDALL (AT&SF) is shown about three miles northeast of Hays on 1909 and 1920 maps.

Otero County

RILEY (AT&SF) is shown about one mile northwest of Fowler on 1916 and 1920 maps.

ROBERTA (AT&SF) is shown about two miles southwest of Swink on 1909 and 1916 maps.

ROBINSON (AT&SF) is shown about nine miles northeast of LaJunta on an 1882 map.

SHELTON (AT&SF) is shown about four miles north of Swink on a 1909 map.

Chapter 24

Phillips County

Still on the Map

Amherst
Haxtun

Holyoke
Paoli

Places in the Past

Bryant
Emerson

Fairfield
Wakeman

Some Railroad Tracks

Burlington Northern Railroad

Some Whistlestops

Reno

PHILLIPS COUNTY

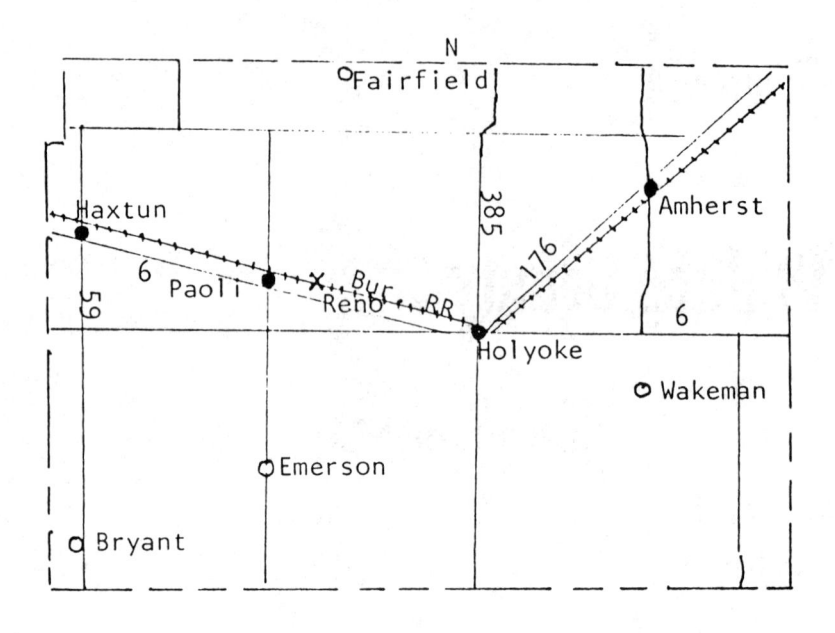

o past   1 inch = 6 miles   x whistlestops
● present   —— main roads

Places on the Colorado Prairie

Still on the Map

AMHERST (platted town) is a Lincoln Land Company town. A town plat was filed for Amherst on July 13, 1888, by the Lincoln Land Company, which platted four towns in Phillips County in conjunction with the building of the Burlington railroad through the county in 1887. Amherst was named after Amherst, Massachusetts, which was the hometown of the person who owned the Amherst site. Amherst almost disappeared in the late 1890s, but was revived in 1907.

HAXTUN (platted town) is another Lincoln Land Company town. A town plat was filed for Haxtun on November 8, 1888, by the Lincoln Land Company and was named after Haxtun Landing on the Hudson River, which was the hometown of a Mr. Emerson who developed the site. The Lincoln Land Company filed plats for Haxtun and Bryant at the same time, but Haxtun has outlived Bryant by almost sixty years.

HOLYOKE (platted town) was named in reference to Holyoke, Massachusetts, and a town plat was filed for Holyoke on December 30, 1887, again by the Lincoln Land Company. Holyoke became the seat of Phillips County when the county was formed in 1889. Holyoke was the first town to be platted in what is now Phillips County; thus, Holyoke's beginning coincided with the building of the Burlington railroad through the area in 1887.

PAOLI (platted town) was the one town in Phillips County which wasn't platted by the Lincoln Land Company; however, Paoli started about the same time as the other four towns. A town plat was filed for Paoli by O. W. Sahn and H. H. Ifee. The town was named after Paoli, Pennsylvania, which was the hometown of a chief engineer for the Burlington Railroad. Paoli almost faded away between 1890 and 1909, but experienced a revival in 1910.

Places in the Past

BRYANT (platted town) was one of several towns that were platted on the Burlington's projected line from Nebraska to Akron;

Phillips County

however, when the project was abandoned, there was little hope for the towns to survive on the prairie. A town plat was filed for Bryant on November 8, 1888, by the Lincoln Land Company, and the town was named after the town's first postmaster, James Bryant. The Bryant post office managed to stay open until 1916, and Bryant stayed on the map until the late 1920s.

EMERSON (rural post office) was located on the Burlington's proposed line to Akron from Holyoke. The Emerson post office stayed open from 1888 to 1890, but Emerson stayed on the map until at least 1916.

FAIRFIELD (place name) is shown on 1940 through 1954 maps and was located about twelve miles northwest of Holyoke. Fairfield was named after Fairfield, Iowa, which was the hometown of a Mrs. Riffenburg, who resided in the area. Fairfield didn't have a post office.

WAKEMAN (rural post office) was located about eight miles southeast of Holyoke, and the Wakeman post office was in operation from 1887 to 1897. Wakeman stayed on the map until at least 1916.

Some Railroad Tracks

BURLINGTON NORTHERN from Nebraska to Logan County:
    1887–1908 Colorado & Wyoming RR
    1908–1970 Chicago, Burlington & Quincy RR
    1970–   Burlington Northern RR

Some Whistlestops

RENO (BN) is shown about seven miles northwest of Holyoke on 1892 through 1902 maps. Reno was located in the same location as Paoli and could have been the siding.

Chapter 25
Prowers County

Still on the Map

Bristol
Carlton
Cheney Center
Granada

Hartman
Holly
Lamar
Wiley

Places in the Past

Albany
Amache
Amity
Ayr
Barton
Big Timbers
Blackwell
Deur
Ella
Kline
Lancaster

McMillan
Mulvane
New Stage Station
Northway
Old Stage Station
Plains
Rowe
Trail City
Verdun
Webb
Wilde

Prowers County

Some Railroad Tracks

Atchison, Topeka & Santa Fe Railway (five parts)

Some Whistlestops

Adams	Kornman
Channing	Manville
Clucas	May Valley
Delite	Millwood
Goodale	Parrish
Karl	Sugardale
Koen	Warwick

Still on the Map

BRISTOL (platted town) began as a Santa Fe railroad town in 1906: The Holly and Swink Railway, a Santa Fe subsidiary, built from Holly to Bristol in 1906. A plat was filed for Bristol by J. Pierce and Frank Butler in the same year. Bristol was named after a railroad official, C. H. Bristol.

CARLTON (platted town) was a post office station on the Santa Fe railroad from 1891 to 1960; a town plat was filed for Carlton on May 20, 1912, by the Colorado Land and Town Company. At one time, the Carlton station was known as "Grote."

CHENEY CENTER (rural post office) is located about fifteen miles south of Holly and provided postal service from 1917 to 1936.

PROWERS COUNTY

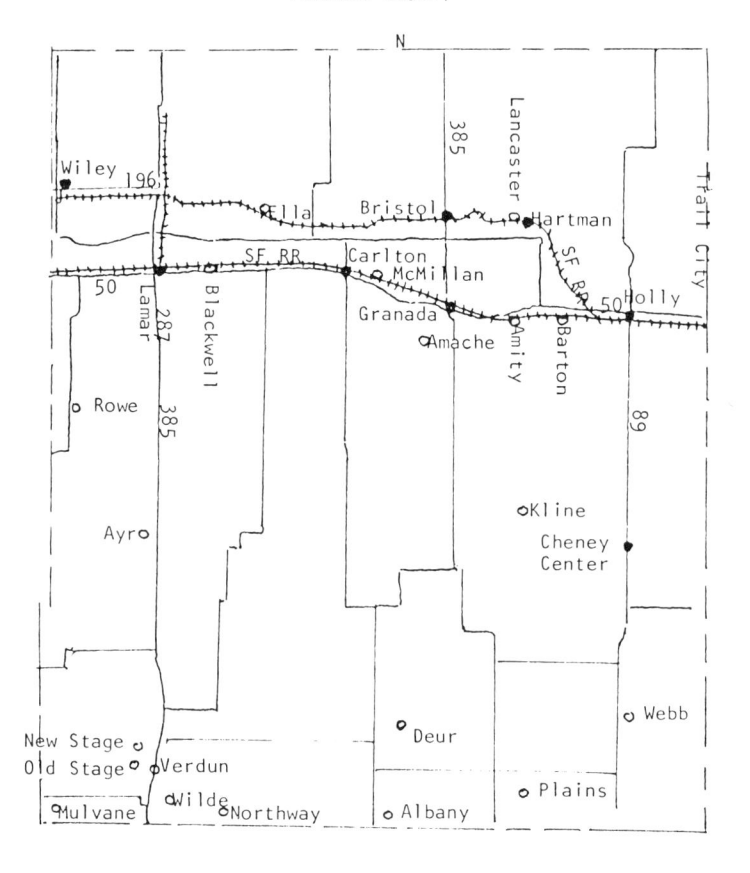

o past
• present

1 inch = 10.6 miles —— main roads

PROWERS COUNTY

x whistlestops   1 inch = 8 miles

Places on the Colorado Prairie

GRANADA (platted town) is the oldest town in Prowers County. Granada began as the temporary terminus of the Santa Fe railroad in 1873, and was named the Spanish word meaning "end of the road." Early Granada was a wild town, but it settled down after the railroad moved on in 1875. A town plat for Granada is on file, but it doesn't contain dates or the name of the person who filed the plat.

HARTMAN (platted town) began much like Bristol, it also was one of the Santa Fe railroad towns that was named after railroad officials. John Duncan filed a plat for Lancaster in 1907; James E. Adamson filed a plat for Hartman in 1908 and located the town in almost the same place as Lancaster. Hartman was named after a railroad official, W. P. Hartman. The town of Hartman was promoted by the Santa Fe Railway. As a result, Lancaster existed only about one year.

HOLLY (platted town) was platted as "Holleys" by N. Coler in 1896, but the town was named after Hiram S. Holly, a pioneer cattleman in the area. After the Holly Sugar Company was built in 1905 and a connecting railroad was started in 1906, Holly's future paralleled the economic status of the sugar industry in southeastern Colorado.

LAMAR (platted town) was established by I. R. Holmes in 1886, and its first order of business was to obtain a government land office; therefore, it was no coincidence that Lamar was named in reference to L.Q.C. Lamar, the Secretary of the Interior at that time. Lamar obtained the land office which gave the town enough import to become seat of Prowers County when it was formed in 1889. It is likely that Lamar was platted during its initial activity in 1886; however, the plat on file was notarized in 1890.

WILEY (platted town) was platted by the Big Bend Town and Improvement Company, and the plat was filed in July of 1906. Wiley was named after W. Wiley, President of the Holly Sugar Company, who promoted the town when the railroad was being built from Holly through the Wiley area in 1906.

Prowers County

Places in the Past

ALBANY (rural post office) was a land boom community of the 1880s. Albany, like so many land boom places, was named after the hometown of many settlers in the area—Albany, New York. The Albany post office was in operation from 1887 to 1891 and from 1897 to 1905, which indicates that Albany had a fleeting rebirth after the drouth of the early 1890s.

AMACHE (internment camp) was used to intern Japanese Americans during World War II. It was unfortunate that "Amache" was chosen as the name for the infamous camp. The camp was named after Amachee Pehee, the Indian princess, who married the noted John Prowers.

AMITY (platted town) means "good will" and was an appropriate name for a town that was started by the Salvation Army. A plat was filed for Amity on August 16, 1905, by the Salvation Army after its unsuccessful attempt to maintain a colony in the area for unfortunates from the eastern United States. The Amity post office was discontinued in 1937, but Amity stayed on the map into the 1960s.

AYR (rural post office) had its beginning during the land boom of the late 1880s and was located at the junction of the wagon roads from Wilde and Mulvane to Lamar. The Ayr post office closed in 1891, but Ayr stayed on the map for at least twenty-five years.

BARTON (railroad post office) was located on the Santa Fe Railroad between Granada and Amity. The Barton post office was in operation from 1895 to 1917; however, a 1902 map shows "Heron" as the railroad station and Barton as the post office.

BIG TIMBERS (landmark) was a large stand of cottonwood trees near the site of Lamar; the grove was noted by Lieutenant Zebulon Pike during his exploration of the area in 1806. Trees on the prairie were worth noting in the 1800s, and they still are, for that matter.

Places on the Colorado Prairie

BLACKWELL (railroad post office) was located about three miles east of the Lamar site on the Santa Fe Railroad, and it preceded Lamar in the area. The Blackwell post office was in operation from 1881 to 1886.

DEUR (rural post office) was located about twenty-five miles south of Granada. The Deur post office was in operation from 1916 to 1920.

ELLA (rural post office) was located at the junction of the Big Sandy and Arkansas Rivers and on the route of the old Santa Fe Trail. Ella is listed as the first post office in what is now Prowers County and was in operation from 1873 to 1876. Ella was located about fifteen miles upstream from Granada and served the traffic on the north side of the Arkansas River while the railroad was stopped at Granada from 1873 to 1875.

KLINE (way-stop) was located on the road from Barton to Minneapolis and is shown on a 1902 map. A post office is not listed for Kline, but there wasn't much happening on the road to Minneapolis, Colorado, in 1902.

LANCASTER (platted town) was the predecessor to Hartman on the Santa Fe Railroad from Holly to Bristol. A town plat was filed for Lancaster on June 29, 1907, by John Duncan; however, a plat was filed for the town of Hartman soon after, and because Lancaster and Hartman were in approximately the same location, something had to give—Lancaster.

MCMILLAN (railroad post office) was located between Granada and Carlton, and the McMillan post office was in operation during 1886; however, McMillan stayed on the map for several years.

MULVANE (platted town) was started during the Baca County land boom of the 1880s, and a town plat was filed for Mulvane on July 22, 1889. The Mulvane post office was discontinued in 1893; thus, Mulvane became one of the typical land-boom towns—short-lived. Mulvane was possibly named after Mulvane, Kansas, because of the many Kansas settlers in the area.

Prowers County

NEW STAGE STATION (stage station) is south of Ayr on a 1916 map and probably refers to the site of a stage station on the road from Lamar to Springfield. Obviously, there must have been an "Old Stage Station" in the area.

NORTHWAY (rural post office) was located near Two Buttes Creek. The Northway post office was in operation from 1916 to 1919.

OLD STAGE STATION (stage station) is shown about two miles south of New Stage Station on a 1916 map. An investigation of the maps does not produce the names of the two stage stations, and perhaps they were called just "Old" and "New."

PLAINS (rural post office) was located about five or six miles south of Webb on the road from Holly to Oklahoma. The Plains post office was in operation from 1908 to 1921. Plains was probably named after its location.

ROWE (rural post office) was the predecessor to Wiley on the old wagon road that paralleled the later route of the Santa Fe railroad. The Rowe post office was in operation from 1898 to 1900.

TRAIL CITY (cattle trail stop) was the prairie's answer to the mining camps—it was one of the wildest places on the Colorado prairie. Trail City offered the cowboys just about everything—except a post office. But Trail City wasn't the kind of place one writes letters about.

VERDUN (rural post office) was located on the road to Springfield form Lamar and was operating in 1920 only.

WEBB (rural post office) was located about seven miles northeast of Plains and was in operation from 1910 to 1919.

WILDE (rural post office) was started in 1887 during the Baca County land boom; however, like many nearby places the drouth stopped any progress by 1893. The Wilde post office was discontinued by 1893, but the name was carried on the maps for

Places on the Colorado Prairie

another twenty years. Therefore, it is likely that Wilde became a landmark location.

Some Railroad Tracks

ATCHISON, TOPEKA & SANTA FE from Holly through Bristol to Bent County:
   Holly to Bristol:
      1906–1912 Holly & Swink Ry.
      1912–   Atchison, Topeka & Santa Fe Ry.
   Bristol to Wilson Junction:
      1908–   Atchison, Topeka & Santa Fe Ry.
   Wilson Junction to Keesee:
      1906–1912 Arkansas Valley Ry.
      1912–   Atchinson, Topeka & Santa Fe Ry.
   Keesee to Bent County:
      1908–   Atchison, Topeka & Santa Fe Ry.

ATCHISON, TOPEKA & SANTA FE from Kansas through Lamar to Bent County:
   Kansas to Granada:
      1873–1900 Colorado & New Mexico RR
      1900–   Atchison, Topeka & Santa Fe Ry.
   Granada to Bent County:
      1875–1900 Pueblo & Arkansas Valley RR
      1900–   Atchison, Topeka & Santa Fe Ry.

ATCHISON, TOPEKA & SANTA FE from Wilson Junction to May Valley:
      1908–   Atchison, Topeka &Santa Fe Ry.

ATCHISON, TOPEKA & SANTA FE from Wiley to Bent County:
      1908–   Atchison, Topeka & Santa Fe Ry.

Prowers County

Atchison, Topeka & Santa Fe from Lamar to Wilson Junction:
    1906–1912 Arkansas Valley Ry.
    1912–   Atchison, Topeka & Santa Fe Ry.

Some Whistlestops

Adams (AT&SF) is shown about three miles southeast of Granada on an 1892 map.

Channing (AT&SF) is shown about three miles east of Kornman on 1909 through 1920 maps.

Clucas (AT&SF) is shown about six miles east of Lamar on a 1968 map. Clucas was formerly called "Morse."

Delite (AT&SF) is shown about three miles northwest of Holly on 1909 through 1920 maps.

Goodale (AT&SF) is shown about six miles west of Bristol on 1909 through 1920 maps.

Karl (AT&SF) is shown about six miles east of Wilson Junction on 1909 through 1920 maps.

Koen (AT&SF) is shown about two miles west of Granada on 1902 through 1920 maps.

Kornman (AT&SF) is shown about three miles north of Lamar on 1909 through 1968 maps.

Manville (AT&SF) is shown about two miles west of Granada on an 1892 map.

May Valley (AT&SF) is shown about seven miles north of Lamar on 1909 through 1968 maps.

Places on the Colorado Prairie

MILLWOOD (AT&SF) is shown about seven miles southeast of Bristol on 1909 through 1920 maps.

PARRISH (AT&SF) is shown about one mile east of Bristol on 1909 through 1920 maps.

SUGARDALE (AT&SF) is shown about two miles east of Wiley on 1909 through 1920 maps.

WARWICK (AT&SF) is shown about one mile east of Bristol on 1916 and 1920 maps.

Chapter 26

Pueblo County

Still on the Map

Avondale
Blende
Boone
Cedarwood
Colorado City
Goodnight
Greenhorn
Lime
Lombardi Village
Marnel

Nepesta
North Avondale
Piñon
Pueblo
Pueblo Ordnance Depot
Stem Beach
Stone City
Swallows
Vineland

Places in the Past

Abbey
Agate
Andersonville

Bessemer
Burnt Mill
Capitol Hill

Pueblo County

Carpenter	Mercier
Central Pueblo	Muddy Creek
Chilcott	Myrtle
Concord	Newport
Crow	Nyberg
Dawkins	Ormandale
Eden	Overton
Edgeplain	Pueblo Air Force Base
Excelsior	Ranch
Fisher	Saint Charles
Fort Pueblo	Salt Creek
Fort Reynolds	Saunders
Fountaine City	Sitton
Graneros	South Pueblo
Granton	Tabor
Grimaldi	Tacony
Harlem	Undercliffe
Hermosillo	Verde
Huerfano	Waremont
Jackson	White Rock
Juanita	Wilson
Lake Minnequa	Wood Valley
Liberty Hill	

Some Railroad Tracks

Atchison, Topeka & Santa Fe Railway (three parts)
Colorado & Southern Railway (two parts)
Colorado & Wyoming Railway
Colorado Railroad

Places on the Colorado Prairie

Denver & Rio Grande Western Railroad (three parts)
Missouri Pacific Railroad

Some Whistlestops

Albia	Greenhorn
Appleton	Hamlet
Baxter	Hayden
Bragdon	Livesly
Brooks	Meadows
Capers	Merrick
Carlisle	Mesa
Carters	Nada
Chico	Nemo
Clay	Riverton
Cuba	San Carlos
Dempsey	Sonora
Devine	Southern Junction
Dundee	Turkey Creek
Erickson Spur	Vegas
Furman	Williams
Goodnight	Zinc Junction
Gravel Spur	

Still on the Map

AVONDALE (platted town) was named after Stratford-On-Avon, England, which was the hometown of Sam Taylor, an early pioneer in the area. The Avondale post office opened in 1892, and a town plat was filed for Avondale on August 19, 1893, by Fred Barndollar.

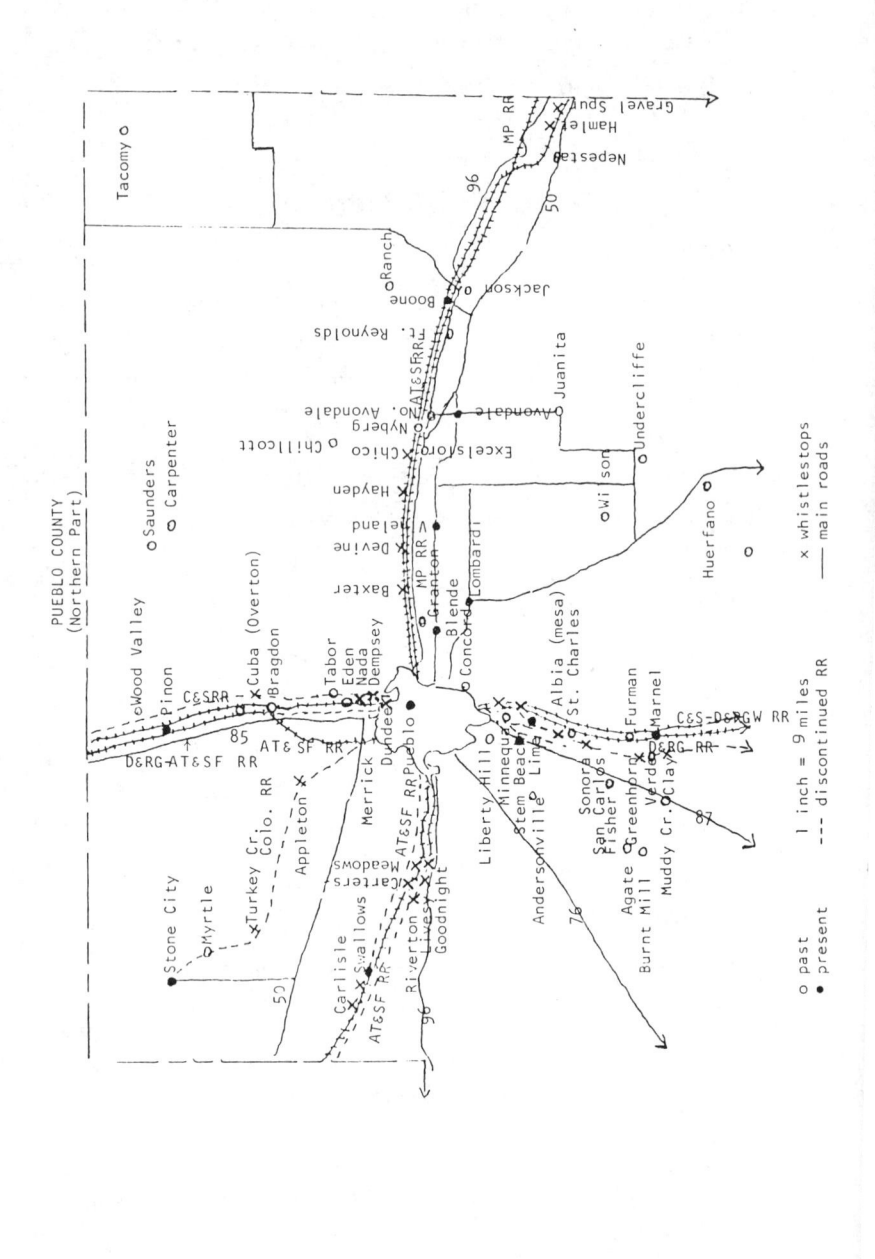

PUEBLO COUNTY (Southern Part)

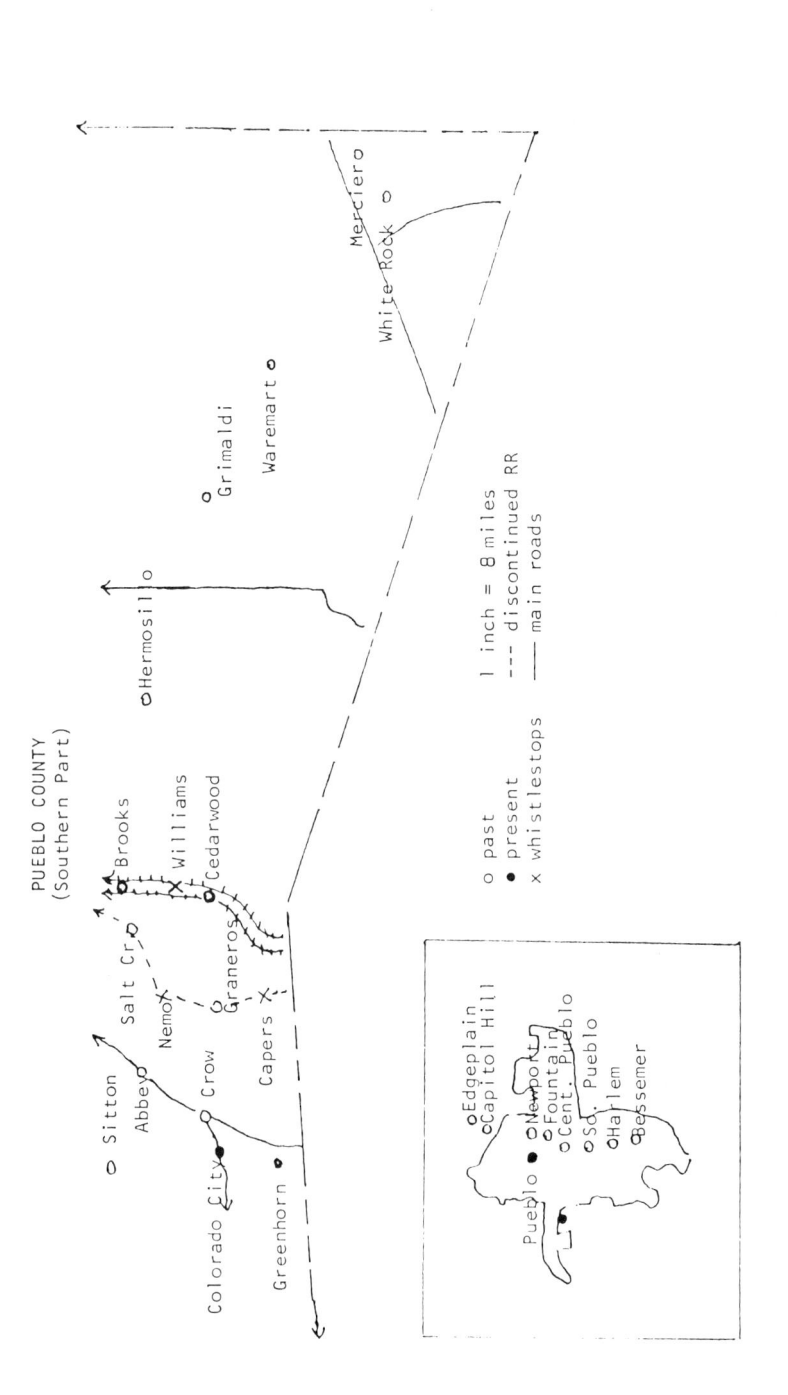

1 inch = 8 miles
--- discontinued RR
—— main roads

o past
● present
x whistlestops

Sitton, Abbey, Crow, Colorado City, Greenhorn, Salt Cr., Nemo, Capers, Graneros, Brooks, Williams, Cedarwood, Hermosillo, Grimaldi, Waremart, White Rock, Merciero

Edgeplain, Capitol Hill, Pueblo, Newport, Fountain, Cent. Pueblo, So. Pueblo, Harlem, Bessemer

Pueblo County

BLENDE (Pueblo suburb) was named after the "sulphide of zinc" because Blende was the site of the zinc smelter established by the United States Zinc Company. Blende's location near Pueblo has resulted in substantial postwar growth.

BOONE (railroad post office) was first called "Booneville" and was named after its founder, A. C. Boone, who was the grandson of Daniel Boone. Boone was a stage station on the Santa Fe Trail route, and the station was at the home of Colonel Boone. The Booneville post office was established in 1863; however, the name was shortened to "Boone" in 1891. The Boone station on the Missouri Pacific railroad was first called "Fosdick."

CEDARWOOD (railroad post office) is located on the Colorado and Southern railroad and about twenty-three miles south of Pueblo. Cedarwood was named after nearby trees. The Cedarwood post office was in operation from 1912 to 1943.

COLORADO CITY (platted town) is a planned community near Greenhorn and Rye. The Colorado City post office was established in 1964. Colorado City is one of the few postwar communities in Colorado that is not a result of urban expansion and is, indeed, some distance from any large city.

GOODNIGHT (unincorporated metropolitan area) is located just west of Pueblo and is shown on a 1975 map.

GREENHORN (rural post office) was named after nearby Greenhorn Mountain and is one of the oldest communities in what is now Pueblo County. The Greenhorn post office was open from 1866 to 1911.

LIME (railroad post office) was named after its function as a supplier of lime to the steel mill in Pueblo. The town of Lime was serviced by the Colorado and Wyoming Railroad from 1907 to 1925, but the Lime post office operated from 1898 to 1943.

Places on the Colorado Prairie

LOMBARDI VILLAGE (place name) is shown about four miles southeast of Pueblo on a 1968 map.

MARNEL (railroad post office) is located on the Colorado and Southern and the Denver and Rio Grande joint railroad line and about seventeen miles south of Pueblo. The Marnel post office was in operation from 1917 to 1923.

NEPESTA (railroad post office) is located on the Atchison, Topeka and Santa Fe railroad and about nine miles southeast of Boone. The Nepesta post office was in operation from 1876 to 1929. Nepesta means "river" in Spanish and refers to the nearby Arkansas River.

NORTH AVONDALE (railroad post office) is located next to the Missouri Pacific and Santa Fe railroads and slightly north of Avondale. The North Avondale post office has been in operation since 1917.

PIÑON (railroad post office) is located on the Rio Grande railroad and about twelve miles north of Pueblo. The Piñon post office was in operation from 1907 to 1921.

PUEBLO (platted town) was named after Fort Pueblo, which was established in the area in 1842. The town of Pueblo was started in the winter of 1859–1860 across Fountain Creek from Fountaine City which had been established a year earlier. South Pueblo was platted next to Pueblo in 1872, and Central Pueblo was platted in 1883; however, all of the "Pueblos" were consolidated into Pueblo in 1886. Pueblo became the "steel city" when General Palmer organized the Colorado Coal and Iron Company and built a steel mill just south of Pueblo in 1881. Pueblo was incorporated in 1885 and has grown to become the second largest city in Colorado.

PUEBLO ORDINANCE DEPOT (federal installation) was established fifteen miles east of Pueblo in 1942. The Pueblo Depot has grown to become one of the largest installations of its kind in the United States.

Pueblo County

STEM BEACH (place name) is shown about ten miles southwest of Pueblo and next to the Saint Charles Reservoir on 1956 and 1968 maps.

STONE CITY (railroad post office) was named after the nearby stone works which were established by the Turkey Creek Stone Company. Stone City was the terminus of the Colorado railroad, and the Stone City post office was in operation from 1912 until 1957, when the railroad was discontinued.

SWALLOWS (railroad post office) is located on the Rio Grande railroad and about eight miles northwest of Livesly. The Swallows post office, named after the many swallows on nearby cliffs, was in operation from 1892 to 1896. The Swallows post office was preceded in the area by the Taylorsville post office, which was in operation from 1875 to 1892.

VINELAND (platted town) was established on the wagon road from Pueblo along the south side of the Arkansas River. A town plat was filed for Vineland on October 29, 1890, by H. S. Van Keuren. Vineland never obtained a post office, but it has managed to stay on the map.

Places in the Past

ABBEY (rural post office) was located about ten miles northwest of Cedarwood, and the Abbey post office was in operation from 1891 to 1914.

AGATE (rural post office) was located about eighteen miles southwest of Pueblo; the Agate post office was in operation from 1880 to 1881.

ANDERSONVILLE (rural post office) was located about seven miles southwest of Pueblo. The Andersonville post office was in operation from 1868 to 1869.

Places on the Colorado Prairie

BESSEMER (platted town) was the community which grew up next to the steel mill in Pueblo and was named after Sir Henry Bessemer, who invented the process of reducing iron ore. A town plat was filed for Bessemer on August 12, 1886, and Bessemer was annexed to Pueblo in 1894.

BURNT MILL (rural post office) was located about ten miles southeast of Goodpasture, and the Burnt Mill post office was in operation from 1911 to 1921. Burnt Mill was preceded in the area by the Kinkel post office, which was in operation from 1907 to 1911.

CAPITOL HILL (platted town) was platted about one mile north of Pueblo; the plat was filed on March 23, 1889, by W. F. Baob. However, Capitol Hill never obtained a post office. It was not shown on the map.

CARPENTER (place name) is shown about thirteen miles east of Piñon on 1882 through 1897 maps.

CENTRAL PUEBLO (platted town) was one of three "Pueblos" which existed next to each other in the 1880s. A town plat was filed for Central Pueblo on March 17, 1883. Central Pueblo, South Pueblo, and Pueblo were consolidated into Pueblo in April of 1886.

CHILCOTT (place name) is shown about fourteen miles northeast of Pueblo on an 1897 map. Another Chilcott was located south of Beulah and is shown on 1884 through 1897 maps. It is probable that both Chilcotts were named after George M. Chilcott, an early settler of Pueblo who became a United States senator.

CONCORD (platted town) was platted in about the same location as Blende and could have been an attempt to locate a town near the Blende Smelter. A town plat was filed for Concord on November 19, 1891, by J. S. Greene; however, Concord did not obtain a post office, and it was not shown on the map.

Pueblo County

CROW (rural post office) was located about five miles northeast of Greenhorn and was named in reference to Matt Crow, who was a former postmaster of Pueblo. The Crow post office was in operation from 1885 to 1891 and from 1896 to 1907.

DAWKINS (railroad post office) was located on the Colorado and Southern railroad and about two miles south of Piñon. The Dawkins post office was in operation from 1885 until it was moved to Piñon in 1907.

EDEN (railroad post office) was located on the Denver and Rio Grande Railroad and about five miles north of Pueblo. The Eden post office was in operation from 1890 to 1914.

EDGEPLAIN (platted town) was platted about one mile north of Pueblo; the plat was filed on October 16, 1889, by George Parsons. However, Edgeplain did not obtain a post office. It was not shown on the map.

EXCELSIOR (rural post office) was located about seventeen miles southeast of Pueblo, and the Excelsior post office was in operation from 1866 to 1871.

FISHER (rural post office) was located about twelve miles southwest of Pueblo. The Fisher post office was in operation from 1895 to 1907.

FORT PUEBLO (trading post) was built by the famous Jim Beckworth and twenty other traders in 1842. Fort Pueblo deteriorated from a trading post to a hangout for many people with dubious reputations. During the Christmas season of 1854, many of the seventeen Mexicans in the fort were celebrating with a brew known as "Taos Lightning." They invited nearby Ute Indians to join their celebration. The Utes turned on their hosts and murdered all but one girl and two children, whom they took with them. The slaughter of 1854 discouraged visitors to the fort, and only crumbling walls remained when Fountaine City was established nearby in 1858.

Places on the Colorado Prairie

FORT REYNOLDS (military fort) was located near the site of Avondale in 1867 and was named after General John F. Reynolds, who died in the battle at Gettysburg. Fort Reynolds was established as an army post for protection of residents along that portion of the Arkansas River. Fort Reynolds was abandoned in 1872.

FOUNTAINE CITY (early settlement) was located near the junction of the Fountain and Arkansas Rivers and on the east side of the Fountain River in 1858. During the winter of 1858–1859, there were thirty cabins in Fountaine City. In the winter of 1859–1860, Pueblo was started across the Fountain River from Fountaine City, and the earlier settlement was soon abandoned in favor of Pueblo.

GRANEROS (railroad post office) was located on the Denver and Rio Grande railroad and about three miles north of Capers. The Graneros post office was in operation from 1889 to 1925 and was named after nearby Graneros Creek.

GRANTON (platted town) was platted about three miles east of Pueblo, and the plat was filed on May 19, 1920, by Robert Grant; however, Granton neither obtained a post office nor was it shown on the map.

GRIMALDI (rural post office) is shown about eighteen miles south of Boone on 1916 through 1934 maps. The Grimaldi post office was in operation from 1913 to 1920.

HARLEM (platted town) was platted just south of South Pueblo, and the plat was filed on March 26, 1889, by the Colorado Fuel and Iron Company, which had established the nearby steel mill. Harlem never obtained a post office, and it was not shown on the map.

HERMOSILLO (rural post office) was located about fifteen miles northeast of Cedarwood, and the Hermosillo post office was in operation from 1867 to 1872. Hermosillo means "something beautiful" in Spanish.

Pueblo County

HUERFANO (rural post office) was located about two miles southeast of the site of Undercliffe and is not to be confused with the town of Huerfano in Huerfano County. Huerfano, named after the nearby Huerfano River, had a post office in operation from 1862 to 1879, when it was moved to nearby Undercliffe.

JACKSON (place name) is shown about two miles south of Boone on 1877 through 1897 maps and was on the wagon road to Undercliffe.

JUANITA (rural post office) was located about ten miles southwest of Boone; the Juanita post office was in operation from 1869 to 1873. However, Juanita stayed on the maps into the 1920s.

LAKE MINNEQUA (platted town) was platted next to Lake Minnequa, and the plat was filed on January 26, 1891, by K. F. Brown and W. C. Cannon. The steel mill at Pueblo was known as "Bessemer" and then "Minnequa" as Gould and Rockefeller took over controlling interests in the steel mill during 1892.

LIBERTY HILL (platted town) was platted about six miles southwest of Pueblo, and the plat was filed on July 11, 1891, by J. S. Smith; however, Liberty Hill did not obtain a post office. It did not appear on the map.

MERCIER (rural post office) was located next to the Otero County line, and the Mercier post office was in operation from 1906 to 1913.

MUDDY CREEK (rural post office) was named after a nearby creek, and the Muddy Creek post office was in operation from 1870 to 1886.

MYRTLE (rural post office) was located about three miles northeast of Stone City, and the Myrtle post office was in operation from 1906 to 1913.

Places on the Colorado Prairie

NEWPORT (platted town) was platted just east of Pueblo, and the plat was filed on December 27, 1890, by G. A. Blackman and others. However, Newport never obtained a post office. It did not appear on the map.

NYBERG (railroad post office) was located on the Santa Fe Railroad and about nine miles northwest of the Boone Station. The Nyberg post office was in operation from 1889 to 1918.

ORMANDALE (platted town) was named after J. B. Orman, who filed the plat for the town on February 24, 1891; however, the land description was not included on the plat, and Ormandale was not shown on the map.

OVERTON (platted town) was platted on the Denver and New Orleans railroad from Falcon to Pueblo, and the plat was filed on August 19, 1891, by the Trine Investment Company. The Overton post office was discontinued in 1900.

PUEBLO AIR FORCE BASE (military installation) was established just outside Pueblo in 1942 and was closed in 1946.

RANCH (place name) is shown about six miles northwest of Boone on an 1897 map.

SAINT CHARLES (rural post office) was located about fifteen miles southwest of Pueblo and was named after the nearby Saint Charles River. The Saint Charles post office was in operation from 1866 to 1881.

SALT CREEK (railroad post office) was located on the Denver and Rio Grande railroad and about four miles northeast of Graneros. The Salt Creek post office was in operation from 1880 to 1908.

297

Pueblo County

SAUNDERS (place name) is shown about twelve miles northeast of Piñon on 1882 through 1897 maps.

SITTON (rural post office) was located about five miles southeast of Goodpasture. The Sitton post office was in operation from 1906 to 1917. Sitton is shown as "Sitton Corner" on a 1956 map.

SOUTH PUEBLO (platted town) was established by William Palmer, and a town plat for South Pueblo was filed on October 27, 1872. South Pueblo was located across the Arkansas River from Pueblo and was started by Palmer as a station for his Denver and Rio Grande railroad. South Pueblo, Pueblo, and Central Pueblo were consolidated into Pueblo in 1886; however, South Pueblo maintained a separate identity after the consolidation.

TABOR (platted town) was platted about eight miles north of Pueblo, and the plat was filed on October 12, 1888, by the Interstate Land Company; however, Tabor did not obtain a post office, and it was not shown on the map.

TACONY (rural post office) was located about eighteen miles northeast of Boone, and the Tacony post office was in operation from 1915 to 1942.

UNDERCLIFFE (rural post office) was located about eleven miles east of Marnel, and the Undercliffe post office was in operation from 1879 to 1925. The Undercliffe post office was preceded in the area by the Huerfano post office which was located just across the Huerfano River from Undercliffe.

VERDE (railroad post office) was located on the Denver and Rio Grande railroad and about seven miles northeast of Salt Creek. The Verde post office was in operation from 1903 to 1912.

Places on the Colorado Prairie

WAREMONT (rural post office) was located about seventeen miles south of Nepesta. The Warmont post office was in operation from 1916 to 1920.

WHITE ROCK (rural post office) was located about twenty-two miles southeast of Nepesta, and the White Rock post office was in operation from 1909 to 1927.

WILSON (platted town) was platted about eleven miles southwest of Avondale, and the plat was filed on January 27, 1911, by the Pueblo–Rocky Ford Land Company. The Wilson post office was discontinued in 1913.

WOOD VALLEY (early post office) was located about fourteen miles north of Pueblo on the stage route to Colorado City. The Wood Valley post office was in operation from 1862 to 1869.

Some Railroad Tracks

ATCHISON, TOPEKA & SANTA FE from El Paso County to Pueblo:
    1887–1900 Denver & Santa Fe RR
    1900–   Atchison, Topeka & Santa Fe Ry.

ATCHISON, TOPEKA & SANTA FE from Otero County to Pueblo:
    1876–1900 Pueblo & Arkansas Valley RR
    1900–   Atchison, Topeka & Santa Fe Ry.

Pueblo County

ATCHISON, TOPEKA & SANTA FE from Pueblo to Fremont County:
- 1878–1878 Cañon City & San Juan RR
- 1878–1900 Pueblo & Arkansas Valley RR
- 1900–1921 Atchison, Topeka & Santa Fe Ry.

COLORADO & SOUTHERN from El Paso County to Pueblo:
- 1881–1886 Denver & New Orleans RR
- 1886–1888 Denver, Texas & Gulf RR
- 1888–1890 Denver, Texas & Fort Worth RR
- 1890–1898 Union Pacific, Denver & Gulf Ry.
- 1898–1915 Colorado & Southern Ry.

COLORADO & SOUTHERN AND DENVER & RIO GRANDE WESTERN from Pueblo to Huerfano County (joint line):
- 1911–   Colorado & Southern Ry. and Denver & Rio Grande Western RR

COLORADO & WYOMING from Pueblo to Lime:
- 1907–1925 Colorado & Wyoming Ry.

COLORADO RAILROAD from Pueblo to Stone City:
- 1910–1912 Kansas-Colorado RR (grading)
- 1912–1938 Colorado-Kansas Ry.
- 1938–1957 Colorado RR

DENVER & RIO GRANDE WESTERN from Pueblo to Fremont County:
- 1872–1886 Denver & Rio Grande Ry.
- 1886–1921 Denver & Rio Grande RR
- 1921–   Denver & Rio Grande Western RR

Places on the Colorado Prairie

DENVER & RIO GRANDE WESTERN from El Paso County to Pueblo:
    1872–1886 Denver & Rio Grande Ry.
    1886–1921 Denver & Rio Grande RR
    1921–   Denver & Rio Grande Western RR

DENVER & RIO GRANDE WESTERN from Pueblo to Huerfano County:
    1876–1886 Denver & Rio Grande Ry.
    1886–1921 Denver & Rio Grande RR
    1921–1924 Denver & Rio Grande Western RR

MISSOURI PACIFIC from Crowley County to Pueblo:
    1887–1909 Pueblo & State Line RR
    1909–1917 Missouri Pacific Ry.
    1917–   Missouri Pacific RR

Some Whistlestops

ALBIA (D&RGW) is shown about six miles south of Pueblo on a 1916 map.

APPLETON (CR) is shown about seven miles northwest of Pueblo on a 1920 map.

BAXTER (AT&SF and MP) is shown about eight miles east of Pueblo on 1882 through 1927 maps.

BRAGDON (AT&SF) is shown about four miles south of Piñon on 1909 through 1968 maps.

Pueblo County

BROOKS (C&S and D&RGW) is shown about four miles southeast of Marnel on 1916 and 1920 maps.

CAPERS (D&RGW) is shown about six miles southwest of Cedarwood on 1916 through 1968 maps.

CARLISLE (D&RGW) is shown about three miles northwest of Swallows on 1909 through 1920 maps.

CARTERS (AT&SF) is shown about one mile northwest of Livesly on 1909 through 1920 maps.

CHICO (AT&SF) is shown about eight miles northwest of Boone on 1882 through 1909 maps.

CLAY (D&RGW) is shown about one mile south of Marnel on a railroad map.

CUBA (D&RGW) is shown about one mile north of Bragdon on 1916 and 1920 maps.

DEMPSEY (D&RGW) is shown about two miles north of Pueblo on a railroad map.

DEVINE (AT&SF) is shown about ten miles east of Pueblo on 1916 through 1968 maps.

DUNDEE (D&RGW) is shown about one mile north of Pueblo on 1892 through 1902 maps.

ERICKSON SPUR (D&RGW) is shown about one mile northwest of Swallows on a 1916 map.

FURMAN (C&S and D&RGW) is shown about five miles northwest of Marnel on 1916 and 1920 maps.

Places on the Colorado Prairie

GOODNIGHT (D&RGW) is shown about four miles southeast of Pueblo on an 1882 map.

GRAVEL SPUR (AT&SF) is shown about four miles southeast of Nepesta on a 1916 map.

GREENHORN (D&RGW) is shown about two miles northwest of Marnel on 1882 through 1897 maps.

HAMLET (AT&SF) is shown about three miles southeast of Nepesta on a 1968 map.

HAYDEN (AT&SF and MP) is shown about three miles east of Devine on a 1916 map.

LIVESLY (AT&SF and D&RGW) is shown about ten miles southwest of Pueblo on 1909 through 1968 maps.

MEADOWS (D&RGW) is shown about ten miles southwest of Pueblo on 1882 through 1892 maps.

MERRICK (AT&SF) is shown about four miles north of Pueblo on 1902 and 1909 maps.

MESA (D&RGW) is shown about six miles south of Pueblo on a 1909 map (in about the same location as Albia).

NADA (D&RGW) is shown about four miles north of Pueblo on an 1897 map.

NEMO (D&RGW) is shown about six miles northwest of Cedarwood on a 1902 map.

RIVERTON (D&RGW) is shown about ten miles southwest of Pueblo on a 1902 map (the same location as Meadows and Livesly).

Pueblo County

SAN CARLOS (D&RGW) is shown about one mile south of Lime on 1882 through 1902 maps.

SONORA (D&RGW) is shown about one-fourth mile north of San Carlos on a 1916 map.

SOUTHERN JUNCTION (D&RGW) is shown about four miles south of Pueblo on a 1916 map.

TURKEY CREEK (CR) is shown about seven miles south of Stone on 1916 and 1920 maps.

VEGAS (D&RGW) is shown about two miles east of Livesly on 1909 and 1916 maps.

WILLIAMS (C&S and D&RGW) is shown about one mile north of Cedarwood on a 1916 map.

ZINC JUNCTION (D&RGW) is shown about one mile south of Southern Junction on a 1916 map.

Places to Visit

Brush, Morgan County

Keota, Weld County

Chapter 27

Sedgwick County

Still on the Map

Julesburg (4th)
Ovid
Sedgwick
Weir (3rd Julesburg)

Places in the Past

Antelope
Flora
Fort Sedgwick
Julesburg (1st)
Julesburg (2nd)

Some Railroad Tracks

Union Pacific Railroad

Some Whistlestops

Adrian
Dorsey
Hitt

SEDGWICK COUNTY

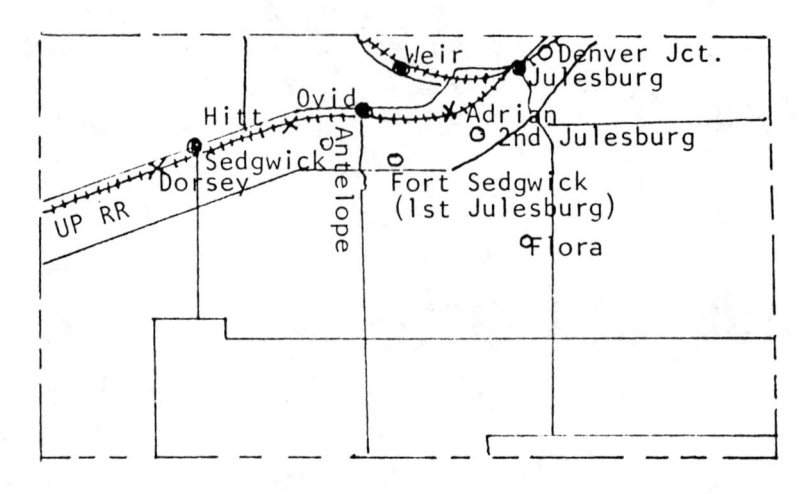

o past   1 inch = 6 miles   x some whistlestops
● present   ——main road

Places on the Colorado Prairie

Still on the Map

JULESBURG (4TH) (platted town) was established when the Union Pacific Railroad moved the Julesburg station in anticipation of a new line to Denver. The fourth Julesburg was first called "Denver Junction," and a town plat was filed for Denver Junction on July 2, 1884, by the Union Pacific Railroad. The name of Denver Junction was changed to "Julesburg" when the town was incorporated in 1886.

OVID (platted town) was named after Ovid, Michigan, which was the birthplace of Ree Parks, a railroad official. A town plat was filed for Ovid on June 19, 1908, by the Ovid Land Company which was headed by a Great Western Sugar Company official, R. K. Marsh. Ovid was incorporated in 1925, and the Great Western Sugar Company built a refinery at Ovid in 1926.

SEDGWICK (platted town) was named after Fort Sedgwick. The Sedgwick post office was first called "Henderson"; however, the name was changed to "Sedgwick" in 1885. A town plat was filed for Sedgwick on April 20, 1887, by John Casey. A replat was filed for Sedgwick in 1906 by the Sedgwick Townsite Company, which was headed by R. K. Marsh of the Great Western Sugar Company.

WEIR (3RD JULESBURG) (railroad post office) was first called "Julesburg" and was established as the terminus of the Union Pacific railroad when it was built into Colorado in 1867. The third Julesburg post office was moved to "Denver Junction" in 1885; however, the original site of the third Julesburg was maintained as a siding on the Union Pacific's main line and was renamed "Weir." The Weir siding was named after James Weir who was a foreman for the Union Pacific Railroad at the Weir site. The Weir post office was in operation from 1889 to 1890; however, the third Julesburg post office had operated from 1869 to 1885.

Sedgwick County

Places in the Past

ANTELOPE (stage station) was located about halfway between the Jules and Spring Hill stations on the Central Overland stage route.

FLORA (rural post office) was located about fourteen miles south of Julesburg. The Flora post office was in operation from 1889 to 1894.

FORT SEDGWICK (military fort) was established in 1864 and was first called "Camp Rankin." The name of Camp Rankin was changed to "Fort Sedgwick," honoring Major General John Sedgwick, who was killed at Spotsylvania during the Civil War. In February 1865, Fort Sedgwick and Julesburg came under siege from the Indians. When the Indians left on the morning of February 3, Julesburg had been burned to the ground. However, the fort survived the siege and remained open until 1871.

JULESBURG (lst) (trading-post community) grew up near the Jules Beni trading post which was established in the 1850s. Jules Beni provided a short route to his post from the Oregon Trail, and soon much of the Oregon Trail traffic was rerouted to include Beni's post. A short time after a stage route was established along the Platte River, Jules Beni's post was made a stage station for the Leavenworth and Pikes Peak Express Company. The first Julesburg was burned to the ground in the Indian siege of 1865, and the residents established a second Julesburg about four miles from the site of the first community.

JULESBURG (2nd) (rural post office) was established after the first Julesburg was destroyed in 1865. Since second Julesburg was obligated to seek a location outside the military reservation, the new community was established about four miles east from the site of the first Julesburg. Shortly after the Union Pacific railroad built into Colorado in 1867, Julesburg was moved to the terminus of the new line.

Places on the Colorado Prairie

Some Railroad Tracks

UNION PACIFIC from Nebraska to Logan County:
    1880–1890 Colorado Central RR
    1890–   Union Pacific RR

Some Whistlestops

ADRIAN (UP) is shown about four miles southwest of Julesburg on 1916 and 1920 maps.

DORSEY (UP) is shown about four miles southwest of Sedgwick on 1916 through 1968 maps.

HITT (BN) is shown about three miles southwest of Ovid on a railroad map.

Chapter 28

Washington County

Still on the Map

Akron
Anton
Cope
Elba
Hyde
Last Chance

Lindon
Otis
Pinneo
Platner
Thurman
Woodrow

Places in the Past

Abbott
Arickaree
Badger
Brunker
Buchanan
Burdett

Corcoran
Curtis
Denova
Dillingham
Easyville
Flat Top

Washington County

Fremont	Plum Bush
Glen	Prairie
Harrisburg	Rago
Henry	Schleyter
Holmesville	Spence
Leslie	Summit Springs
Lone Star	Townsend
Meekton	Wagner
Messex	Waitley

Some Railroad Tracks

Burlington Northern Railroad
Union Pacific Railroad

Some Whistlestops

Xenia

Still on the Map

AKRON (platted town) was named by a Mrs. Calvert, wife of a railroad official, in reference to their hometown, Akron, Ohio. A town plat was filed for Akron on July 1, 1882, by the Lincoln Land Company after the arrival of the Burlington railroad in 1881. Akron was made the county seat when Washington County was formed from a part of Weld County in 1887.

ANTON (rural post office) is located about twenty-four miles northwest of Cope, and the Anton post office was in operation from 1916 to 1928 and was reopened in 1934.

WASHINGTON COUNTY
(Northern Part)

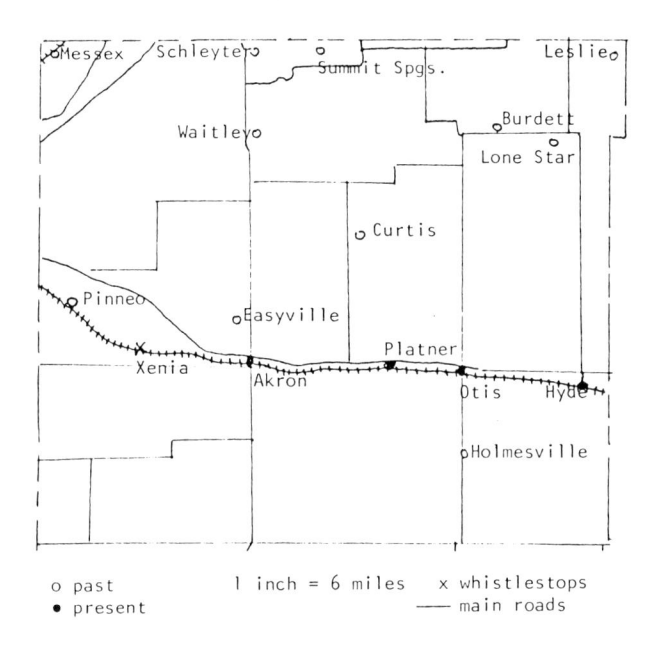

Map showing locations: Messex, Schleyter, Summit Spgs., Leslie, Waitley, Burdett, Lone Star, Curtis, Pinneo, Easyville, Platner, Xenia, Akron, Otis, Hyde, Holmesville.

- o past
- • present
- 1 inch = 6 miles
- x whistlestops
- — main roads

WASHINGTON COUNTY
(Southern Part)

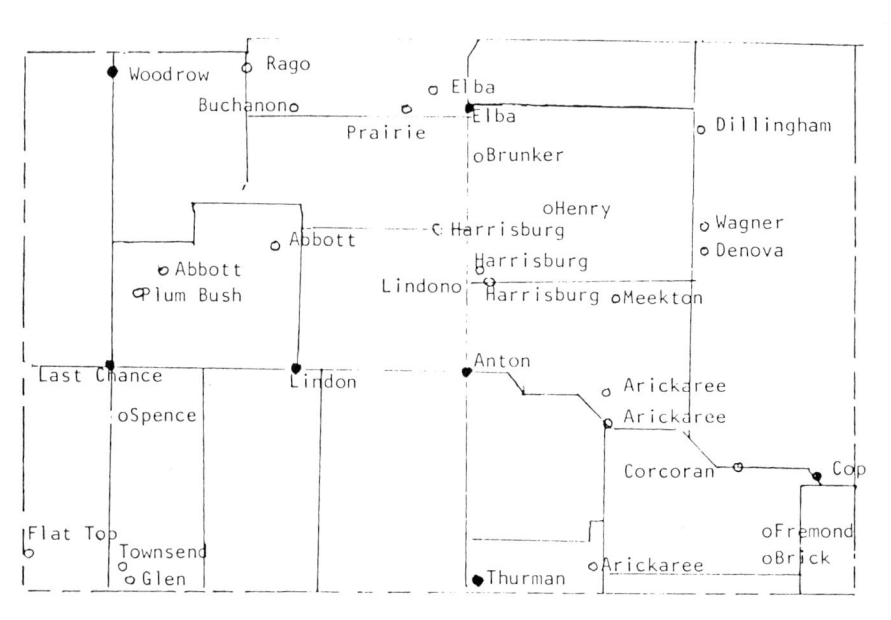

Map showing locations: Woodrow, Rago, Buchanon, Elba, Prairie, Dillingham, Brunker, Henry, Harrisburg, Wagner, Denova, Abbott, Plum Bush, Lindon, Harrisburg, Meekton, Last Chance, Spence, Lindon, Anton, Arickaree, Arickaree, Corcoran, Cop, Flat Top, Townsend, Glen, Thurman, Arickaree, Fremond, Brick.

- o past
- • present
- 1 inch = 8 miles
- — main road

Washington County

COPE (platted town) was first called "Gray," and the Gray post office was in operation from 1888 to 1889. The name of the Gray post office was changed to "Cope" in 1889 after Jonathan Cope, who homesteaded the site. A town plat was filed for Cope on February 11, 1921, by the Colorado Farm Lands Company.

ELBA (rural post office) is located about fifteen miles south of Akron, and the Elba post office was in operation from 1910 to 1958.

HYDE (platted town) was another of the Burlington's railroad towns, and a town plat was filed for Hyde on March 18, 1886, by the Lincoln Land Company; however, the Hyde post office opened in 1882. Hyde was replatted in 1919, and the plat for "New Hyde" was filed in 1919 by W. H. Smith. The Hyde post office closed in 1940.

LAST CHANCE (highway way-stop) is located on Highway 36 about twenty miles west of Anton and is shown on 1956 and 1968 maps.

LINDON (rural post office) is located about ten miles west of Anton, and the Lindon post office has been in operation since 1888. Lindon was named in reference to L. J. Lindbeck, an early resident in the area. The Lindon area was settled in part by Danish farmers.

OTIS (platted town) was reportedly named after an early settler in the area, but this needs verification. A town plat was filed for Otis on December 1, 1887, by an unnamed person. Otis almost died out during the drouth of the 1890s; however, its strategic location between Akron and Yuma gave Otis a chance to survive.

PINNEO (platted town) was named after B. F. Pinneo, a law enforcement officer of note. A town plat was filed for Pinneo on September 25, 1888, by the Lincoln Land Company; however, the Pinneo post office opened in 1883 and closed in 1898. The Pinneo post office was reopened in 1920 and closed in 1931.

Places on the Colorado Prairie

PLATNER (platted town) was first called "Millett," and the Millett post office was in operation in 1890. The Platner post office opened in 1892, and a town plat was filed for Platner on April 13, 1917, by Esther Smith, Hayward Rice, and Benjaman Shannon. The Platner post office closed from 1903 to 1909 and again in 1955.

THURMAN (rural post office) is located about ten miles south of Anton, and the Thurman post office was in operation from 1888 to 1953. Thurman was first called "Stone City" and was renamed "Thurman" after an army officer.

WOODROW (rural post office) is located about eighteen miles north of Last Chance. The Woodrow post office has been in operation since 1913.

Places in the Past

ABBOTT (rural post office) is shown about ten miles northwest of Lindon on 1892 through 1916 maps and about six miles north of Lindon on 1920 through 1940 maps; Abbott was moved in 1918 because the drouth of the 1890s practically devastated the area. The Abbott post office was in operation from 1887 to 1920 and was named after Albert Abbott who was head of a land company which speculated in the area.

ARICKAREE (rural post office) was first located about ten miles northwest of the site of Lindon and near the site of Duck Springs, a watering place for buffalo. The first Arickaree was established by James Ulwinick in 1877, and the Arickaree post office opened in 1888. Sometime between 1916 and 1920, the Arickaree post office was moved to Highway 36 about six miles southwest of Anton. The third site of the Arickaree post office was about one mile north of the second site and is shown on a 1956 map. The Arickaree post office was closed in 1961. Arickaree was named after the nearby Arickaree River.

Washington County

BADGER (rural post office) was located about seventeen miles southwest of Anton. The Badger post office was in operation from 1890 to 1891 and from 1893 to 1894.

BRUNKER (rural post office) was located about twelve miles south of Akron, and the Brunker post office was in operation from 1907 to 1917.

BUCHANAN (place name) is shown about fifteen miles southwest of Akron on 1892 and 1902 maps.

BURDETT (rural post office) was located about fifteen miles north of Otis and next to a proposed route of the Burlington Railroad that was never constructed. The Burdett post office was in operation from 1888 to 1940.

CORCORAN (rural post office) was located about six miles west of Cope; the Corcoran post office was in operation from 1889 to 1894.

CURTIS (rural post office) was located about seven miles north of Platner, and the Curtis post office was in operation from 1888 to 1901. Curtis was one of several places established along a proposed route of the Burlington Railroad which was left unbuilt.

DENOVA (rural post office) was located about twenty miles south of Otis, and the Denova post office was in operation from 1916 to 1953. Denova was named after the Spanish word meaning "new."

DILLINGHAM (rural post office) was located about twenty miles southwest of Otis; the Dillingham post office was in operation from 1911 to 1920.

EASYVILLE (platted town) did not obtain a post office. It did not appear on the map, either—maybe Easyville did not live up to its name. A town plat for Easyville was filed by Cyrus Tripp on March 27, 1899. The town was platted about seven miles northwest of the site of Anton.

Places on the Colorado Prairie

FLAT TOP (rural post office) was located about eleven miles south of the site of Last Chance: the Flat Top post office was in operation from 1915 to 1921.

FREMONT (rural post office) was located about seven miles southwest of Cope; the Fremont post office was in operation from 1908 to 1914.

GLEN (rural post office) was located about twenty-seven miles northeast of Limon, and the Glen post office was in operation from 1905 to 1920.

HARRISBURG (rural post office) is shown about nine miles northwest of the site of Anton on 1892 through 1911 maps, about twelve miles north of the site of Anton on 1916 through 1932 maps, and about four miles north of the site of Anton on 1939 through 1956 maps. The Harrisburg post office was in operation from 1887 to 1953.

HENRY (rural post office) was located about fourteen miles southeast of Akron, and the Henry post office was in operation from 1907 to 1917.

HOLMESVILLE (place name) is shown about six miles south of Otis on an undated map.

LESLIE (platted town) was one of several towns which were established on the proposed route of the Burlington railroad; however, the line was not constructed, and most of the towns faded away. A town plat was filed for Leslie on November 13, 1888, by the Lincoln Land Company. The Leslie post office closed in 1896.

LONE STAR (place name) is shown about fifteen miles northwest of Hyde on a 1942 map.

MEEKTON (rural post office) was located about nine miles northeast of Anton, and the Meekton post office was in operation from 1910 to 1918.

Washington County

MESSEX (platted town) was the only town in Washington County located on the Union Pacific railroad. (The Union Pacific just touches Washington County in the northwest corner.) A town plat was filed for Messex on May 7, 1909, by Ernest Hart. The Messex post office closed in 1942.

PLUM BUSH (rural post office) was located about ten miles northwest of Lindon, and the Plum Bush post office was in operation from 1910 to 1918. The town was named after nearby Plum Bush Creek.

PRAIRIE (rural post office) was located about twelve miles southwest of Akron, and the Prairie post office was in operation between 1910 and 1920.

RAGO (rural post office) was located about sixteen miles southwest of Akron; the Rago post office was in operation between 1912 and 1951.

SCHLEYTER (rural post office) was located about eighteen miles northwest of Platner, and the Schleyter post office was in operation about 1912 to 1913.

SPENCE (rural post office) was located about seven miles southeast of Last Chance; the Spence post office was in operation from 1910 to 1920.

SUMMIT SPRINGS (Indian battleground) was the site of the last important Indian battle which was fought in northeastern Colorado. On July 11, 1869, a large band of Cheyenne Indians, led by Chief Tall Bull, encountered 285 white scouts and troopers along with their Pawnee allies. The troopers, who were led by General Carr, were victorious, and Chief Tall Bull and 52 Cheyenne Indians were killed.

TOWNSEND (rural post office) was located about thirteen miles southwest of Lindon, and the Townsend post office was in operation from 1890 to 1893.

Places on the Colorado Prairie

WAGNER (place name) is shown about nineteen miles south of Otis on a 1942 map.

WAITLEY (rural post office) is shown about twelve miles southeast of Messex on 1934 and 1940 maps.

Some Railroad Tracks

BURLINGTON NORTHERN from Yuma County to Morgan County:

    1881–1908 Burlington & Colorado RR

    1908–1970 Chicago, Burlington & Quincy RR

    1970–   Burlington Northern RR

UNION PACIFIC from Logan County to Morgan County:

    1880–1890 Colorado Central RR

    1890–   Union Pacific RR

Some Whistlestops

XENIA (BN) is shown about six miles west of Akron on 1909 through 1968 maps.

Places to Visit

Adena, Morgan County

Northeast of Waterton, Jefferson County

Chapter 29

Weld County

Still on the Map

Ault	Fosston
Barnesville	Frederick
Briggsdale	Galeton
Buckingham	Garden City
Carr	Gilcrest
Cornish	Gill
Crest	Gowanda
Dacona	Greeley
Dearfield	Grover
Dover	Hardin
Eaton	Hereford
Erie	Hudson
Evans	Ione
Firestone	Johnston
Fort Lupton	Keenesburg

Weld County

Keota	Prospect Valley
Kersey	Purcell
Kuner	Rinn
LaSalle	Rockport
Lucerne	Roggen
Masters	Rosedale
Mead	Saint Vrains
Milliken	Severence
New Raymer	South Roggen
Nunn	Stoneham
Omar	Vollmar
Peckham	Wattenburg
Pierce	Windsor
Platteville	

Places in the Past

Avalo	Gearhart
Camfield	Geary's Ranch
Chapleton	Graham
Coleman	Green City
Eagle's Nest	Highland Lake
Flemming's Ranch	Houston
Fort Jackson	Kalous
Fort Junction	Kauffman
Fort Latham	Kelim
Fort Lupton	Koening
Fort Saint Vrain	Latham
Fort Vasquez	Osgood
Gault	Poudre City

Places on the Colorado Prairie

Puritan
Sligo
Twenty-Five Mile House
Vim
Wentz

Wetchel
Whitman
Youngstown
Zilar

Some Railroad Tracks

Burlington Northern Railroad (three parts)
Colorado Central Railroad
Colorado & Southern Railway (two parts)
Denver, Laramie & Northwestern Railroad
Denver, Utah & Pacific Railroad
Great Western Railroad (five parts)
Union Pacific Railroad (seven parts)

Some Whistlestops

Ady
Alden
Athol
Auburn
Avery
Black Hollow
Blandin
Boyds
Bracewell
Bruce
Buda
Bunyun
Clark
Cloverly

Comer
Decker
Dent
Dick
Dixon
Dixon's Mill
East LaSalle
Elm
Farmers
Glick
Greeley Junction
Hardman
Harney
Hodgson

Weld County

Hurrich	Plumbs
Idaho Creek	Powars
Irvington	Pulliam
Jessum	Ragans
Johnson	Sheehan
Johnson's	Sloan
Kerns	Sublette
Kirkland	Summit
Kluver	Tampa
Krauss	Tonvill
Lone Tree	Tracyville
Mathews	Walker
Mitchell	Warren
Moore	Welty
Ogilvy	Wildcat
Parkdale	Yoxall

Still on the Map

AULT (platted town) was first called "McAllister," and then it was called " Burgdorf." The Ault post office was established in 1898, and the town plat for Ault was filed on November 26, 1901, by R. L. Pence and John Hayden. Ault was named after Alexander Ault who purchased much of the grain in the area before silos were built for grain storage.

BARNESVILLE (platted town) was named after its founder, Charles E. Barnes, who filed the town plat on June 11, 1910. The Barnesville post office was discontinued in 1935; however, Barnesville has managed to stay on the map as a siding.

BRIGGSDALE (platted town) was established when the Union Pacific Railroad built a stubline to the site in 1910. A town plat was

WELD COUNTY
(Southwestern Part)

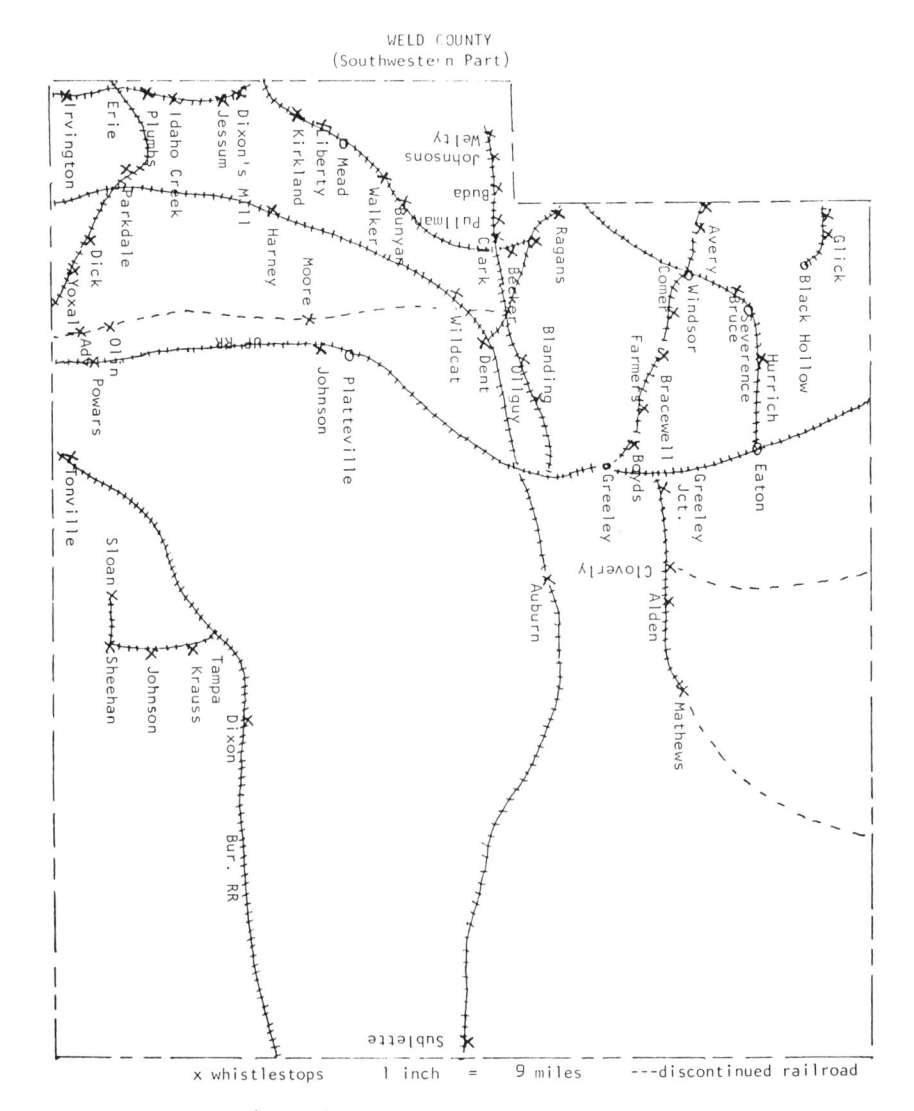

x whistlestops 1 inch = 9 miles --- discontinued railroad
—— main roads

WELD COUNTY
(Northeastern Part)

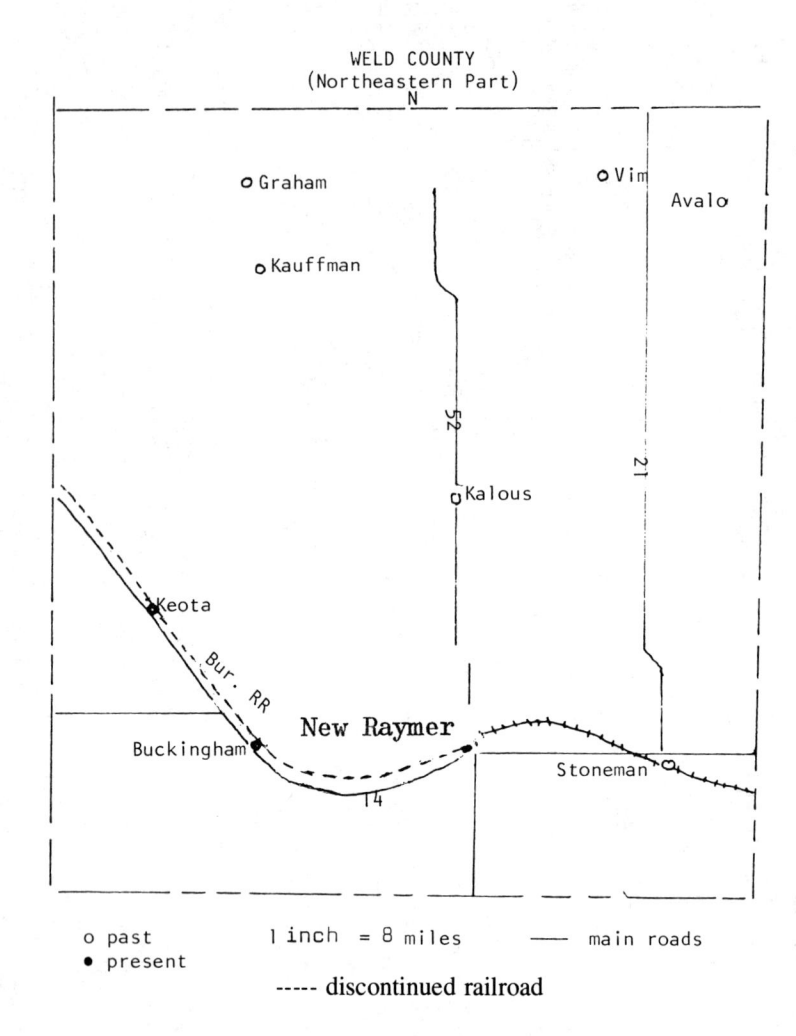

o Graham
o Kauffman
o Vim
Avalo
52
o Kalous
21
Keota
Bur. RR
Buckingham
New Raymer
14
Stoneman

o past
● present

1 inch = 8 miles

——— main roads
----- discontinued railroad

WELD COUNTY
(Northwestern Part)

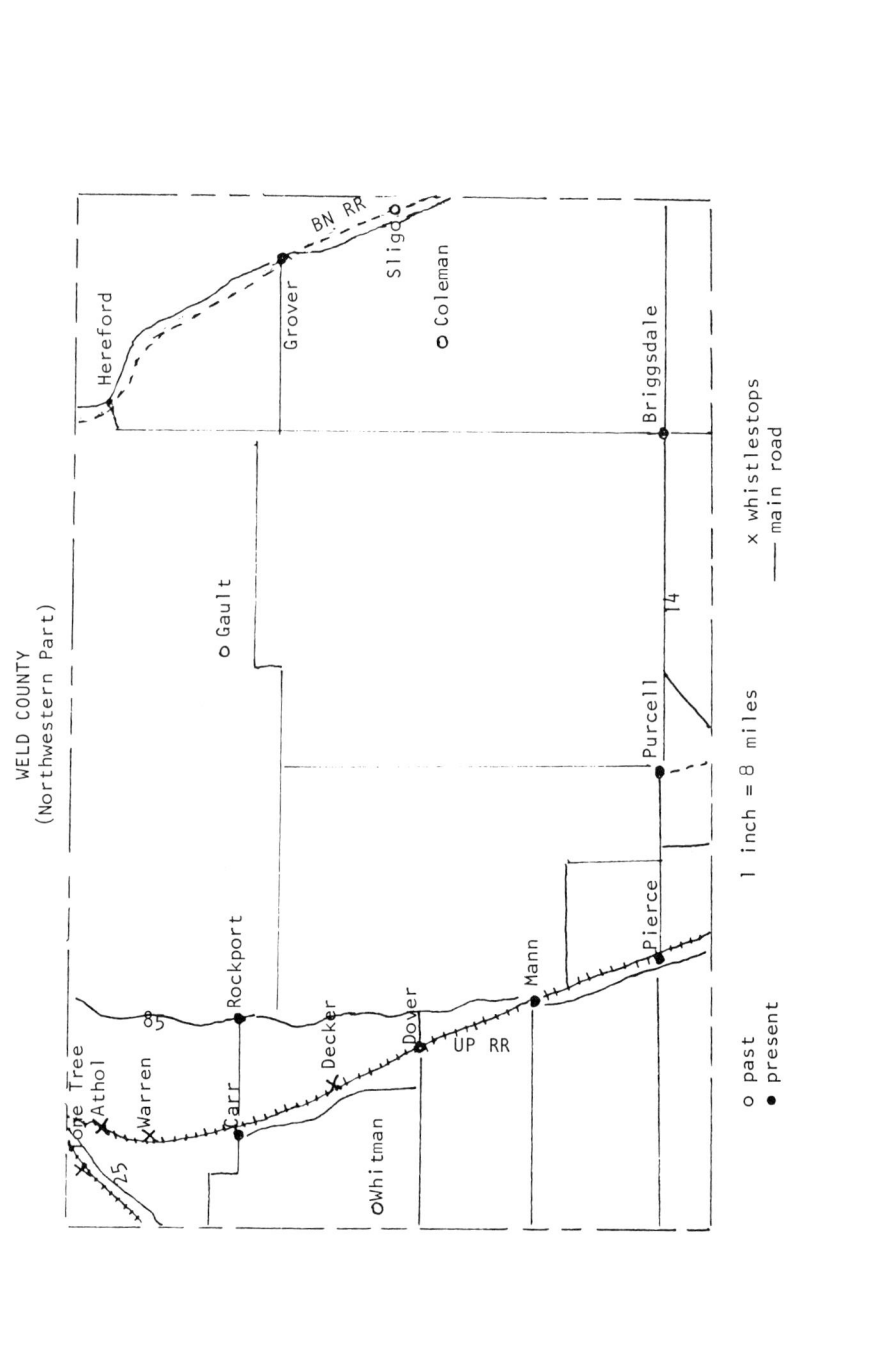

1 inch = 8 miles

x whistlestops
— main road

o past
• present

WELD COUNTY
(Southwestern Part)

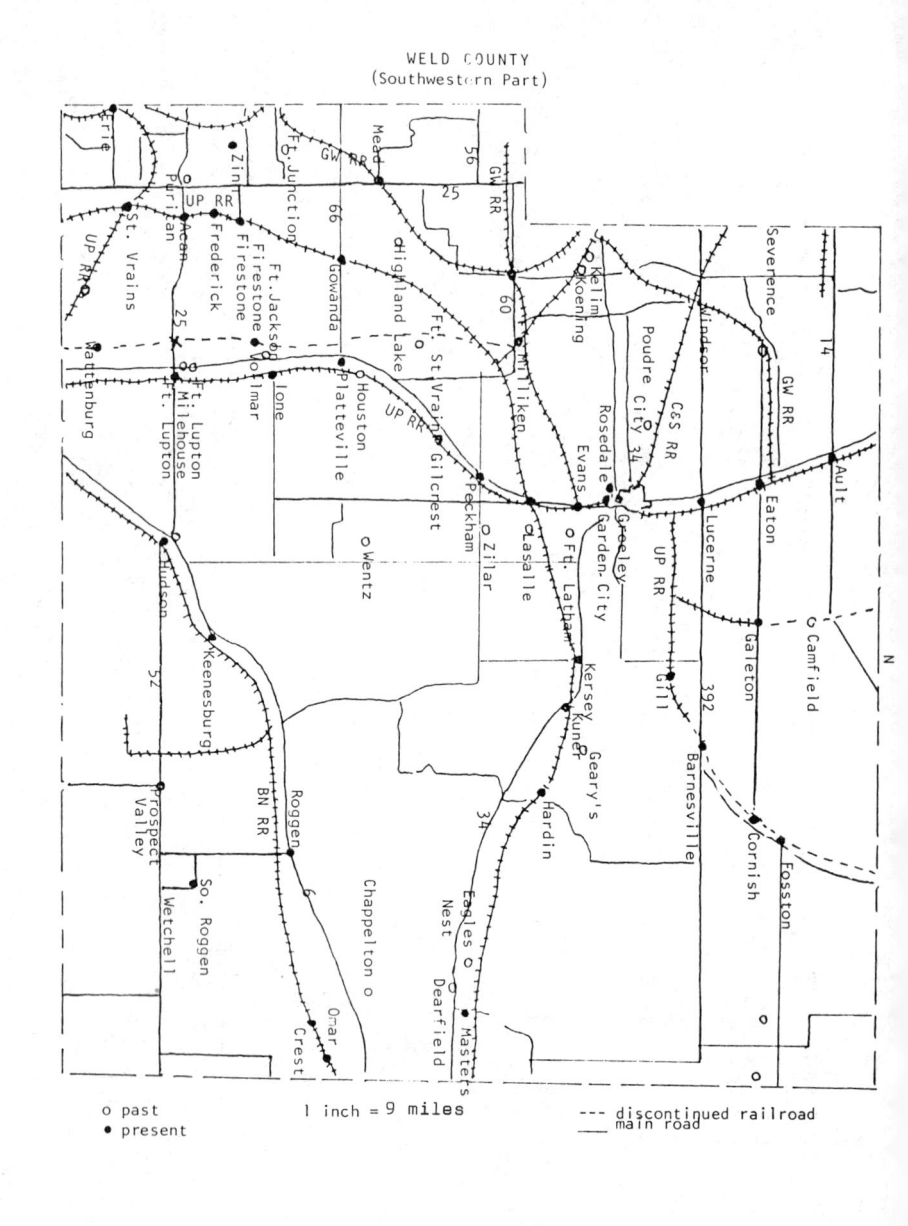

Places on the Colorado Prairie

filed for Briggsdale on May 24, 1910, by Frank N. Briggs who named the town for himself. The stubline from Briggsdale to Barnesville was abandoned in 1965.

BUCKINGHAM (platted town) was named after C. D. Buckingham, who was superintendent of the McCook Division of the Burlington Railroad, which built the line to the site of Buckingham in 1888. The Buckingham post office began upon the arrival of the railroad; however, a town plat wasn't filed for Buckingham until Frank L. Doty filed one on February 7, 1914. The Buckingham post office was closed in the 1960s.

CARR (platted town) was named after Robert Carr, who was the fifth president of the Denver Pacific Railroad, which built to the site of Carr in 1869. A post office was established at Carr in the 1870s, but a town plat was filed for Carr on July 13, 1907, by S. W. McGuire and others.

CORNISH (platted town) was the last of eight towns to be platted along the Union Pacific's spur lines northeast of Greeley in the early 1900s. A town plat was filed for Cornish on September 18, 1911, by Henry Breder, and the town was named after either a Mr. Cornish, who was a civil engineer for the Union Pacific Railroad, or a William Cornish who was president of the Union Pacific Land Company. The Cornish post office was closed shortly after the spur line was discontinued in 1965.

CREST (platted town) was established on the Burlington Railroad between Roggen and Wiggins in 1907. A town plat was filed for Crest on October 1, 1921, but the Crest post office closed two years later.

DACONA (platted town) was the second in a trio of coal-mining towns which were platted just northeast of Erie in the early 1900s. A town plat was filed for Dacona on June 10, 1907 by the Dacona Landsite Company.

DEARFIELD (platted town) was platted by a Negro, O. Jackson, who wanted to establish a farming community for Negroes.

Weld County

Jackson filed a plat for Dearfield on January 14, 1914, and named the town in connection with the idea that "work would make the fields dear to those who worked in them." Dearfield is still on the map, but there is little remaining of the all-Negro community.

Dover (platted town) began as a siding on the Union Pacific Railroad. A post office was established at Dover in 1905, and a town plat was filed for the town on July 29, 1913, by Elmer Merritt. The Dover post office closed in 1913.

Eaton (platted town) was named after the fourth governor of Colorado, Benjamin Eaton. The Eaton post office opened in 1882 under the name of "Eatonton"; however, the name was changed to "Eaton" a year later. The town plat for Eaton was filed on July 8, 1889, by Aaron and Benjaman Eaton. The Great Western Sugar Company built a refinery at Eaton in 1902.

Erie (platted town) began as a coal camp in 1870, and was named after Erie, Pennsylvania. The Denver-Boulder Valley Railroad built a line to the Erie coal field in 1870, and a town plat was filed for Erie on May 20, 1871, by the Colorado Coal Company.

Evans (platted town) was named after John Evans, third president of the Denver Pacific Railroad. A plat was filed for Evans on November 22, 1869, and a replat in 1891. Evans competed with Greeley for a while but was eventually overshadowed by its neighbor to the north.

Firestone (platted town) was the third of three coal mining towns which were platted just northeast of Erie. A town plat was filed for Firestone on September 13, 1907, by the Denslow Coal and Land Company. Firestone was named after Jacob Firestone who owned the site.

Fort Lupton (platted town) took the name of the fort which was established just north of the townsite in 1836 by Lieutenant Lancaster Lupton. The Fort Lupton post office opened in 1869; however, the town plat for Fort Lupton wasn't filed until June 16, 1882, by W. J. Winbourn. The Great Western Sugar Company built a refinery at Fort Lupton in 1921, and Kuner later established a vegetable-canning factory there. The sugar refinery has since been dismantled.

FOSSTON (platted town) was named after H. W. Foss who filed a plat for Fosston on September 25, 1909. Fosston was one of nine platted towns along the Union Pacific's two stublines northeast of Greeley. The Fosston post office closed in 1941.

FREDERICK (platted town) was first called "McKissick," but the name was changed to "Frederick" after the owner of the townsite, Frederick Clark. A town plat was filed for Frederick on May 16, 1907, by Mary Clark, Maud Clark Reynolds, and Mary Clark Steele. Frederick, Firestone, and Dacona were platted within a few miles of each other in 1907.

GALETON (platted town) was platted as "Zita" along the Union Pacific's stubline to Purcell, and the plat was filed on April 14, 1909, by George Musburger. Galeton became the terminus of the stubline when the line was abbreviated in 1943.

GARDEN CITY (platted town) was platted just south of Greeley, and the town plat was filed on September 4, 1935, by Ida H. Wray. Garden City was given the nickname for Greeley and was incorporated in 1936.

GILCREST (platted town) was named after a Mr. Gilcrest, and the town plat was filed on March 6, 1907, by G. A. Starbird and W. K. Starbird. Gilcrest became noted for the potatoes grown in and shipped from the area.

GILL (platted town) was named after William Gill, who filed a plat for the town under the name of the Gill-Decker Improvement Company on April 8, 1909. Gill was platted next to the Union Pacific's stubline to Briggsdale.

GOWANDA (platted town) was platted in anticipation of the Union Pacific railroad which was constructed from Firestone through the Gowanda site in 1911. A town plat was filed for Gowanda on

Weld County

September 11, 1910, by Fred W. Carruth. Gowanda and most of the other towns just west of the Platte in Weld County were unable to compete against the more established towns on the eastern side of the river, and the Gowanda post office closed in 1930.

GREELEY (platted town) was established as the "Union Colony" in 1870 and was headed by Nathan Meeker who represented Horace Greeley of the New York *Tribune*. Henry West, Union Colony representative, filed a town plat for the Union Colony on June 29, 1871, but the Colony was referred to as "Greeley," its post office name. Greeley grew rapidly and was made county seat in 1877. A town plat was filed for Greeley on March 25, 1887, by Nathan Meeker and William Post.

GROVER (platted town) was established as a post office in 1885, and the Lincoln Land Company filed a town plat for Grover on November 10, 1888. Grover was preceded in the area by "Chatoga," which was established by the Nebraska and Colorado Townsite Company. The Lincoln Land Company was seldom denied its choice of townsites; thus, Grover represented the area after the Burlington railroad was built through the area in 1887.

HARDIN (platted town) was first called "Eagle's Nest" and was a station on the Central Overland stage route. The Hardin site was next called "Platte Valley" in the 1860s, and a post office was established at Platte Valley in 1876. The Platte Valley post office became the "Hardin" post office in 1881, which was about the time that the Union Pacific railroad was built through the area. A town plat was filed for Hardin on May 28, 1906, by Louise Von Richthofen.

HEREFORD (platted town) was named after the nearby Hereford Ranch which initiated the town as a shipping station for its cattle. A town plat was filed for Hereford on August 16, 1909, by Richard G. Piper, and a post office was established for the town in the same year.

HUDSON (platted town) was named after the Hudson City Land and Improvement Company, which developed the site. A town

Places on the Colorado Prairie

plat was filed for Hudson on February 2, 1888, by John Lapp. Hudson is located halfway between Fort Morgan and Denver on the Burlington Railroad.

IONE (railroad post office) is located about four miles north of Fort Lupton on the Union Pacific railroad. The Ione post office was in operation from 1927 to 1958.

JOHNSTON (platted town) was named after John W. Paprish who was the son of the founder, Harvey J. Paprish. Johnstown was platted on the Great Western railroad to Longmont and Loveland, and the plat was filed on November 8, 1902, by Harvey J. Paprish. The Great Western Sugar built a refinery at Johnstown in 1926.

KEENESBURG (platted town) was first called "Keene" in reference to the Keene Improvement Company which developed the town. A town plat was filed for Keene in 1906, but the name was changed to "Keenesburg" in order to avoid postal confusion with Keene, Nebraska. A town plat was filed for Keenesburg on May 11, 1908, by John J. O'Hara.

KEOTA (platted town) was named after the Indian word meaning "the fire has gone out" and was established by the Lincoln Land Company, which filed a town plat for Keota on November 10, 1888. The Colorado and Wyoming Railroad built the line through the Keota area in 1887, and Keota grew to provide a hotel and other services for the railroad. However, the "fire has gone out" in Keota.

KERSEY (platted town) was first called "Orr," and the town plat for Orr was filed in 1894. The name was changed to "Kersey," and a town plat was filed on November 25, 1896, by Jesse K. Painter. Kersey was named after the maiden name of Jesse Painter's mother. Kersey received its major impetus from the nearby Union Pacific Railroad.

KUNER (platted town) was named after the Kuner Pickle Company which operated a receiving station at the site until 1936. A town plat was filed for Kuner on June 19, 1908, by E. F. Cottingham and

Weld County

V. W. Conner. The Kuner post office was discontinued in 1920, but the Kuner siding continued to be serviced by the Union Pacific Railroad.

LaSalle (railroad post office) was named after LaSalle, Illinois, which was the hometown of an early resident in the area. The LaSalle post office has been in operation since 1886. LaSalle is the junction for the Union Pacific from northern and eastern Colorado.

Lucerne (railroad post office) was named after the alfalfa which was grown in the area. The Lucerne post office was established in 1892 on the Denver-Pacific Railroad, about six miles north of Greeley.

Masters (railroad post office) is located on the Burlington Railroad about seven miles west of Orchard. The Masters post office has been in operation since 1900 and was named after a foreman on the nearby 4-Bar cattle ranch.

Mead (platted town) was named after Dr. Martin Mead, who homesteaded the site in 1886. The town plat for Mead was filed on February 19, 1906, By Paul Mead and Louis Roman. The plat for Mead was filed shortly after the Great Western Sugar Company built a railroad from Loveland through the Mead site to Longmont.

Milliken (platted town) was first called "Hillsborough" after George Hill who owned a ranch and stage stop on the site. The Hillsborough post office was established in 1871, and the name was shortened to "Hillsboro" in 1891. A town plat was filed for Hillsboro by Mary Knowlton in 1905. The town plat for Milliken was filed on July 23, 1909, and it included the Hillsboro site. The Milliken plat was filed by the Northwestern Land and Iron Company; the town was named after the president of the Company, John R. Milliken.

New Raymer (platted town) was first called "Raymer" and was named after George Raymer, an engineer for the Burlington Railroad. The town plat for Raymer was filed in 1889 by the Lincoln Land Company. Raymer began to fade near the turn of the

Places on the Colorado Prairie

century; however, a town plat was filed for "New Raymer" on July 23, 1910, by W. W. Baldwin and W. E. Whittier, and the town began to revive for a while.

NUNN (platted town) was named after a local hero, Tom Nunn, who prevented a train wreck on the Union Pacific railroad when he flagged down the train before it crashed into a sunken culvert. The town plat for Nunn was filed on June 1, 1906, by H. L. Murray and Lincoln Bancroft.

OMAR (railroad post office) is located on the Burlington railroad about thirteen miles northeast of Roggen. The Omar post office was in operation from 1915 to 1917 and in 1922 and 1923.

PECKHAM (railroad post office) is located on the Union Pacific railroad about two miles northeast of Gilcrest. Peckham was first called "Nantes," but the Peckham post office was established in 1898. The Peckham post office closed in 1911 for five years and closed permanently in 1934.

PIERCE (platted town) began as a switch and water tank on the Union Pacific railroad and was named after General John Pierce, president of the Denver Pacific Railroad. The Pierce post office was established in 1903, and the town plat for Pierce was filed in 1907 by the Shafer brothers.

PLATTEVILLE (platted town) was named after the nearby Platte River. The plat for Platteville was filed on July 17, 1871, by the Platte River Land Company; thus, Platteville is one of the oldest communities in Weld County. The Platteville post office didn't begin operation until 1875, which indicates that Platteville wasn't a smashing success when it was first platted.

PROSPECT VALLEY (place name) is a small farming center located about twelve miles east of Hudson. Prospect Valley has been on the map since the 1950s.

Weld County

PURCELL (platted town) was named after Lawrence Purcell, who founded the town. It is located about nine miles east of Pierce. Purcell was the terminus of one of the Union Pacific's stublines.

RINN (rural post office) began as a post office community in 1901; even though the post office closed in 1907, Rinn has survived as a service community to local farmers. The Rinn blacksmith shop is one of the oldest businesses in the area.

ROCKPORT (place name) is located about five miles east of Carr and is shown on a 1968 map.

ROGGEN (platted town) was first called "Blair," but the name was changed because of the postal conflict with Blair, Nebraska. The Roggen post office was established in 1883, and was named after either the Nebraska Secretary of State, Edward Roggen, or a surveyor for the Burlington Railroad named Roggen. A town plat was filed for Roggen by the Last Springs Ranch Company on June 17, 1908.

ROSEDALE (platted town) is the sister town of Garden City, and both are located next to Greeley. A town plat for Rosedale was filed on May 16, 1939, by an unnamed person. The economy of Rosedale and Garden City received a boost from the fact that Greeley was a "dry" town until 1969, and its suburbs provided substantial refreshment.

SAINT VRAINS (railroad post office) emerged as a stop on the Denver–Boulder Valley railroad in the 1880s. The Saint Vrains post office was in operation from 1915 to 1918.

SEVERENCE (platted town) was first called "Tailholt," but the name was changed to "Severence" when a post office was established in the community in 1894. Severence was named after D. F. Severence, who filed the town plat for the town on July 12, 1906. Severence experienced a recession in the late 1890s, but was revitalized when the Great Western railroad was built to the town in 1905.

Places on the Colorado Prairie

SOUTH ROGGEN (place name) is located about five miles southeast of Roggen and five miles northeast of Prospect Valley. It is shown on a 1968 map.

STONEHAM (platted town) was established by the Lincoln Land Company when the Burlington Railroad built to the site in 1888. The Lincoln Land Company filed a town plat for Stoneham on September 5, 1889.

VOLLMAR (platted town) was named after George Vollmar who owned the townsite. The Denver, Laramie, and Northwestern Railroad built a line to Vollmar in 1908, and the town plat for Vollmar was filed on May 21, 1910, by the Denver-Laramie Realty Company. The Vollmar post office closed in 1912, and the railroad was discontinued in 1917; thus, Vollmar's heyday was short-lived.

WATTENBURG (platted town) was established when the Denver, Laramie, and Northwestern railroad built to the site in 1909. The town plat for Wattenburg was filed on August 30, 1909, by Christine and Caroline Wattenburg, and the town was named for their family. Wattenburg never obtained a post office, probably because of its proximity to Brighton and Fort Lupton.

WINDSOR (platted town) was named after Reverend A. S. Windsor, who was a friend of Edward Hollister, the town's founder. Windsor was first called "New Liberty," and the New Liberty post office opened in 1876; however, the name was changed to "Windsor" when Edward Hollister and the Lake Supply Ditch Company filed a town plat for Windsor on July 19, 1883. The Greeley, Salt Lake, and Pacific Railroad built a line through the site of Windsor in 1881, and the Great Western Sugar Company built a factory with an adjoining railroad at Windsor in 1905.

Weld County

Places in the Past

AVALO (rural post office) was located about eight miles northwest of Westplains and is shown on 1902 through 1940 maps. The Avalo post office was in operation from 1898 to 1936. Avalo was located in the most desolate part of Weld County.

CAMFIELD (platted town) was one of the many towns which were platted along the Union Pacific's stublines to Purcell and Briggsdale. The town plat for Camfield was filed on May 17, 1909, by the Camfield Town and Improvement Company, and the town was named after a Greeley hotel man. The Camfield post office closed in 1925, and the stubline through Camfield was discontinued in 1943.

CHAPLETON (rural post office) was located about eight miles west of Wiggins and is shown on 1924 through 1940 maps. The Chapleton post office was in operation from 1917 to 1940.

COLEMAN (rural post office) was located about ten to twelve miles southwest of Sligo and is shown on 1916 and 1920 maps. The Coleman post office was in operation from 1915 to 1919, and was named in reference to R. Coleman, who homesteaded the site.

EAGLE'S NEST (stage station) was located between the Fremont and Latham stations on the Central Overland stage route.

FLEMMING'S RANCH (rural post office) is shown about five miles east of the site of Longmont on an 1866 map. Flemming's Ranch could have been a stage station. The Flemming's Ranch post office was in operation from 1863 to 1875.

FORT JACKSON (trapper's fort) was established by Henry Fraeb and Peter Sarpy in 1837 and was located near Ione. Fraeb and Sarpy were agents for a St. Louis fur-trading company. Fort Jackson was abandoned in about 1844.

Places on the Colorado Prairie

FORT JUNCTION (home-guard fort) was established by a home-guard during the Indian uprising of 1864, and was named after its location near the junction of the Boulder and the Saint Vrain Rivers.

FORT LATHAM (temporary fort) was established at the Latham stage station during the Indian uprising of 1864. Both the station and fort were named after Milton Latham, an early-day senator from California. The Indian uprising led to the establishment of several military forts along the South Platte River; however, temporary defenses at stage stations, such as Latham, comprised the major portion of defense installations.

FORT LUPTON (trapper's fort) was established in 1836 by Lieutenant Lancaster Lupton who came west with the Colonel Dodge expedition in 1835. Lieutenant Lupton obtained a leave from the army, returned to the Rocky Mountains, and established a trading post about one mile south of the site of present-day Fort Lupton. The post was first called "Fort Lancaster" but was changed to "Fort Lupton" before it was abandoned in 1844.

FORT SAINT VRAIN (trapper's fort) was first known as "Fort George" and was established as a trapper's trading fort in 1837 by Marcelline and Cezan St. Vrain. The St. Vrains established the fort in conjunction with the American Fur Company. Fort Saint Vrain was abandoned in 1844; the fort was used later, however, to form the first county government in northern Colorado.

FORT VASQUEZ (trader's fort) was located about one mile south of present-day Platteville and was established in 1836 by Louis Vasquez and Andrew Sublette. Fort Vasquez was operated by Locke and Randolph in the early 1840s, when Indians half-destroyed the fort and caused its abandonment. The remains of Fort Vasquez were used as a temporary fortress during the Indian uprising of 1864.

GAULT (rural post office) was located about twelve miles southwest of Hereford and is shown on 1902 through 1920 maps. The Gault post office was in operation from 1900 to 1916, and was

Weld County

named after James Gault who homesteaded and taught school in the area.

GEARHART (place name) was located about thirteen miles east of Cornish and is shown on a 1934 map.

GEARY'S RANCH (rural post office) was located about ten miles southeast of Greeley and is shown on 1882 through 1902 maps. The Geary's Ranch post office was in operation from 1888 to 1894. The Union Pacific railroad to Denver from Julesburg crossed the Platte River at Hardin; thus, Geary's Ranch was in a position to serve the traffic from Hardin to Greeley, which was northwest of the Union Pacific's cutoff line to Denver.

GRAHAM (rural post office) was located in an isolated area about sixteen miles northeast of Grover and is shown on a 1916 map. The Graham post office was in operation from 1911 to 1918.

GREEN CITY (platted town) was named after D. S. Green, who promoted the Southwestern Colony for which Green City was to be the center. A town plat was filed for Green City on June 22, 1871, by a person not named. The colonists of the Southwestern Colony were enticed west with glowing promises from D. S. Green; however, the colony failed to prosper and didn't even rate a post office three years after it was founded.

HIGHLAND LAKE (rural post office) was located about two miles northwest of Mead and is shown on 1884 through 1920 maps. The Highland Lake post office was in operation from 1885 to 1910, and was next to the popular recreation area of Highland Lake.

HOUSTON (railroad post office) was located on the Union Pacific railroad and just north of Platteville. The Houston post office was in operation from 1910 to 1913.

KALOUS (rural post office) was located about twelve miles north of New Raymer and is shown on 1920 through 1940 maps. The Kalous post office was in operation from 1915 to 1931, and was named after the Kalous family, who operated a gas pump on the site.

Places on the Colorado Prairie

KAUFFMAN (rural post office) was located about thirteen miles east of Grover and is shown on 1920 through 1940 maps. The Kauffman post office was in operation from 1914 to 1934.

KELIM (platted town) was named after its founder, Lee J. Kelim, who filed a plat for the town on March 15, 1907. Lee Kelim was a pioneer in the area, and he built and ran the first electric plant in Loveland, Colorado. Kelim received its impetus from the Great Western railroad, which was built to the townsite in 1907. The Kelim post office closed in 1923.

KOENING (railroad post office) was located on the Great Western Railroad and about seven miles northwest of Milliken. The Koening post office was in operation from 1913 to 1930 and was named after the Koening family, who were prominent in the area.

LATHAM (stage station) was first named ''Cherokee City'' and was established by John Rollins in 1861; however, the name was changed to ''Latham'' when a stage station was located on the site in 1863. The Latham station was named after Milton Latham, an early-day senator from California. Latham became known as ''Fort Latham'' during the Indian uprising. It was county seat from 1864 to 1870.

OSGOOD (rural post office) was located in the area which is known as ''Greasewood Flats'' and is shown about eight miles east of Cornish on 1916 through 1934 maps. The Osgood post office was in operation from 1910 to 1928 and took its name from a local rancher.

POUDRE CITY (platted town) was named after its location adjacent to the Cache La Poudre River. A town plat for Poudre City was filed by Edwin H. Brown on February 8, 1909; however, a post office wasn't opened for Poudre City, nor was it shown on the map.

PURITAN (platted town) was named after the nearby Puritan Coal Mine, and the town plat for Puritan was filed on July 1, 1947. The Union Pacific Railroad built a spur line to the Puritan Mine in

Weld County

1908, and the mining activity stimulated the nearby community; however, the spur line to Puritan was discontinued in 1956, and Puritan was not shown on the map by the late 1960s.

SLIGO (platted town) was named after Sligo, Ireland, and was established next to the Colorado and Wyoming Railroad when it was built from Sterling to Cheyenne in 1887. A town plat for Sligo was filed on November 30, 1908, by the Lincoln Land Company. Sligo had lost much of its importance to the railroad by the late 1930s, and the post office was discontinued in 1951.

TWENTY-FIVE MILE HOUSE (stage station) was located about a mile southwest of the Fort Lupton townsite. Twenty-Five Mile House was located on the Central Overland route and was named after its distance from Denver.

VIM (rural post office) was located in the Pawnee Buttes area and is shown on a 1927 map. Vim was preceded by the "Spurgin" post office, which was in operation from 1916 to 1927. The Vim post office was in operation from 1927 to 1944, but it is shown as "Spurgin" on 1920 through 1940 maps, except for 1927.

WENTZ (rural post office) was located about ten miles north of the Hudson townsite and is shown on 1897 through 1902 maps. The Wentz post office was in operation from 1891 to 1903 and served the traffic along the wagon road from Hudson to Evans. The Milton Reservoir covers the site of Wentz now.

WETCHEL, or WATCHEL (place name) was located about twelve miles southeast of Roggen and is shown on a 1916 map.

WHITMAN (rural post office) was located about seven miles northeast of Carr and is shown on an 1884 map. The Whitman post office was in operation during 1882 only and served the traffic along the wagon road from Wellington to Cheyenne.

YOUNGSTOWN (platted town) was platted to include the town of Hudson, and the town plat for Youngstown was filed on July 2,

1859, by W. B. Russell. The platting of Youngstown was probably an attempt to absorb and expand Hudson, but the Youngstown plat didn't hold up to the well-established Hudson.

ZILAR (rural post office) was located about six miles southeast of Greeley and is shown on a 1902 map. The Zilar post office was in operation from 1892 to 1894 and served the road from Hudson to Evans.

Some Railroad Tracks

BURLINGTON NORTHERN from Boulder County through Erie and back to Boulder County:
    1889–1908 Denver, Utah and Pacific RR
    1908–1970 Chicago, Burlington & Quincy RR
    1970–   Burlington Northern RR

BURLINGTON NORTHERN from Morgan County to Adams County:
    1881–1908 Burlington & Colorado RR
    1908–1970 Chicago, Burlington & Quincy RR
    1970–   Burlington & Northern RR

BURLINGTON NORTHERN from Tampa to Sloan:
    1925–1970 Chicago, Burlington & Quincy RR
    1970–   Burlington Northern RR

BURLINGTON NORTHERN from Logan County to Wyoming:
    1887–1908 Colorado & Wyoming RR
    1908–1970 Chicago, Burlington & Quincy RR
    1970–1975 Burlington Northern RR
    1975   (Line from Wyoming to New Raymer removed.)

Weld County

COLORADO CENTRAL from Wyoming to Weld County:
> 1877–1890 Colorado Central RR
> 1890–1890 Union Pacific, Denver & Gulf Ry.

COLORADO & SOUTHERN from Black Hollow to Larimer County:
> 1906–   Colorado & Southern Ry.

COLORADO & SOUTHERN from Greeley to Larimer County:
> 1881–1890 Greeley, Salt Lake & Pacific Ry.
> 1890–1898 Union Pacific, Denver & Gulf Ry.
> 1898–   Colorado & Southern Ry.

DENVER, LARAMIE & NORTHWESTERN from Greeley to Elm:
> 1910–1917 Denver, Laramie & Northwestern RR

DENVER, UTAH & PACIFIC from Boulder County to Adams County:
> 1881–1889 Denver, Utah & Pacific RR

GREAT WESTERN from Elm to Adams County:
> 1909–1917 Denver, Laramie & Northwestern RR
> 1917–1947 Great Western Ry.

GREAT WESTERN from Larimer County to Boulder County:
> 1901–   Great Western Ry.
>> 1901 Constructed to Johnstown
>> 1905 Constructed to Mead
>> 1906 Constructed to Boulder County

GREAT WESTERN from Johnstown to Welty:
> 1902 –   Great Western Ry.
>> 1902 Constructed to Buda
>> 1903 Constructed to Welty

GREAT WESTERN from Milliken to Johnstown:
- 1904– Great Western Ry.

GREAT WESTERN from Eaton to Boulder County:
- 1905– Great Western Ry.
    - 1905 Constructed to Windsor
    - 1907 Constructed to Boulder County

UNION PACIFIC from Greeley Junction to Purcell and Briggsdale:
- 1910– Union Pacific RR
    - 1943 Discontinued to Galeton
    - 1965 Discontinued to Barnesville

UNION PACIFIC from Adams County to Boulder County:
- 1870–1874 Denver–Boulder Valley RR
- 1874–1880 Denver Pacific Ry.
- 1880–1898 Union Pacific Ry.
- 1898– Union Pacific RR
    - 1966 Discontinued to St. Vrains

UNION PACIFIC from LaSalle to Adams County:
- 1909– Union Pacific RR
    - 1909 Constructed to Firestone
    - 1911 Constructed to LaSalle

UNION PACIFIC from Morgan County to Adams County:
- 1880–1890 Colorado Central RR
- 1890–1898 Union Pacific, Denver & Gulf Ry.
- 1898– Union Pacific RR

UNION PACIFIC from Wyoming to Adams County:
- 1869–1880 Denver Pacific Ry.
- 1880–1898 Union Pacific Ry.
- 1898– Union Pacific RR

Weld County

UNION PACIFIC from St. Vrains to the Grant Mine:
    1908–   Union Pacific RR

UNION PACIFIC from Parkdale to Puritan:
    1908–   Union Pacific RR

Some Whistlestops

ADY (GW) is shown about three miles north of Brighton on a 1916 map.

ALDEN (UP) is shown about two miles west of Gill on a railroad map.

ATHOL (UP) is shown near the Wyoming state line on 1882 through 1902 maps.

AUBURN (UP) is shown about five miles west of Kersey on 1916 and 1920 maps.

AVERY (C&S) is shown about two miles northwest of Windsor on 1909 through 1920 maps. Avery was named after Frank Avery who came to the area with the Union Colony.

BLACK HOLLOW (C&S) is shown about eight miles west of Ault on 1902 through 1968 maps.

BLANDIN (DL&NW) is shown about two miles southwest of Evans on a 1916 map.

BOYDS (C&S) is shown about one mile northwest of Greeley on 1909 through 1920 maps. Boyds was named after Robert Boyd, who settled in the area before the Union Colony was established in 1870.

BRACEWELL (C&S) is shown about seven miles northwest of Greeley on 1909 through 1968 maps.

Places on the Colorado Prairie

BRUCE (GW) is shown about two miles south of Severence on a 1909 map.

BUDA (GW) is shown about three miles west of Johnstown on a railroad map.

BUNYUN (GW) is shown about two miles north of Walker on a 1920 map.

CLARK (GW) is shown about two miles west of Johnstown on a 1909 map.

CLOVERLY (UP) is shown about four miles west of Gill on a railroad map.

COMER (C&S) is shown about three miles south of Windsor on 1909 through 1920 maps.

DECKER (UP) is shown about four miles south of Carr on 1909 through 1956 maps.

DENT (UP) is shown about twelve miles southwest of Greeley on 1916 through 1970 maps.

DICK (UP) is shown about six miles northwest of Brighton on a railroad map.

DIXON (BN) is shown about six miles east of Roggen on 1882 through 1902 maps and was located in the same vicinity as Crest, which was platted in the 1920s.

DIXON'S MILL (BN) is shown about eight miles north of Erie on 1909 through 1920 maps; also shown in Boulder County.

EAST LA SALLE (UP) is shown about one mile east of LaSalle on a 1950 map.

ELM (GW) is shown about three miles northeast of Milliken on 1909 through 1968 maps.

349

Weld County

FARMERS (C&S) is shown about five miles northwest of Greeley on 1909 through 1968 maps.

GLICK (C&S) is shown about three miles west of Black Hollow on a 1916 map.

GREELEY JUNCTION (UP) is shown about two miles north of Greeley on a railroad map.

HARDMAN (GW) is shown about two miles north of Johnstown on 1909 through 1920 maps.

HARNEY (UP) is shown about three miles north of Firestone on a 1968 map.

HODGSON (GW) is shown about four miles northwest of Platteville on 1916 and 1920 maps. Hodgson was named after George Hodgson, a pioneer in the area.

HURRICH (GW) is shown about five miles west of Eaton on a 1968 map.

IDAHO CREEK (BN) is shown about five miles north of Erie on 1909 through 1920 maps.

IRVINGTON (BN) is shown about two miles south of Erie on 1909 through 1920 maps.

JESSUM (BN) is shown about seven miles north of Erie on 1909 through 1920 maps.

JOHNSON (UP) is shown about three miles south of Platteville on an 1882 map.

JOHNSON (BN) is shown about two miles northwest of Prospect Valley on a 1924 map.

Places on the Colorado Prairie

JOHNSON'S (GW) is shown about two miles east of Welty on 1909 through 1920 maps.

KERNS (C&S) is shown about four miles northwest of Windsor on 1909 through 1920 maps.

KIRKLAND (GW) is shown about six miles northeast of Longmont on 1909 through 1920 maps.

KLUVER (C&S) is shown about five miles northeast of Timnath on a 1916 map; it is also shown in Larimer County.

KRAUSS (BN) is shown about three miles northwest of Prospect Valley on a 1924 map.

LONE TREE (CC) is shown near the Wyoming state line on 1882 through 1902 maps.

MATHEWS (UP) is shown about two miles northeast of Gill on a railroad map.

MITCHELL (BN) is shown about one mile south of Erie on 1892 and 1902 maps. Mitchell was actually on the Denver, Utah and Pacific line.

MOORE (GW) is shown about two miles southwest of Platteville on 1916 and 1920 maps.

OGILVY (UP) is shown about two miles northeast of Dent on a 1920 map.

PARKDALE (UP) is shown about three miles east of Erie on 1916 and 1920 maps.

PLUMBS (BN) is shown about four miles north of Erie on 1909 through 1920 maps.

POWARS (UP) is shown about three miles south of Fort Lupton on a 1920 map. Powars was named after Forrest Powars, a landowner nearby.

Weld County

PULLIAM (GW) is shown about two miles west of Johnstown on 1909 through 1920 maps.

RAGANS (GW) is shown about twelve miles southwest of Greeley on 1909 through 1920 maps.

SHEEHAN (BN) is shown about two miles southwest of Prospect Valley on a 1924 map.

SLOAN (BN) is shown about four miles southwest of Prospect Valley on a 1924 map.

SUBLETTE (UP) is shown about three miles southwest of Orchard on a railroad map.

SUMMIT (UP) is shown about two miles south of the Wyoming state line on an 1887 map. Summit appears to be in the same location as Athol.

TAMPA (BN) is shown about four miles southwest of Roggen on 1909 through 1968 maps.

TONVILLE (BN) is shown about five miles southwest of Hudson on 1916 through 1968 maps.

TRACYVILLE (DL&NW) is shown about two miles west of Fort Lupton on a 1969 map.

WALKER (GW) is shown about four miles northeast of Mead on 1909 through 1968 maps.

WARREN (UB) about two miles south of the Wyoming state line on 1909 through 1920 maps. Warren appears to have been in the same location as Summit and Athol.

WELTY (GW) is shown about six miles west of Johnstown on 1909 through 1940 maps.

Places on the Colorado Prairie

WILDCAT (UP) is shown about eleven miles southwest of LaSalle on 1916 through 1968 maps.

YOXALL (UP) is shown about seven miles east of Erie on 1909 through 1920 maps.

Places To Visit

Weldona, Morgan County

West of Ramah, El Paso County

Chapter 30

Yuma County

Still on the Map

Abarr
Armel
Beecher Island
Clarkville
Eckley
Hale
Heartstrong
Idalia
Joes
Kirk

Laird
Mildred
Robb
Schramm
Vernon
Wages
Wauneta
Wray
Yuma

Places in the Past

Alvin
Avoca

Bolton
Condon

Yuma County

Ford	Logan
Fox	Ludlam
Friend	Newton
Gurney	Rogers
Hermes	Shields
Hughes	Steffens
Landsman	Wales
Lansing	Witherbee

Some Railroad Tracks

Burlington Northern Railroad

Some Whistlestops

None Listed

Still on the Map

ABARR (platted town) was first called "Brownsville," and a plat was filed for the town on May 17, 1922, by Silas E. Hoffman. The name of Brownsville was changed to "Abarr" in 1923, honoring the wife of Silas Hoffman, Ethel Abarr Hoffman. The Abarr post office was discontinued in 1948.

ARMEL (rural post office) is located about twelve miles northeast of Idalia. The Armel post office was in operation from 1903 to 1958.

BEECHER ISLAND (battleground and later post office) took its name from the Battle of Beecher Island in 1868. One thousand Indians led by Chief Roman Nose laid siege to the camp of

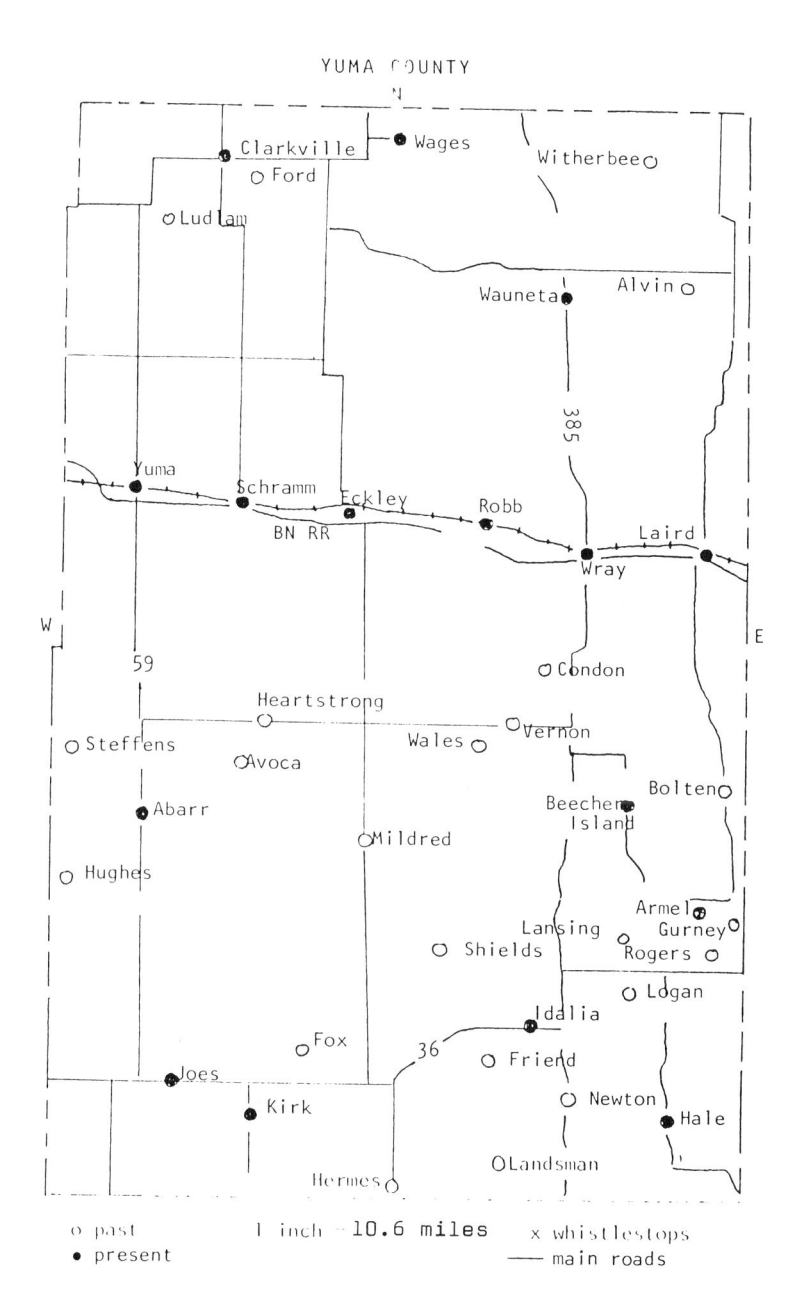

YUMA COUNTY

○ past • present 1 inch = 10.6 miles x whistlestops — main roads

Yuma County

fifty-one Kansas scouts on September 17. The scouts made a retreat to a small island in the middle of the nearby Arickaree River; thus, the stage was set for the Battle of Beecher Island. Four volunteers made it to Fort Wallace and reinforcements reached the island which had been under attack for five days. The Indians were successfully driven off, but the battle at Beecher Island had taken many lives, including those of Chief Roman Nose and Lieutenant Fred Beecher, who was honored by having the battle named after him. A memorial was erected at the site of Beecher Island in 1905, and a post office was established at the site in 1925; however, a flood in 1935 washed away the memorial, graves, and markers. The Beecher Island post office, which was first called "Glory" was closed in 1958.

CLARKVILLE (rural post office) is located about twenty miles northeast of Yuma, and the Clarkville post office was in operation from 1938 to 1954.

ECKLEY (platted town) started as a Burlington Railroad town in the early 1880s; however, a town plat wasn't filed until May 30, 1890, by the Lincoln Land Company. Eckley was named after Adams Eckles, a foreman on a local cattle ranch.

HALE (rural post office) is located about eleven miles southeast of Idalia, and the Hale post office has been in operation since 1905. Hale began as a way-stop on the wagon road from Jaqua, Kansas, to Tuttle, Colorado.

HEARTSTRONG (rural post office) replaced the post office in the platted town of Happyville. The Happyville post office began in 1910, and a town plat was filed for Happyville on January 17, 1921, by C. L. Mason and Clarence Gilmore. The Happyville post office was changed to the "Heartstrong" post office in 1922; however, the maps continued to carry the name of "Happyville" into the 1950s. The Heartstrong post office was discontinued in 1940. Happyville denotes much optimism, but Heartstrong is a more practical name for that part of the prairie.

IDALIA (rural post office) is reported to have been a platted town;

however, there is no plat on file at the Yuma County or Washington County courthouses. The Idalia post office was preceded by the Alva post office which was in operation from 1887 to 1888. The Idalia post office began in 1888 and was named after Edaliah Helmich, who was the wife of Idalia's founder, John Helmick.

JOES (rural post office) is probably one of the most well-known little places in Colorado because of the success which its high school basketball team attained in national competition during the 1920s. Joes was named after three early settlers who were all named Joe, including Joe White. The Joes post office began operation in 1912.

KIRK (rural post office) was named after its founder, George Niekirk, who established the Kirk post office in 1887. The original Kirk post office was located four miles north of the present site.

LAIRD (platted town) was named after Congressman James Laird of Nebraska. A town plat was filed for Laird on October 7, 1887, by the See-Bar-See Land and Cattle Company which also filed the first plat for Wray. Like most of the platted towns in Yuma County, the impetus for Laird came from the Burlington railroad which was built through the area in 1881. The Laird post office was called "See-Bar-See" in the 1890s.

MILDRED (rural post office) was located about twelve miles northwest of Idalia, and the Mildred post office was in operation from 1910 to 1954.

ROBB (platted town) is shown on an 1884 map; however, the Robb post office wasn't established until five years later. A town plat was filed for Robb on February 7, 1890, by G. M. Boss and C. G. Smyth, and the town's impetus came from the Burlington railroad.

SCHRAMM (platted town) was named after R. Von Hormon Schramm who started the town after he became disenchanted with Yuma and moved his buildings. A town plat was filed for Schramm on July 6, 1922, by R. F. Reynolds; however, Schramm had moved to the site in 1892. The post office at Schramm was in operation in 1913 and 1914 and from 1922 to 1925.

VERNON (rural post office) is located about eight miles northwest of Beecher Island. The Vernon post office began operation in 1892 when it replaced the postal service of nearby Condon.

WAGES (platted town) was named after an early settler in the area, Mid Wages. A town plat was filed for Wages on June 5, 1920, by Robert L. Johnson, but the Wages post office had started three years earlier. The post office at Wages was closed in 1950, but Wages is still on the map.

WAUNETA (place name) is located about sixteen miles north of Wray on United States Highway 385. Wauneta is shown on 1956 and 1968 maps.

WRAY (platted town) was named after John Wray, who was a foreman on the nearby I. "Print" Olive ranch; the operation of this spread almost equated that of cattle ranches in the heyday of the industry. A town plat was first filed for Wray by the See-Bar-See Land and Cattle Company on July 31, 1886. A second town plat was filed for Wray on October 2, 1886, by the Lincoln Land Company. Wray became county seat in 1902, after contesting the position with Yuma, which had been the county seat since 1889.

YUMA (platted town) was named after the Yuma Indians. A town plat was filed for Yuma on January 8, 1886, by George F. Weed; however, a fire destroyed the fledgling town about one year later, and it had to start over. Yuma was named county seat of Yuma County when the county was formed in 1889, but the rapidly growing Wray wrested the seat from Yuma in 1902.

Places in the Past

ALVIN (rural post office) was located about fifteen or sixteen miles northeast of Wray on Red Willow Creek. The Alvin post office was in operation from 1910 to 1929.

Places on the Colorado Prairie

AVOCA (rural post office) was almost isolated as the terminus of a wagon road from Yuma which was fifteen miles to the north. The Avoca post office was in operation only a few years around 1890, but Avoca managed to stay on the map until the twentieth century.

BOLTON (rural post office) was located next to Kansas on a wagon road from Haigler, Kansas, to Idalia. The Bolton post office lasted just a few years near the turn of the century. Most of the wagon roads in early Yuma County were directed south to the Rock Island railroad.

CONDON (rural post office) took over the postal operations from the nearby Wales post office in 1888 and serviced the area southwest of Wray until 1892. Condon was known as "Condon Corners" because of its location at the junction of two wagon roads.

FORD (rural post office) was located about eighteen miles north of Schramm, and the Ford post office was in operation from 1909 to 1917.

FOX (rural post office) was located about twelve miles west of Idalia on the wagon road from Friend to Kirk. The Fox post office was in operation from 1890 to 1912.

FRIEND (rural post office) was named after Friend, Nebraska, which was the hometown of many residents in the area. Friend was first called "Frontier Legion" and was homesteaded by S. M. Weaver in 1886. The Friend post office was in operation from 1887 to 1901 and was located at the junction of wagon roads to Kirk and Fox.

GURNEY (rural post office) was located about eight or nine miles southeast of Beecher Island, and the Gurney post office was in operation from 1907 to 1923 in Colorado (right next to the Kansas border).

HERMES (rural post office) was located about twenty-one miles northwest of Joes; the Hermes post office was in operation from 1908 to 1919.

Yuma County

HUGHES (rural post office) was located about twelve miles northwest of Joes; the Hughes post office was in operation from 1913 to 1954.

LANDSMAN (rural post office) was located about ten miles south of Idalia on the wagon road from Newton to Tuttle. Landsman was named after nearby Landsman Creek, and the Landsman post office was in operation from 1883 to 1918; also shown in Kit Carson County.

LANSING (rural post office) was located about ten miles northeast of Idalia on the wagon road from Kansas to Idalia. The Lansing post office was in operation from 1886 to 1910.

LOGAN (rural post office) was located about five miles northeast of Idalia and just south of the wagon road to Idalia from Lansing. The Logan post office was in operation from 1887 to 1901.

LUDLAM (rural post office) was located about eight miles northeast of Yuma on the wagon road from Rockland to Yuma, and the Ludlam post office operated from 1889 to 1890.

NEWTON (rural post office) was located on the wagon road from Hale to Landsman, and the Newton post office was in operation from 1889 to 1918.

ROGERS (rural post office) was located about eight miles southeast of Beecher Island, and the Rogers post office was in operation from 1886 to 1888. It becomes evident that Yuma County consisted mostly of platted towns along the railroad or of rural post offices.

SHIELDS (rural post office) was named after Daniel Shields, who obtained the post office which was in operation from 1887 to 1894. Shields was located about seven miles northwest of Idalia on the wagon road which paralleled the Arickaree River.

STEFFENS (rural post office) was located about fifteen miles southwest of Yuma; the Steffens post office was in operation from 1915 to 1919.

Places on the Colorado Prairie

WALES (rural post office) was named after a Mr. Wales who established the post office in 1888; although Wales stayed on the map for thirty years or more, the post office lasted only about one year.

WITHERBEE (rural post office) was named after John Witherbee who obtained and ran the post office.

Some Railroad Tracks

BURLINGTON NORTHERN from Nebraska to Washington County:

    1881–1908 Burlington & Colorado RR

    1908–1970 Chicago, Burlington & Quincy RR

    1970– Burlington Northern RR

Some Whistlestops

None shown on the map.

Selected Bibliography

Articles

Colorado Writer's Project. Work Projects Administration, "The Names of Colorado Towns," *Colorado Magazine*, January 1940–May 1943.

Public Documents

State of Colorado. *Yearbook of the State of Colorado*. Denver: Colorado State Planning Commission, 1959–1961.

U.S. Post Office Department. *United States Official Postal Guide*. Washington, D.C.: U.S. Government Printing Office, 1920–1945.

Books

Bancroft, Caroline. *Colorful Colorado*. Boulder, Colorado: Johnson Publishing Company, 1966.

Bauer, William H., James L. Ozment, and John H. Willard, *Colorado Postal History*. Crete News, Inc., 1971.

Colorado State Business Directory. Denver: J. A. Blake, 1875–1882; James R. Ives and Company, 1883–1893; Colorado Directory Publishing Company, 1894–1895; Gazetteer Publishing Company, 1886–1935, 1937, and 1939.

Colorado State Historical Association. *The Encyclopedia of Colorado*. Denver: Colorado State Historical Association, no date.

Crofutt, George A. *A Grip-Sack Guide of Colorado*. Reprint by Cubar Associates, Golden, Colorado (first published in Omaha: Overland Publishing Company, 1885).

Davis, E. O. *The First Five Years of the Railroad Era in Colorado*. Denver: Sage Books, Inc., 1948.

Dawson, Frank. *Place Names in Colorado*. Lakewood, Colorado: Printed by the Jefferson Record, 1954.

Griswold, Don and Jean. *Colorado's Century of Cities*. Denver: Printed by Smith-Brooks Printing Company, 1958.

LeMassena , R. A. *Colorado's Mountain Railroads*. Vols. I–V. Golden, Colorado: Smoking Stack Press, 1963–1966.

Lavender, David. *Bent's Fort*. Garden City, New York: Doubleday and Company, Inc., 1954.

Long, Margaret. *The Smoky Hill Trail*. 2nd edition; Denver: Printed by W. H. Kistler Stationery Company, 1947.

Ormes, Robert M. *Railroads and the Rockies*. Denver: Sage Books, Inc., 1963.

State Historical Society of Colorado. *Point of Interest*. Denver: State Historical Society of Colorado, 1972.

Stone, Wilbur F. *History of Colorado*. Chicago: S. J. Clark Publishing Company, Vols. I–III, 1918; Vol. IV, 1919.

Writer's Program, Work Projects Administration. *Colorado, a Guide to the Highest State*. New York: Hastings House, 1941.

Maps

Adams, George H. and Sons. *Colorado*. New York: George H. Adams and Son, 1884.

Continental Oil Company. *Official Road Map of Colorado*. Chicago: H. M. Gousha Company, 1927.

Continental Oil Company. *Touraide Map of Denver, Colorado Springs, and Pueblo*. New York: Rand McNally and Company, 1970.

Continental Oil Company. *Touraide Road Map of Colorado*. San Jose, California, 1970.

Elbert, Frederick (under the direction of Governor William Gilpin). *Map of Colorado Territory*. Denver: G. W. and C. B. Cotton and Company, 1866.

Intermountain Chapter, National Railway Historical Society, Inc. *Railroads in the State of Colorado*. Golden, Colorado: Colorado Railroad Museum, 1969.

Latest Map of Colorado. Denver: G. S. Clason, 1909.

Nell, Louis. *Topographical and Township Map of the State of Colorado*. Denver: Chain and Hardy, 1882.

Nell, Louis. *Topographical Map of Colorado*. Denver: E. Besley and Company, 1892.

Nell, Louis. *Topographical Map of Colorado*. Denver: Hamilton and Kendrick, 1902.

New Map of Colorado. Denver: H. S. Thayer, 1877.

Rocky Mountain Railroad Club. *Map of Colorado*. Denver: Clason Map Company, 1913. Updated by E. J. Haley for Hotchkiss Company, 1968.

State Board of Immigration of Colorado (no title on copy). Denver: Clason Map Company, 1920.

State Game and Fish Department of Colorado. *Map of Colorado*. Denver: Daniel-Smith Company, 1940.

State Highway Commission of Colorado. *Map of the State Highways of Colorado*. Denver: Clason Map Company, 1916.

Thayer, H. S. *Map of Colorado*. Denver: Richards and Company, 1873.

U.S. Department of the Interior, General Land Office Maps.
State of Colorado. 1897
State of Colorado. 1924.

U.S. Department of the Interior, Geological Survey Maps:

Albany, Colorado Quadrangle. 30 Min., 1893. Reprint 1946.

Apishipa, Colorado Quadrangle. 30 Min., 1897. Reprint 1948.

Arvada, Colorado Quadrangle. 7-½ Min., 1965.

Big Springs, Colorado Quadrangle. 30 Min., 1893. Reprint 1948.

Colorado, Mining Districts, Transmission Lines, and Water Power Plants. 1924.

Colorado Topographical. 1934.

Colorado Topographical. 1956.

Colorado Topographical. 1968.

Commerce City, Colorado Quadrangle. 7-½ Min., 1965.

El Moro, Colorado Quadrangle. 30 Min., 1897. Reprint 1949.

Englewood, Colorado Quadrangle. 7-½ Min., 1965.

Fort Collins, Colorado Quadrangle. 15 Min., 1905. Reprint 1960.

Fort Logan, Colorado Quadrangle. 7-½ Min., 1965.

Higbee, Colorado Quadrangle. 30 Min., 1893. Reprint 1948.

Mesa de Maya, Colorado Quadrangle. 30 Min., 1893. Reprint 1948.

Mount Carrizo, Colorado Quadrangle. 30 Min., 1892. Reprint 1948.

Springfield, Colorado Quadrangle. 30 Min., 1893. Reprint 1943.

Timpas, Colorado Quadrangle. 30 Min., 1893. Reprint 1948.

Two Buttes, Colorado Quadrangle. 30 Min., 1893. Reprint 1948.

Vilas, Colorado Quadrangle. 30 Min., 1892. Revised 1949.

Other Sources

Town plats which were on file in the county clerk's office for each of the counties which are included in this book.

Interviews with residents, especially county clerks, in the counties which are included in this book.

Interviews with personnel of the Burlington Northern Railroad, the Railroad Museum, and the Atchison, Topeka & Santa Fe Railway.

Field trips to the counties included in this book, with points of emphasis on "places in the past" and on the retracing of stage routes and discontinued railroad routes.

Index of Places

Aaby, Che., 80
Abarr, Yum., 356
Abbey, Pue., 292
Abbott, Was., 317
Abeyta, L.A., 223
Acequia, Dou., 108
Ackerman, Log., 244
Acme, L.A., 223
Adams, Baca, 46
Adams, Pro., 282
Adams City, Ada., 15
Adena, Mor., 248
Adria, Sed., 311
Ady, Wel., 348
Aetna, E.P., 141
Agate, Elb., 116
Agate, Pue., 292
Aguilar, L.A., 205
Air Force Base, E.P., 134
Akron, Was., 314
Albano, E.P., 134
Albany, Pro., 278
Albia, Pue., 301
Alcott, Den., 92
Alcreek, L.A., 213
Alden, Wel., 348
Alexander, Ote. (see Fowler)
Alexandria, Ara., 34
Alfalfa, Lar., 198
Alfalfa, L.A., 213
Alkalai, Bent, 57
Alkalai Springs, L.A., 213
Allan Ranch, E.P., 134
Altona, Bou., 68
Alvin, Yum., 360
Amache, Pro., 278
American Ranch, Log., 241
Amherst, Phi., 271
Amity, Pro., 278
Amo, E.P., 134
Amy, Lin., 231
Anderson Dale, Ote., 263
Andersonville, Pue., 292
Andrix, L.A., 209
Angora, Ote., 263
Annandale, Den., 92
Antees, Ada., 24
Antelope, Sed., 310
Antelope Springs, Mor., 252
Antees, Ada., 24
Antero, Ada., 19
Anton, Was., 314
Apache, Hue., 150
Apishipa, L.A., 213
Appleton, Pue., 301

Applewood, Jef., 160
Arapahoe, Che., 78
Arapahoe City, Jef., 165
Archers, Jef., 165
Arden, Kio., 176
Arena, Che., 78
Arena, Jef., 170
Argo, Den., 92
Arickaree, Was., 317
Arkins, Lar., 193
Arlington, Kio., 174
Arnel, Yum., 356
Armstrong, Log., 241
Arnold, Log. (see Willard)
Aroya, Che., 78
Arriba, Lin., 228
Arvada, Jef., 163
Ascalon, Che., 82
Ashland, Kit., 182
Athens, Den., 93
Athol, Wel., 348
Atlanta, Baca, 46
Atwell, L.A., 213
Atwood, Log., 238
Auburn, Wel., 348
Ault, Wel., 326
Auraria, Den., 93
Auraria, Den., 100
Aurora, Ada., 15
Aurora, Ara., 28
Avalo, Wel., 340
Avendale, Kit., 182
Avery, Wel., 348
Avoca, Yum., 361
Avoca City, Ada., 19
Avondale, Pue., 287
Ayer, Ote., 261
Aylmer, L.A. (see Bowen)
Ayr, Pro., 278
Badger, Was., 318
Badger, Was., 318
Bagdad, Lin., 234
Baker, Bac., 46
Balzac, Mor., 256
Barela, L.A., 209
Barnes, L.A., 223
Barnes, Lar. (see Barnett)
Barnes Junction, L.A., 223
Barnesville, Wel., 326
Barnett, Lar., 198
Barnum, Den., 93
Barnwell, Elb., 123
Barr, Ada., 15
Barlett, Bac., 42
Barton, Pro., 278

371

Index

Bashor, Ada., 19
Bassetts Mill, E.P., 134
Baxter, Pue., 301
Beaver, Mor., 253
Beaverton, Kit., 182
Beecher Island, Yum., 356
Beethurst, Bent, 59
Beetland, Log., 238
Bellvue, Lar., 191
Beloit, Kit., 182
Benham, Ara., 34
Benham Springs, Elb., 119
Bennett, Ada., 15
Benson, Lar., 198
Bent Canyon, L.A., 213
Benton, Ote., 266
Bent's Road Crossing, Che., 80
Bent's Fort, Bent, 54
Bent's Fort, Ote., 263
Berkeley, Den., 93
Berkeley, Jef., 165
Berlin, Ada., 19
Berthoud, Lar., 191
Beshoar, L.A., 209
Bessemer, Pue., 293
Beta, Log., 244
Bethune, Kit., 180
Beuck, Elb. (see Buick)
Bierstadt, E.P., 141
Big Bend, Bent, 59
Big Sandy, E.P., 134
Big Springs, Che., 81
Big Timbers, Pro., 278
Bijou, Ara. (see Byers)
Bijou, Mor., 253
Bijou, Mor., 256
Bijou Basin, Elb., 120
Bijou Creek, Elb., 120
Bijou Springs, Ara., 34
Bijouview, Mor., 253
Bird, Ada., 19
Bisonte, Baca, 51
Blackwell, Pro., 279
Blaine, Baca, 44
Black Canyon, 155
Black Hollow, Wel., 348
Blair, Wel. (see Roggen)
Bland, Elb., 120
Blandin, Wel., 348
Blende, Pue., 290
Bloom, Ote., 264
Bluebell, Elb., 120
Boaz, L.A., 223
Boettcher, Bou., 73
Boettcher, Lar., 198
Boggsville, Bent, 57
Bolton, Yum., 361
Boner Springs, Lar., 194

Bonney, Kit., 182
Boone, Pue., 290
Boone's, Bou., 68
Booneville, Pue. (see Boone)
Borsts, E.P. (see Southwater)
Boston, Baca, 46
Boulder, Bou., 64
Boulder City, Bou. (see Boulder)
Bovina, Lin., 228
Bowen, L.A., 209
Bowser, Kit., (see Flagler)
Box Elder, Ada., 19
Box Elder, Ara., 34
Box Elder, Lar., 194
Boyd, Lar., 198
Boyds, Wel., 348
Boyero, Lin., 228
Bracewell, Wel., 348
Bragdon, Pue., 301
Braidwood, Lar., 198
Brandon, Kio., 174
Branson, L.A., 209
Breed, E.P., 141
Breen, Hue., 155
Briggsdale, Wel., 326
Brighton, Ada., 16
Bristol, Lar., 194
Bristol, Pro., 274
Broadhead, L.A., 213
Broadmoor, E.P., 127
Broadway Estates, Ara., 28
Brookfield, Baca, 46
Brooklyn, Ara., 34
Brooks, Pue., 302
Broomfield, Boul., 66
Bronco, Mor., 256
Brookside, E.P., 134
Brownard, Log., 244
Brownsville, Yum. (see Abarr)
Bruce, Wel., 349
Brunker, Was., 318
Brush, Mor., 248
Bryant, Phi., 271
Buchanan, Log., 244
Buchanan, Was., 318
Buchtel, Ote., 267
Buckeye, Baca, 47
Buckeye, Lar., 191
Buckingham, Wel., 331
Buckley Naval Air Station, Ara., 31
Buda, Wel., 349
Buffalo, Log. (see Merino)
Buick, Elb., 118
Bulger, Lar., 191
Bulger City, Lar. (see Bulger)
Bunell, Ada., 20
Bunyan, Wel., 349
Bunker Hill, Hue (see Lester)

Places on the Colorado Prairie

Burdett, Was., 318
Burgdorf, Wel. (see Ault)
Burlington, Bou., 68
Burlington, Kit., 180
Burnham, Den., 100
Burnt Mill, Pue., 293
Burt, E.P., 134
Buster, L.A., 213
Butte City, Baca (see Minneapolis)
Buttes, E.P., 130
Byers, Ara., 31

Caddel, Hue., 150
Caddoa, Bent, 54
Calhan, E.P., 130
California Ranch, Dou. (see Franktown)
Camden, Mor., 256
Cameron, Elb., 123
Cameron, Hue., 155
Camfield, Wel., 340
Camp Carson, E.P. (see Fort Carson)
Camp Collins, Lar. (see Fort Collins)
Camp George West, Jef., 163
Camp Rankin, Sed. (see Fort Sedgwick)
Camp Shumway, Hue., 150
Camp Tyler, Mor. (see Fort Morgan)
Campion, Lar., 198
Campo, Baca, 44
Canfield, Bou., 68
Capers, Pue., 302
Capitol Hill, Bou., 69
Capitol Hill, Pue., 293
Carbonado, Hue., 149
Carey, Kit., 182
Carlisle, Kit., 183
Carlisle, Pue., 302
Carlton, E.P., 142
Carlton, Pro., 274
Carpenter, Pue., 293
Carr, Mor. (see Bijou)
Carr, Wel., 331
Carr Crossing, Lin., 231
Carriso, Bac., 47
Carrizo, Baca, 47
Carrizo Springs, Baca, 47
Carters, Pue., 302
Case, Ote., 267
Case, Dou., 108
Castiel, Ote., 267
Castle Rock, Dou., 104
Catherine, Ote., 267
Catlin, Ote. (see Manzanada)
Cedar Point, Elb., 120
Cedar Point, Elb., 123
Cedarhurst, L.A., 214

Cedarwood, Pue., 290
Celeryville, Ada., 24
Central Pueblo, Pue., 293
Champion, Hue., 155
Channing, Pro., 282
Chapleton, Wel., 340
Chapin, Kit., 183
Chapman, Bou., 73
Chatfield, Ara., 38
Chatoga, Wel. (see Grover)
Chelsea, Log., 244
Chemung, Che., 81
Cheney Center, Pro., 274
Chenoa, Log., 241
Chenoweth, Elb., 120
Cheraw, Ote., 261
Cherokee, Lar. (see Stonewall)
Cherokee City, Wel. (see Latham)
Cherry, Dou., 108
Cherry Creek, Ara., 35
Cherry Hills, Ara., 31
Cherry Knolls, Ara., 31
Cherry Valley, 35
Cherrylyn, Ara., 34
Cherrywood, Ara., 31
Cheyenne Wells, Che., 78
Cheyenne Wells, Che., 81
Chicago Colorado Colony, Bou. (see Longmont)
Chico, Pue., 302
Chico Basin, E.P., 134
Chicosa, L.A., 214
Chicosa Junction, L.A., 223
Chilcott, Pue., 293
Childs, Jef. (see Church's)
Chilili, L.A., 214
Chivington, Kio., 174
Church's, Jef., 165
Church's, Jef., 170
Church's, Jef., 170
Church's, Jef., 170
Cimmaron City, Baca, 47
Cimmaron Hills, E.P., 130
Citadel, Dou., 111
Clanda, L.A., 214
Claremont, Kit (see Stratton)
Clark, Wel., 349
Clark Colony, Ara., 35
Clarkston, Bou., 69
Clarkville, Yum., 358
Claud, Elb., 120
Clay, Pue., 302
Clay Pit, Dou. (see Larkspur)
Clear Creek Junction, Jef., 170

373

Index

Clemmons, Elb. (see Schley)
Clermont, Elb., 120
Clifford, Lin., 234
Clifton, Bou., 73
Cloverly, Wel., 349
Clucas, Pro., 282
Clyde, Baca, 47
Coal Creek, Ara., 35
Coal Creek, Jef., 170
Cole, Kit., 183
Coleman, Wel., 340
Colfax, Den., 93
College Hill, Jef., 170
Colorado City, E.P., 135
Colorado City, Pue., 290
Colorado Springs, E.P., 130
Columbia, Kit., 183
Columbine, Ara., 31
Columbine Valley, Ara., 31
Comanche, Ada., 20
Comer, Wel., 349
Commerce City, Ada., 16
Concord, Hue. (see Lascar)
Concord, Pue., 293
Condon, Yum., 361
Condon Corners, Yum. (see Condon)
Connell Creek, Lin., 231
Consul, Hue., 155
Coon Creek, Lin., 231
Coon Valley, Kio., 176
Cooper, Mor., 256
Cope, Was., 316
Corcoran, Was., 318
Cornelia, Bent, 59
Cornish, Wel., 331
Corona, Mor. (see Wiggins)
Coronado, Ada., 16
Coronado, Che., 82
Coronado, Den., 100
Corrinth, Baca, 47
Cotsworth, Mor., 253
Cowan, Jef., 170
Cowans, Lin., 231
Cox, Ada., 24
Creech, Lin. (see Genoa)
Crest, Wel., 331
Crews, E.P. 142
Croft, Cro., 88
Crook, Log., 238
Crouse, Lar., 199
Crow, Pue., 294
Crowley, Cro., 87
Crows Roost, E.P. 135
Crystal Springs, Kit., 183

Cuba, Pue., 302
Cucharas, Hue., 150
Curtis, Was., 318
Cuthbertson, Lar., 199

Dacano, Wel., 331
Dairy Place, Ada., 20
Dalerose, L.A., 209
Dalley, Log., 238
Damascus, Lin., 232
Darlow, Ada., 25
Davidson, Bou., 69
David's Wells, Che., 81
Dawkins, Pue., 294
Dayton, Kio., 176
Dearfield, Wel., 331
Decatur, Baca, 48
Decker, Wel., 349
Deerings Well, Che., 81
Deer Trail, Ara., 32
Delcarbon, L.A., 149
Delhi, L.A., 209
Delite, Pro., 282
Dempsey, Pue., 302
Dennisons, Log., 241
Dent, Wel., 349
Denova, Was., 318
Denver, Den., 90
Denver City, Den. (see Denver)
Denver Junction, Sed. (see 4th Julesburg)
Denver Mills, Den. (see Sheffield)
Deora, Bac., 44
Derby, Ada., 20
Deuel, Mor., 253
Deur, Pro., 279
Devine, Pue., 302
Dick, Wel., 349
Dillingham, Was., 318
Dillview, L.A., 214
Diston, Kio., 177
Divide, E.P. (see Palmer Lake)
Dixon, Lar., 199
Dixon, Wel., 349
Dixon's Mill, Bou., 73
Dixon's Mill, Wel., 349
Doby, Elb., 123
Dodd, Mor., 253
Dorsey, Sed., 311
Double Adobe, Cro., 87
Douglas, Dou., 108
Dover, Wel., 332
Downer, Bou., 73
Downing, L.A., 214
Drake, Lar., 191
Dream House Acres, Ara., 32

374

Drennan, E.P., 135
Dresden, Hue., 155
Druce, L.A., 214
Dubois, Che., 81
Duff, Ada., 20
Dundee, Pue., 302
Dupont, Ada., 16

Eads, Kio., 174
Eagle's Nest, Wel., 340
Earl, L.A., 210
East LaSalle, Wel., 349
Eastlake, Ada., 16
Easton, E.P. (see Eastonville)
Eastonville, E.P., 130
Easyville, Was., 318
Eaton, Wel., 332
Eatonton, We. (see Eaton)
Eckley, Yum., 358
Eden, Pue., 294
Edgarton, E.P., 135
Edgeplain, Pue., 294
Edgewater, Jef., 163
Edison, E.P., 135
Edler, Baca, 44
El Moro, L.A., 210
El Paso, E.P., 135
El Paso, E.P. (see Buttes)
Elba, Was., 316
Elbert, Elb., 118
Elder, Ote., 267
Eldorado Springs, Bou., 66
Elizabeth, Elb., 118
Ella, Pro., 279
Ellicott, E.P., 131
Elm, Wel., 349
Elphis, Kit., 183
Elsmere, E.P., 135
Elyria, Den., 93
Emerson, Phi., 272
Engle, L.A., 214
Engleville, L.A. (see Engle)
Englewood, Ara., 32
Eno, Ada., 25
Ensign, Mor. (see Bijou)
Ent Air Force Base, E.P., 131
Enterprize, Jef. (see Waterton)
Erie, Wel., 332
Erickson Spur, Pue., 302
Eskdale, Ada., 20
Estelene, Baca, 48
Eureka, Che., 81
Eureka, Che., 82
Evans, Wel., 332

Eversman, Bou., 73
Excelsior, Pue., 294
Fairfield, Phi., 272
Fairmount, Elb., 120
Fairmont, Ote. (see Swink)
Falcon, E.P., 131
Farmers, Wel., 350
Farr, Hue., 151
Federal Heights, Ada., 16
Fenton, Ote., 267
Fergus, Kio. (see Hawkins)
Fife, Lar., 199
Firestone, Wel., 332
Firstview, Che., 80
Fisher, Bou., 73
Fisher, Pue., 294
Fisk Orchard Place, Jef., 165
Fisk's Broadway Gardens, Ara., 35
Fisk's Gardens, Ara. (see Englewood)
Fitzsimons, Ada., 16
Flagler, Kit, 180
Flat Top, Was., 319
Fleming, Log., 238
Flemmings Ranch, Wel., 340
Flora, Sed., 310
Flues, L.A., 215
Fondis, Elb., 118
Forbes Junction, L.A., 223
Ford, Log., 244
Ford, Yum., 361
Forder, Lin., 232
Forks, Lar., 191
Fort Carson, E.P., 131
Fort Chambers, Bou., 69
Fort Collins, Lar., 192
Fort Collins, Lar., 194
Fort George, Wel. (see Fort St. Vrain)
Fort Jackson, Wel. 340
Fort Junction, Wel., 341
Fort Lancaster, Wel. (see Ft. Lupton)
Fort Latham, Wel. 341
Fort Logan, Den. 92
Fort Lupton, Wel. 332
Fort Lupton, Wel. 341
Fort Lyon 1st, Bent 54
Fort Lyon 2nd, Bent, 56
Fort Morgan, Mor., 251
Fort Morgan, Mor., 253
Fort Pueblo, Pue., 294
Fort Reynolds, Pue., 295
Fort St. Vrain, Wel., 341
Fort Sedgwick, Sed., 310
Fort Vasquez, Wel., 341
Fort Wicked, Log. (see Godfrey's)

375

Index

Fosdick, Pue. (see Boone)
Fossil Creek, Lar., 199
Fosston, Wel., 333
Fountain, E. P., 131
Fountaine City, Pue., 295
Four Corners Crossing, Bent, 56
Four Mile House, Den., 94
Fowler, Ote., 261
Fox, Yum., 361
Franceville, E.P., 135
Franceville Junction, E.P., 136
Franktown, Dou., 104
Frederick, Wel., 333
Fredonia, Bent, 57
Fremont, Mor., 254
Fremont, Was., 319
Fremont's Orchard, Mor. (see Orchard)
Frick, Baca, 51
Friend, Yum., 361
Frontier City, Lin., 232
Frontier Legion, Yum. (see Friend)
Frost, Ada., 20
Frys, Lar., 199
Fulton, Ada., 20
Furman, Pue., 302

Galatea, Kio., 175
Galeton, Wel., 333
Galien, Log., 244
Gallup, Ada., 25
Garcia, L.A., 223
Garden City, Wel., 333
Gann, Dou., 112
Gary, Mor., 251
Gate City, Jef., 166
Gault, Wel., 341
Gearhart, Wel., 342
Geary's Ranch, Wel., 342
Gem, Bent, 57
Genoa, Lin., 230
Giddings, Lar., 199
Giese, Mor., 256
Gilchrest, Wel., 333
Gill, Wel., 333
Gillette, L.A., 215
Gilman, Jef., 166
Gilpin, Bent, 59
Girard, Lin., 232
Glade, Dou., 112
Gleaneth, E.P., 136
Glencoe, Jef., 170
Glendale, Ara., 32
Glen, Was., 319
Glenn, E.P., 136
Glick, Wel., 350

Glider Training School, 254
Globe, Hue., 155
Globeville, Den., 94
Glory, Yum. (see Beecher)
Godfrey, Elb. (see Buick)
Godfrey's, Log., 241
Goff, Kit., 183
Golddale, Dou., 108
Golden, Jef., 163
Golden City, Jef. (see Golden)
Gomer's Mills, Elb., 121
Goodale, Pro., 282
Goodnight, Pue., 290
Goodnight, Pue., 303
Goodrich, Mor., 251
Gordon, Hue., 151
Gorham, Bou. (see Marshall)
Gotera, L.A., 215
Gowanda, Wel., 333
Graceland, Elb., 121
Grady's, Che., 81
Graft, Baca, 48
Grafton, Den., 94
Graham, Wel., 342
Grahame Ranch, Mor., 254
Gramercy Park, Ada., 20
Granada, Pro., 277
Graneros, Pue., 295
Granger, E.P., 136
Granton, Pue., 295
Graves, Lar. (see Teds)
Grahame Ranche, Mor., 254
Gravel Spur, Pue., 303
Gray, Was. (see Cope)
Graycreek, L.A., 215
Graylin, Log., 241
Gray's Landing, L.A., 215
Greeley, Wel., 334
Greeley Junction, Wel., 350
Green City, Wel., 342
Green Canyon, L.A., 215
Green Knoll, Lin., 232
Greenfield, L.A., 215
Greenhorn, Pue., 290
Greenhorn, Pue., 303
Greenland, Dou., 107
Greenwood, Ara., 32
Greys, Lar., 199
Griffin, Mor., 256
Grimaldi, Pue., 295
Grinnell, L.A., 215
Grote, Pro. (see Carlton)
Grover, Wel., 334
Gurney, Yum., 361

376

Places on the Colorado Prairie

Gwilliamsville, E.P., 136
Hadfield's Island, Log., 242
Hadley, Bent, 59
Hale, Yum., 358
Hall, E.P., 142
Hall, Log., 244
Hall Station, Lin., 232
Hallack Junction, Jef., 171
Hamlet, Pue., 303
Hanover, E.P., 136
Happyville, Yum. (see Heartstrong)
Harboard, Baca, 51
Harbourville, Bent, 57
Hardin, Wel., 334
Hardman, Wel., 350
Hargisville, Elb., 121
Harlem, Pue., 295
Harman, Den., 94
Harmony, Lar., 199
Harney, Wel., 350
Harris, Ada. (see Westy)
Harris Park, Ada. (see Westy)
Harrisburg, Ada. (see Westy)
Harrisburg, Was., 319
Hartman, Pro., 277
Hasty, Bent, 56
Haswell, Kio., 175
Hathaway's Quarry, Duo., 112
Hawkins, Kio., 175
Hawley, Ote., 267
Hawthorn, Ara., 35
Haxtun, Phi., 271
Hayden, Pue., 303
Hayford, Log., 244
Hazeltine, Ada., 21
Heartstrong, Yum., 358
Hedinger Lake, Lin., 232
Henderson, Ada., 17
Henderson, Sed. (see Sedgwick)
Henderson's Island, Ada. (see Henderson)
Henkel, E.P. 142
Henry, Was., 319
Henry's, E.P. (see Monument)
Hereford, Wel., 334
Hermes, Yum., 361
Hermosillo, Pue., 295
Hermes, Yum., 361
Heron, Pro. (see Barton)
Hester, Cro., 87
Heston, Lar., 199
Hezron, Hue., 155
Hezron Junction, Hue., 155
Higbee, Ote., 264
Higgins, L.A., 223

Highland, Bou., 73
Highland Lake, Wel., 342
Highlands, Den., 94
Hillrose, Mor., 251
Hillsboro, Wel. (see Milliken)
Hillsborough, Ada., 21
Hillsborough, Wel. (see Milliken)
Hillside, Ara., 35
Hilltop, Dou., 108
Hilton, Bent, 59
Hitt, Sed., 311
Hodgson, Wel., 350
Hoehne, L.A., 210
Hoehne, L.A., 216
Hog Back, L.A., 216
Hogan, Lin., 232
Hohnville, Ada., 21
Hole-in Prairie, L.A., 216
Hole-in Rock, L.A., 216
Holly, Pro., 277
Holmes, E.P., 142
Holmes City, Baca, 48
Holmesville, Was., 319
Holtwold, Elb., 121
Holtwold, E.P., 136
Holyoke, Phi., 271
Home Place, Ote., 264
Hoopup, L.A., 216
Houghton, L.A., 224
Houston, Wel., 342
Hoyt, Kit., 183
Hoyt, Mor., 251
Hudson, Wel., 334
Huerfano, Pue., 296
Hughes, Ada. (see Brighton)
Hughes, Yum., 362
Hugo, Lin., 230
Hugo Springs, Lin., 232
Huntsville, Dou., 109
Hurley, Mor., 256
Hurrich, Wel., 350
Husted, E. P., 136
Hyde, Was., 316
Hygiene, Bou., 66

Idaho Creek, Wel., 350
Idalia, Yum., 358
Ideal, Hue., 151
Iliff, Log., 239
Independence, Den., 94
Indianapolis, L.A., 216
Ingleside, Lar., 199
Inman, Kio., 177
Ione, Wel., 335
Iron Springs, Ote., 264

377

Index

Iron Springs, Ote. (see Bloom)
Irondale, Ada., 17
Irving, Dou., 109
Irvington, Bou., 69
Irvington, Wel., 350
Irwin Canyon, L.A., 216
Island Station, Ada. (see Henderson)
Ivywild, E.P., 131

Jackson, Pue., 296
Jansen., L.A., 210
Jessica, Log., 244
Jessum., Wel., 350
Jimmy Camp., E.P., 137
Jimmy Camp., E.P., 142
Joew, Yum., 359
Johnson, Wel., 33
Johnson., Wel., 350
Johnson, Wel., 350
Johnson, Wel., 351
Johnstown, We., 335
Joliet, Kio. (see Arlington)
Jones, Jef., 171
Joycoy, Baca, 48
Jones, Jef., 171
Juanita, Pue., 296
Juchem, Jef., 171
Julesburg 1st, Sed., 310
Julesburg 2nd, Sed., 310
Julesburg 3rd, Sed., 309
Julesburg 4th, Sed., 309
Junction, Ara., 38
Junction House, Mor., 254

Kalous, Wel., 342
Kanza, Elb., 121
Karl, Pro., 282
Karval, Lin., 230
Kassler, Jef., 163
Kauffman, Wel., 343
Kazan, L.A., 216

Keenesburg, Wel., 335
Keesee, Bent, 59
Kelim, Wel., 343
Kelker, E.P., 137
Kelley, Log., 242
Kelley's, Log. (see American Ranch)
Kendrick, Lin., 232
Kenwood, Ara., 38
Kenyon Corner, Lar., 192
Keota, Wel., 335
Kerns, Lar., 200
Kerns, Wel., 351
Kersey, Wel., 335
Keysor, Elb., 121

Kilburn, Kio., 176
Kim, L.A., 210
King, Dou., 112
King Center, Cro., 88
King's Ferry, Ote., 264
Koen, Pro., 282
Koening, Wel., 343
Konnantz, Baca, 48
Kornman, Pro., 282
Krauss, Wel., 351
Kravig, Lin. (see Karval)
Kremis, Ote., 267
Kreybill, Bent, 60
Kuhn's Crossing, Elb., 121
Kuner, Wel., 335
Kutch, Elb., 118

La Plaza de Las Leones, Hue. (see Walsenburg)
La Vergne, E.P., 137
Lafayette, Bou., 66
Lafayette, Ote., 267
Laird, Yum., 359
La Junta, Ote., 262
La Junta Air Force Base, Ote., 264
Lake, Lin., 234
Lake Minnequa, Pue., 296
Lakeside, Bou., 69
Lakewood, Jef., 163
Lamar, Pro., 277
Lamb, Mor., 256
Lamport, Baca, 49
Lancaster, Pro., 279
Landsman, Yum., 362
Landsman, Kit., 183
Langford, Bou., 69
Lansing, Yum., 362
Laporte, Lar., 192
Larimer, Hue., 151
Larkspur, Dou., 107
Las Animas, Bent, 56
LaSalle, Wel., 336
Lascar, Hue., 149
Last Chance, Was., 316
Latham, Wel., 343
Laub, L.A., 217
Laura, Log., 242
Leader, Ada., 17
Lee's Siding, Jef., 171
Leetsdale, Den., 95
Lehigh, Dou., 112
Leroy, Log., 242
LeRoy, Log. (see Leroy)
Leslie, Was., 319
Lester, Hue., 151

Places on the Colorado Prairie

Leyden, Jef., 164
Liberty Hill, Pue., 296
Liggett, Bou., 73
Lillian Springs, Log., 242
Lime, Pue., 290
Limon, Lin., 230
Lindon, Was., 316
Linwood, L.A., 217
Little Buttes, E.P., 137
Little Thompson, Lar., 194
Littleton, Ara., 32
Littleville, Mor., 254
Livesly, Pue., 303
Living Springs, Ada., 21
Lockwood, L.A., 217
Loco, Kit., 183
Lodi, Mor., 256
Log Lane, Mor., 251
Logan, Log., 244
Logan, Yum., 362
Logantown, Ara., 36
Lolita, Cro., 88
Loma Park, Hue., 131
Lombardi Village, 291
Lone Star, Was., 319
Lone Tree, Wel., 351
Longmont, Bou., 66
Loraine, E.P., 137
Lords, Lar., 200
Louisville, Bou., 67
Louviers, Dou., 107
Love, E.P., 137
Loveland, Lar., 192
Lowell, Kit. (see Old Burlington)
Lowery, Lar., 200
Lowland, Elb., 123
Lowry Air Force Base, Ara., 33
Lubers, Bent, 60
Lucerne, Wel., 336
Ludlam, Yum., 362
Ludlow, L.A., 210
Lyons, Bou., 67
Lycan, Baca., 44
Lyman, Ada., 21
Lynn, L.A., 224
Lytle, E.P., 137

MacRose, Ara., 39
Madge, Dou., 112
Magee, Ada., 25
Maine Ranch, Ben., 58
Maitland, Hue., 151
Majors, E.P., 138
Malaby's, Lar., 200
Maldanado, L.A. (see San Miguel)

Malowe, Kit. (see Flagler)
Manchester, Mor., 256
Manila, Ada., 25
Manville, Pro., 282
Manzanola, Ote., 262
Marcott, Log., 244
Margueritte, L.A., 217
Marion, Lar., 200
Marlman, Bent, 60
Marnel, Pue., 291
Marshall, Bou., 67
Martin, Bent, 60
Masters, Wel., 336
Matheson, Elb., 119
Mathews, Baca., 49
Mathews, Wel., 351
Mattison, Elb. (see Matheson)
Maudru, Mor., 257
Maxey, Baca., 49
May Valley, Pro., 282
Mayfield, E.P. (see Peyton)
Mayne, Hue., 152
Mayville, Che., 81
McClave, Bent, 56
McClellands, Lar., 200
McConnelisville, E.P., 142
McDonald, L.A., 217
McFerran, E.P. (see Newfield)
McGuire, Hue., 152
McMillen, Pro., 279
Mead, Wel., 336
Meadows, Bent (see Prowers)
Meadows, Pue., 303
Medford Springs, Bent, 58
Media, L.A., 217
Medill, Che., 82
Meekton, Was., 319
Melonfield, Bent, 60
Melvin, Ara., 36
Memphis, Kio. (see Towner)
Mercer, Log. (see Peetz)
Mercier, Pue., 296
Merino, Log., 239
Merrick, Pue., 303
Mesa, Ada., 25
Mesa, Pue., 303
Messex, Was., 320
Midway, Baca., 44
Mildred, Yum., 359
Military Park, Ara., 36
Millett, Was. (see Platner)
Milliken, Wel., 336
Millwood, Pro., 283

379

Index

Mindeman, Ote., 262
Miner, Lar., 200
Minneapolis, Baca, 49
Minto, Log., 245
Mirage, Lin. (see Clifford)
Mitchell Camp, Bent, 58
Mitchell, Bou., 73
Mitchell, Wel., 351
Model, L.A., 211
Model City, L.A. (see Model)
Modoc, Bou., 70
Monon, Baca, 49
Monson, Hue., 156
Montana Diggins, Ara., 36
Monument, E.P., 132
Moore, Wel., 351
Mooreville, Ara., 39
Morey, Bou., 73
Morningside, Jef., 166
Morris, Kit., 184
Morse, Pro. (see Clucas)
Morrison, Jef., 164
Mosby, E.P., 138
Moseley, Mor., 256
Mount Carbon, Jef., 171
Mount Olivet, Jef., 171
Mount Pearl, Che., 82
Mount Vernon, Jef., 166
Mountclair, Den., 95
Mountain View, Jef., 164
Muddy Creek, Pue., 296
Mulvane, Pro., 279
Munroe Park, Ada., 21
Muriel, Hue., 152
Muskoka, Kit., 185
Mustang, Hue., 149
Myrtle, Pue., 296

Nada, Pue., 303
Namaqua, Che., 83
Namaqua, Lar., 194
Narrows, Mor., 257
Nelson, Mor., 257
Nemo, Pue., 303
Nepasta, Pue., 291
New Haven, Log., 242
New Hyde, Was. (see Hyde)
New Liberty, Wel. (see Windsor)
New Memphis, Dou., 109
New Raymer, Wel., 336
New Stage Station, Pro., 280
Newdale, Ote., 267
Newfield, E.P., 138
Newport, Pue., 297
Newton, Yum., 362

Nichols, Hue., 156
Ninaview, Bent, 56
Nine Mile Bottom, Ote. (see Higbee)
Nine Mile House, Ada., 21
Nine Mile House, Ara., 36
Niwot, Bou., 67
Nob Hill, Ara., 33
Nola, L.A., 224
Noland, Bou., 70
N.O.R.A.D., E.P., 132
Norfolk, Lar., 200
North Avondale, Pue., 291
North Denver, Den. (see Berkeley)
North Fort Morgan, Mor., 257
North Washington, Ada., 17
Northern Swansea, Ada., 22
Northglenn, Ada., 17
Northrop, Bou., 70
Northway, Pro., 280
Norton, Elb., 122
Norwood, Jef., 166
Nowlinsville, Baca, 49
Numa, Cro., 88
Nunn, Wel., 337
Nyberg, Pue., 297

O.Z., E.P. (see Ramah)
Oaksdale, Ara., 36
Obrien, Dou., 112
Officer, L.A., 217
Officer, Lar., 200
Oglivy, Wel., 351
Oklarado, Baca, 49
Old Burlington, Kit., 184
Old Stage Station, Pro., 280
Oleson, Ada., 22
Olney Springs, Cro., 87
Omar, Wel., 337
Omega, Lar., 200
Omer, Ote., 264
Onine, L.A., 217
Opal, Bent, 58
Orchard, Mor., 251
Orchard Place, Ara. (see Englewood)
Orchard Place, Ote., 264
Orcutt, Lar., 200
Ordway, Cro., 87
Oriska, Kit., 184
Orlando, Hue., 156
Ormandale, Pue., 297
Ormega, Ote., 267
Orr, Wel. (see Kersey)
Orsburn, Elb., 122
Osgood, Wel., 343
Otero, Ote. (see La Junta)

Otis, Was., 316
Overton, Pue., 297
Ovid, Sed., 309
Owl Canyon, Lar., 200
Oxford, Ote. (see Fowler)

Padroni, Log., 239
Palmer Lake, E.P., 132
Paoli, Phi., 271
Papeton, E.P., 138
Park Creek, Lar., 194
Parkdale, Wel., 351
Parker, Dou., 107
Parrish, Pro., 283
Pate, Ada., 25
Patches, L.A., 217
Patron, Ada., 25
Patt, L.A., 218
Pauley, Hue., 152
Pawnee, Mor., 254
Pearl Mack, Ada., 17
Peckham, Wel., 337
Peconic, Kit., 185
Peetz, Log., 239
Pella, Bou., 70
Peoria, Ara., 33
Perry's Corner, Kit., 184
Petersburg, Ara., 36
Peterson Field, E.P. (see Ent)
Petra, Lar., 194
Peyton, E.P., 132
Pictou, Hue., 149
Piedmont, E.P., 138
Pierce, Wel., 337
Pierson, Ada., 22
Pikeview, E.P., 132
Pine Grove, Dou., 109
Pinneo, Was., 316
Piñon, Pue., 291
Piñon Springs, L.A., 218
Placita, L.A., 218
Plains, Pro., 280
Plainview, Jef., 164
Plateau, Doug., 112
Platner, Was., 317
Platte Canyon, Jef. (see Waterton)
Platte Valley, Wel. (see Hardin)
Platteville, Wel., 337
Player, Bent, 60
Pleasant View, Jef., 164
Plum, Dou. (see Sedalia)
Plumb Bush, Was., 320
Plumb Valley, L.A., 218
Plumbs, Wel., 351
Plummers, Lar., 201

Plymouth, Baca, 49
Pollack, Lar., 195
Portner, Lar., 201
Poso, L.A. (see Model)
Poudre, Lar., 201
Poudre City, Wel., 343
Powars, Wel., 351
Powell, Log., 245
Prairie, Was., 320
Pride, Baca, 50
Pring, E.P., 142
Pritchett, Baca, 44
Proctor, Log., 239
Progress, Baca, 50
Prospect Valley, Wel., 337
Prowers, Bent, 56
Pryor, Hue., 149
Pueblo, Pue., 291
Pueblo Air Force Base, 297
Pueblo Ordinance Depot, 291
Pulaski, L.A., 218
Pulliam, Wel., 352
Pullman Shops, Den., 100
Pultney, Cro., 87
Punkin Center, 231
Purcell, Wel., 338
Puritan, Wel., 343
Puttney, Cro., 87

Queen Beach, Kio., 176
Quimby, Ada., 22
Quimby Sta., Ada., 25
Ragans, Wel., 352
Rago, Was., 320
Ralston, Jef., 167
Ralston, Jef., 171
Ralston Creek, Jef. (see Arvada)
Ramah, E.P., 133
Ranch, Pue., 297
Randall, Ote., 267
Rapson, L.A., 218
Rattlesnake Butte, Hue., 152
Ravenwood, Hue., 149
Raybal, Hue., 152
Raymer, Wel. (see New Raymer)
Red Lion, Log., 240
Red Rock, L.A., 218
Redmond, Lar., 201
Reed's Springs, Elb., 122
Regneir, Baca, 50
Remmington, Lar., 201
Rene, Ote., 265
Reno, Phi., 272
Resolis, Elb., 119
Rex, Lar., 201

Index

Richards, Baca, 50
Ridge, Jef., 171
Ridgeview, Ara., 33
Rifle Range, Jef., 171
Riley, Ote., 268
Rinn, Wel., 338
Rio de Las Animas, L.A. (see Trinidad)
Ripple, Lar., 201
River Bend, Elb., 119
Rivera, L.A., 224
Riverdale, Bent, 60
Riverton, Pue., 303
Rixey, Bent, 58
Robb, Yum., 359
Roberts, Lar., 201
Roberta, Ote., 268
Robinson, Ote., 268
Rock Butte, Elb., 123
Rock Creek, Mor., 254
Rockford, Dou., 109
Rockland, Log., 242
Rockport, Wel., 338
Rockridge, Dou., 109
Rocky Ford, Ote., 262
Rocky Mountain Arsenal, Ada., 17
Rodley, Baca, 50
Rogers, Yum., 362
Roggen, Wel., 338
Rolla, Ada., 25
Roof, Hue., 156
Root, Hue., 156
Rose Hill, Ada., 22
Rosedale, Hue., 152
Rosedale, Wel., 338
Roswell, E.P., 138
Round Corral, Dou. (see Sedalia)
Round Oak, Hue., 152
Rouse, Hue., 153
Rouse Junction, Hue., 156
Rowe, Pro., 280
Roydale, Den., 100
Ruff, Baca, 50
Rugby, L.A., 218
Rule, Bent, 58
Running Creek, Elb., 122
Rush, E.P., 133
Rush Creek, Che., 83
Russellville, Dou., 109
Ruxton, Bent, 60
Rysby, Bou., 70

Sable, Ada., 22
Saint Charles, Den. (see Denver)
Saint Charles, Pue., 297
Saint Louis, Lar., 195

Saint Petersburg, Log., 240
Saint Vrain, Bou., 70
Saint Vrains, Wel., 338
Salem, Ara., 36
Salis, Che., 83
Salt Creek, Pue., 297
Salt Springs, Kio., 176
San Antonia, L.A. (see Apishipa)
San Carlos, Pue., 304
San Isidro, L.A. (see Abeyta)
San Jose, L.A. (see Grinnell)
San Joseville, Ote., 265
San Miguel, L.A., 218
Sanborn, Lin., 233
Sand Arroya, Baca, 50
Sand Creek, Ada. (see Nine Mile House)
Sand Creek, Che., 83
Sand Creek, Kio., 176
Sand Creek Junction, Ada., 25
Sandown, Den., 100
Sandy, Hue., 156
Saugus, Lin., 231
Santa Clara, Hue. (see Rouse)
Santa Clara Junction, Hue., 156
Santisma Trinidad, L.A. (see Trinidad)
Sarinda, Log., 242
Saunders, Pue., 298
Schley, Elb., 122
Schleyter, Was., 320
Schramm, Yum., 359
Schulter Plaza, L.A. (see Aguilar)
Schuyler, Ada. (see Sable)
Scott, Lar., 195
Scranton, Ada., 22
Security, E.P., 133
Sedgwick, Sed., 309
Sedalia, Dou., 107
See-Bar-See, Yum. (see Laird)
Segreganset, Kio., 177
Seibert, Kit., 180
Selma, Log., 245
Semper, Jef., 167
Seton, Baca (see Setonsburg)
Setonsburg, Baca, 50
Seventeen Mile House, Ara., 37
Severence, Wel., 338
Shaw, Lin., 231
Shaw Heights, Ada., 18
Shaw Heights Mesa, Ada., 18
Sheehan, Wel., 352
Sheffield, Den., 95
Shelton, Ote., 268
Sheridan, Ara., 33
Sheridan Lake, Kio., 175

Places on the Colorado Prairie

Sheridan Park, Ara., 37
Sherman Spur, L.A., 224
Sherrelwood, Ada., 18
Sherwin, Log., 245
Shields, Yum., 362
Sidney, Elb., 123
Silva, L.A., 224
Silvia, L.A., 224
Simla, Elb., 119
Simpson, Ada., 23
Simpson, L.A., 224
Sinnard, Lar., 201
Sitton, Pue., 298
Skinners, E.P., 142
Sligo, Wel., 344
Sloan, Wel., 352
Snyder, Mor., 251
Sommers, E.P., 142
Sonora, Pue., 304
Sopris, L.A., 211
Sorrento, Che., 82
South Denver, Den., 95
South Platte, Log., 243
South Pueblo, Pue., 298
South Roggen, Wel., 339
South Side, Ote., 265
South Wind, Ara., 33
Southern Junction, Pue., 304
Southglenn, Ara., 33
Southwater, E.P., 138
Southwestern Colony, Wel. (see Green City)
Southwood, Ara., 33
Spence, Was., 320
Spring Bottom, Ote., 265
Spring Canyon, Lar., 195
Spring Hill, Log., 243
Spring Valley, Dou., 109
Springfield, Baca, 45
Spruce, Dou., 112
Spurgin, Wel. (see Vim)
Squirrel Creek, E.P., 139
Stage Canyon, L.A., 218
Stage Canyon, L.A., 219
Standley Lake, Jef., 171
Station #21, Kit., 184
Station #22, Kit., 184
Station #23, Kit., 184
Station #24, Lin., 233
Steffens, Yum., 362
Stein, Log., 245
Stem Beach, Pue., 292
Sterling, Log., 240
Stevenson, Baca, 50
Stockville, L.A., 219

Stone City, Pue., 292
Stone City, Was. (see Thurman)
Stoneham, Wel., 339
Stonewall, Lar., 195
Stonington, Baca, 45
Story, Mor., 257
Stout, Lar., 195
Strasburg, Ada., 18
Strasburg, Ara., 34
Stratmoor Hills, E.P., 133
Stratmoor Valley, E.P., 133
Straton Meadows, E.P., 133
Stratton, Kit., 182
Strouseville, Jef., 167
Stuart, Kio., 175
Struby, Dou., 112
Sublette, Wel., 352
Suffield, L.A., 224
Suffolk, E.P., 139
Sugar City, Cro., 87
Sugardale, Pro., 283
Sullivan, Ara., 37
Sulpher Gulch, Dou., 110
Summit, Wel., 352
Summit Springs, Was., 320
Sunshine, Hue., 156
Superior, Bou., 68
Surber, E.P., 139
Swallows, Pue., 292
Sweetwater, Kio., 177
Swift, Lin., 233
Swimford, Ada., 23
Swink, Ote., 263
Symons, Ote. (see Mindeman)

Table Rock, Dou., 110
Table Rock, E.P., 139
Tabor, Pue., 298
Tacony, Pue., 298
Tailholt, Wel. (see Severence)
Tampa, Wel., 352
Taylor, Lar., 201
Teachouts, E.P., 139
Ted's Place, Lar., 201
Ten Mile House, Lar. (see Stonewall)
Tennessee Colony, Wel. (see Green City)
Thatcher, L.A., 211
Thedalund, Ada., 23
Thomas, Jef., 171
Thornton, Ada., 18
Thurman, Was., 317
Timmath, Lar., 193
Timpas, Ote., 263
Timpas, Ote., 265
Tioga, Hue., 153

383

Index

Tip Top, E.P., 142
Tobe, L.A., 211
Toben, Log., 245
Toll Gate, Ara., 37
Toltec, Hue., 156
Tomah, Dou., 112
Tonvill, Wel., 352
Toonerville, Bent, 57
Tower Junction, Bou., 73
Towner, Kio., 175
Townsend, Was., 320
Tracyville, Wel., 352
Trail City, Pro., 280
Trilby, Lar., 201
Trinchera, L.A., 211
Trinchera Plaza, L.A., 212
Trinidad, L.A., 212
Trowell Ranch, Mor., 257
Troy, L.A., 212
Truckton, E.P., 133
Tubs, Baca (see Carrizo Springs)
Tuna, Hue., 156
Turkey Creek, Pue., 304
Tuttle, Kit., 184
Twelve Mile House, Ara., 37
Twelve Mile House, Jef. (see Church's)
Twenty Mile House, Dou., 110
Twenty Mile Siding, Log. (see Fleming)
Twenty Five Mile House, Wel., 344
Two Buttes, Bac., 45
Tyrone, L.A., 212

Uncle Jack Moores, Ote., 265
Undercliffe, Pue., 298
Union, Mor. (see Pawnee)
Union Colony, Wel., 344
Union Hill, E.P., 139
U.S.A.F. Academy, E.P., 133
University Park, Den., 95
Utah Junction, Ada., 25
Utleyville, Baca, 45

Valentine, Lar., 201
Vallery, Mor., 255
Valley, Kit., 184
Valley, Log., 243
Valmont, Bou., 68
Valverde, Den., 95
Van's Point, Kit., 185
Vegas, Pue., 304
Verde, Pue., 298
Verdum, Pro., 280
Vernon, Yum., 360
Viena, Baca, 51
Vilas, Baca, 45

Villa Park, Den., 96
Villegreen, L.A., 212
Vim, Wel., 344
Vineland, Pue., 292
Virginia, Dou., 110
Virginia Dale, Lar., 193
Virginia Dale, Lar., 195
Vogel, Ote., 265
Vollmar, Wel., 339
Vona, Kit., 182
Vroman, Ote., 263

Wages, Yum., 360
Wagner, Was., 321
Waitley, Was., 321
Wakeman, Phi., 272
Wales, Yum., 363
Walker, Wel., 352
Wallett, Kit., 185
Walsen, Hue., 153
Walsenburg, Hue., 150
Walsh, Baca, 45
Ward, Bou., 74
Waremont, Pue., 299
Warren, Wel., 352
Warwick, Pro., 283
Washburn, Ada. (see Hazeltine)
Washburn, Lar., 195
Watchel, Wel., 344
Water Valley, Kio., 177
Waterton, Jef., 167
Watervale, L.A., 212
Watkins, Ada., 18
Wattenburg, Wel., 339
Wauneta, Yum., 360
Waveland, Bent, 60
Waverly, Lar., 193
Wayne, E.P., 139
Webb, Pro., 280
Weissport, E.P., 139
Weitzer, Ote. (see Vroman)
Welby, Ada., 18
Weldon, Mor. (see Weldona)
Weldona, Mor., 251
Wellington, Lar., 193
Wellons, Lin., 233
Well's Ranch, Elb., 122
Welty, Wel., 352
Wentworth, Baca, 51
Wentz, Wel., 344
West Las Animas, Bent (see Las Animas)
Western Hills, Ada., 18
Westminster, Ada., 18
Westplains, Log., 240
Wetchel, Wel., 344

Places on the Colorado Prairie

Wezel, Lin., 233
Wheatfield, E.P., 139
Wheatland, Lar., 196
Wheatridge, Jef., 165
White, More., 257
White Rock, Pue., 299
Whiterock, Bou., 74
Widefield, E.P., 139
Widefield, E.P., 142
Wiggins, Mor., 251
Wigwam, E.P., 133
Wild Horse, Che., 80
Wildcat, Wel., 352
Wilde, Pro., 280
Wilds, Lar., 193
Wiley, Pro., 274
Willam Springs, E.P., 140
Willard, Log., 240
Williams, Pue., 304
Williams Fort, Ote. (see Bents Fort)
Willow Springs, Lin., 233
Wilson, Pue., 299
Winchell, Hue., 156
Windsor, Wel., 339
Winona, Lar., 196
Winston, Log., 241
Witherbee, Yum., 363

Wolf Creek, Elb., 122
Wolhurst, Ara., 39
Wood Valley, Pue., 299
Woodburn, E.P., 140
Woodmen, E.P., 142
Woodrow, Was., 317
Woods, Lar., 201
Wormington, L.A., 219
Wray, Yum., 360
Wyman, Jef., 171
Wynetka, Ara., 37

Xenia, Was., 321

Yachita, L.A., 219
Yale, Kit., 185
Yeiser, L.A., 219
Yetta, L.A. (see Tyrone)
Yoder, E.P., 133
Youngstown, Wel., 344
Yoxall, Wel., 352
Yuma, Yum., 360

Zilar, Wel., 345
Zinc Junction, Pue., 304
Zita, Wel. (see Galeton)

Index of Railroads

American Smelting & Refining Co., 223
Arkansas Valley Ry., 58, 82, 177, 265, 266, 281, 282
Associated Railroads, 96, 168
Atchison, Topeka & Santa Fe Ry., 38, 58, 96, 110, 140, 141, 219, 266, 281, 282, 299, 300
Bear Canon RR, 221
Burlington & Colorado RR, 23, 96, 255, 321, 345, 363
Burlington Northern RR, 23, 71, 96, 168, 243, 255, 272, 321, 345, 363
Canon City & San Juan RR, 300
Canon de Agua RR, 221
Carlton Interests, 141
Chicago, Burlington & Quincy RR 23, 71, 96, 168, 243, 255, 272, 321, 345, 363
Chicago, Kansas & Nebraska Ry., 97, 123, 140, 185, 233
Chicago, Rock Island & Pacific Ry., 97, 123, 140, 185, 233

Chicosa Canon Ry., 222
Colorado & New Mexico RR, 281
Colorado & Southeastern RR, 221
Colorado & South Eastern Ry., 221
Colorado & Southern Ry., 23, 38, 71, 72, 97, 98, 111, 123, 140, 141, 153, 168, 196, 197, 219, 220, 221, 300, 346
Colorado & Wyoming RR, 222, 243, 272, 345
Colorado & Wyoming Ry., 222, 300
Colorado Central RR 23, 24, 71, 72, 97, 168, 197, 198, 243, 255, 311, 321, 346, 347
Colorado Eastern RR, 24, 97
Colorado Eastern Ry., 24, 97
Colorado-Kansas Ry., 300
Colorado Midland Ry., 141
Colorado Railroad, 153, 300
Colorado Railroad Co., 196, 197
Colorado Springs & Cripple Creek District Ry., 140

385

Index

Cripple Creek & Colorado Springs RR, 140
Denver & Berkeley Park Rapid Transit, 99
Denver & Boulder Valley RR, 72
Denver & Intermountain RR, 99, 167, 169
Denver & Intermountain Ry., 96, 167, 169
Denver & Interurban RR, 24, 72, 98, 168
Denver & Middle Park RR
Denver & Montana RR, 255
Denver & New Orleans RR, 38, 97, 111, 122, 140, 300
Denver & Northwestern Ry. 99, 169
Denver & Rio Grande RR, 38, 98, 111, 141, 153, 154, 155, 222, 223, 300, 301
Denver & Rio Grande Ry., 38, 98, 111, 141, 153, 154, 222, 300, 301
Denver & Rio Grande Western RR, 38, 98, 100, 141, 153, 154, 155, 169, 222, 223, 300, 301
Denver & Salt Lake RR, 98, 169
Denver & Santa Fe RR, 38, 96, 110, 140, 299
Denver & Westside Cable Ry., 99
Denver-Boulder Valley RR, 347
Denver Circle RR, 96
Denver City RR #2, 99
Denver City Ry., 99
Denver City Cable Ry., 99
Denver City Electric Rys., 99
Denver City Traction Co., 99
Denver City Tramway Co., 96, 99, 167, 169
Denver City Tramway #2, 99
Denver City Tramway Corp., 169
Denver Consolidated Tramway, 99
Denver, Golden & Morrison RR, 169
Denver Horse RR, 99
Denver, Lakewood & Golden RR, 96, 167, 169
Denver, Laramie & Northwestern RR, 24, 98, 346
Denver, Laramie & Northwestern Ry., 98
Denver, Leadville & Gunnison Ry., 38, 97, 168
Denver, Longmont & Northwestern RR, 71
Denver, Marshall & Boulder Ry., 23, 24, 72, 98, 168
Denver, Northwestern & Pacific RR, 98, 169

Denver Pacific Ry., 72, 100, 347
Denver Railroad & Land Co., 24, 97
Denver Railroad Land & Coal Co., 24, 97
Denver, South Park & Pacific Ry., 38, 97, 168
Denver, Texas & Ft. Worth RR, 97, 140, 220, 221, 300
Denver, Texas & Gulf RR, 38, 97, 111, 123, 140, 300
Denver Tramway Co., 96, 99, 168, 169
Denver Tramway Corp., 96, 99, 168, 169
Denver Tramway Extension Co., 99
Denver, Utah & Pacific RR, 24, 71, 98, 168, 169, 345, 346
Denver Western & Pacific Ry., 98
Dodge City & Cimmaron Valley Ry., 51
Eldorado Springs Ry., 72
Florence & Cripple Creek Ry., 140
Ft. Collins Development Ry., 196, 197
Golden, Boulder & Caribou RR, 72
Golden Cycle Mining & Milling Co., 141
Great Western Ry., 197, 346, 347
Greeley, Salt Lake & Pacific RR, 196, 197
Highland Street RR, 99
Holly & Swink Ry., 266, 281
Intermountain Ry., 96, 167, 169
Kansas-Colorado RR, 300
Kansas Pacific Ry., 24, 82, 100, 123, 234
Longmont & Erie RR, 71
Metro Ry., 99
Metro Transit, 99
Midland Terminal Ry., 141
Missouri Pacific RR, 88, 177, 266, 301
Missouri Pacific Ry., 100, 177, 266, 301
Park Ry., 99
Pueblo & Arkansas Valley RR, 219, 266, 281, 299, 300
Pueblo & State Line RR, 88, 266, 301
Rio Grande Western Ry., 141
Road Canon RR, 220
South Denver Cable Ry., 99
Trinadad & Denver RR, 222
Union Pacific RR, 24, 72, 82, 100, 123, 197, 198, 234, 243, 255, 311, 321, 347
Union Pacific Ry., 100, 123, 234, 347
Union Pacific, Denver & Gulf Ry., 23, 38, 71, 72, 97, 98, 140, 153, 168, 196, 197, 198, 219, 220, 221, 222, 243, 255, 300, 346, 347
University Park Ry., 99
Victor Fuel Co., 221
West End RR, 99